# DRO

(Drastamat Kanayan)
Armenia's First Defense Minister of
the Modern Era

Author
ANTRANIG CHALABIAN

Translated from Armenian by
JACK CHELEBIAN, M.D.

**DRO** (Drastamat Kanayan):  Armenia's First Defense Minister of the Modern Era

Indo-European Publishing

For information and contact visit our website at:
IndoEuropeanPublishing.com


Cover Design by Alfred Aghajanian

ISNB: 978-1-60444-078-2

IndoEuropean
Publishing.com
Los Angeles, CA, USA

# DEDICATION

What could I dedicate this monograph to, written for the sake of immortalizing the memory of dauntless Dro, but to the Armenian Revolutionary Federation, which granted to the nation fedayeen like Andranik, Dro, *Aghbiur* (Spring) Serob, Gevorg *Chavush* (Policeman), Hrair-*Dzhoghk* (Hell) (Armenak Ghazarian), Murat (Khrimian) of Sebastia, Dono Makar, Nikol Duman (Nikoghayos Ter Hovannesian), *Keri* (Uncle) (Arshak Galfayan), Vartan of Khanasor, Hamazasb (Srvandzian), Torgom (Tuman Tumiants), Sebuh (Arshak Nersesian), Smbad (Baroyan), Dashnak Khecho, Martiros Charukhjian, and many, many more. There are as well female warriors, about whom the reader can learn in my *Revolutionary Figures* book. They armed and taught martial skills to the Armenian serf *(raya)*; forestalled the great slaughter of Eastern Armenians in the eight victorious battles of the year-and-a-half-long 1905–1906 Armeno-Tatar War, and reached out with helping hands to the Eastern Armenians being massacred in Baku, in September 1918, where the great warrior Murat of Sebastia fell in those battles "on the rocky hills of Baku." Crowning this, the ARF forged in fire the fame and glory of the Armenian people in the May 1918 battles, particularly through the efforts of steadfast Aram (Manukian), ingenious military man Movses Silikian, and lionhearted Drastamat Kanayan, on the plains of Sartarabad and Bash-Aparan.

Eternal glory to the Armenian martial organization!

A. C

# TRANSLATOR'S NOTE
# AND
# ACKNOWLEDGMENTS

My interest in history dates back to my latency years when I was an avid reader of Armenian history through books I found at our home, at neighbors' and relatives' homes, and at school.

When I was in high school, I recall my father asked me about my interests for college. I mentioned history but he was quick to dissuade me from that. Eventually I ended up finding my niche in medicine, particularly in the specialty of psychiatry, which traditionally emphasizes the history as well as the social and cultural context of illness. Years later it was with a mix of irony and admiration that I witnessed my father become an accomplished historian, author of several valuable books, and recipient of a doctorate in history from the Armenian Academy of Sciences, in 1994, at the age of seventy-two! It follows that embarking on the translation of his last book, *Dro,* from the original Armenian into English felt like coming home full circle.

Being a translator means making difficult decisions. One of these is determining how much, or how many features, of the original language should be allowed to show through, since the price, paid by the reader, of such allowance is having to hesitate and perhaps regroup when encountering the occasional odd word choice, phrase, or construction. I have chosen to have the English translation reflect a good deal of the original Armenian, in part because I believe that in doing so there is less opportunity to unwittingly stray from the original, and also because I suspect that many readers, although certainly not all, will have some familiarity with the original language.

In the United States the word *brave* was used over many decades to describe young men of Native American tribes in the role of warrior. In Armenian the equivalent word has the same two meanings, that of warrior or fighter, and one who has the quality of bravery. While some readers may stumble in encountering this term, it is so laden a word that any substitution would do a disservice to the writer, the reader, and the men whom the term signifies.

A similarly loaded word is *fedayee,* a term borrowed from Persian, common in Arabic, understood in Armenian. It means "he who is committed" or "he who is sacrificed." Over many decades in the last century it referred to freedom fighters (and guerillas, insurgents, partisans, terrorists, revolutionaries—the choices are many) from Iran to Algeria to Palestine in the Muslim world, and most recently in this century to the dictator Saddam Hussein's "*fedayeen* Saddam." But in Armenian folk memory, the revolutionary movement is identified with the *fedayee* movement.[1]

Last, but not least, I am deeply grateful to Ms. Berdjouhi Esmerian and Tom Gift, M.D., for their invaluable editorial and technical input and assistance.

Jack Chelebian, M.D.

---

[1] *Nationalism and Socialism in the Armenian Revolutionary Movement,* Anaide Ter Minassian, Zoryan Institute, 1984.

# CRANES

Oh cranes, cranes,
From which shore are you coming,
From that place where the chiming
Springs are crying?

> We are coming from Sassun,
> Erzrum and Van
> From our parched
> Lake Sevan.

Oh cranes, cranes,
Whence you come vexed;
From those mountains where there are fearless
Fedayeen and struggle?

> Where Andranik with his band,
> *Aghbiur* Serob and Sosé,
> Have again climbed the mountains,
> To commune with lightnings.

Oh cranes, cranes,
Come down near us, come down.
We need Kevork *Chavoush*
And General Andranik.

SERO ANTONIAN
(excerpts)

# EMIGRANT'S SONG

Leaving behind my home and hearth
I was blown in the wind,
I cried my heart out,
Spring season left my heart.

Play the strings, brother singer,
Let the songs speak sweetly
Oh, it has been a while since
I cried from my heart, dear brother. . . .

Armenian folksong

# TABLE OF CONTENTS

# INTRODUCTION

A few incidents prompted me to undertake the preparation of this manuscript about brave Dro's adventurous yet fruitful life, despite the fact that after the publication of my last book (in English in 1999), *Armenia After the Coming of Islam,* which in the end was satisfactory but very time consuming, I had decided not to write any other books. Indeed, that 608-page book with 10 maps and 24 pictures, and complex content, had taken a year longer than my 760 pages long book titled *General Andranik and the Armenian Revolutionary Movement,* which was well received by the public with five printings in many thousands.

While I was busy with the 2nd printing of *Armenia After the Coming of Islam,* I received a booklet about Dro, 60 pages long, with pictures. The author was familiar to me from Beirut—the well-known writer Armen Donoyan.

I read with interest Donoyan's booklet. My curiosity about Dro was not quenched with that booklet, and it became the spur and beginning of my research.

I started browsing my personal library comprising a few thousand volumes in two rooms. Encouraged by the information I uncovered in Simon Vratsian's *Along Life's Pathways* 6-volume collection and other books, I continued my search in Armenian historiography and my work began to grow.

Gerald Ottenbreit, Jr., of the Armenian Research Center at Michigan University (Dearborn), and an American historian with some knowledge of Armenian, brought to my attention a 174-page book titled *Dro,* published in Yerevan

1

in 1991, the author being Hamlet Gevorgian.

Aside from these positive developments, the main driving force in this work was my curiosity about the enigmatic but also popular hero named Dro. I wanted to uncover the truth about the hero's political and military activities, not by words, but by hard evidence. Dro has been much maligned, critiqued, and even accused of treason. Even some delegates at ARF General Assemblies did not understand him. Moreover, in the ARF Bureau, Ruben and Hamo Ohandjanian, for example, had tried to expel him from the ranks—as you will read in my book—as a "collaborator with Bolshevism and Nazism," but Vahan Navasardian, who adored Dro, had defended him.

The reason for all these contradictions and misunderstandings was Dro's unassuming and modest temperament. Narcissism, megalomania, vanity, and self-praise were never a part of his character. He did not speak or brag about himself or his intrepid deeds. On one occasion in Warsaw during WWII, he had said to Aram Dabaghian, "Didn't I tell you there is the hand of the Turks in this issue?" As soon as he said it the hero recognized the self-praise involved and without waiting for Aram's response, quickly changed the subject with, "Hey, tell me, do you have any update on the refugee situation?"

They say that grandeur lies in modesty.

I saw Dro once in Beirut, for a few seconds, but that moment and the impression it left on me remain imprinted in my mind forever. Having emerged from my home, which was very close to the Neshan Palanjian Academy, I was walking east on the sidewalk. When I reached the Academy's main gate, Dro and Simon Vratsian emerged from the side door next to the gate and immediately headed west, toward their residence, without looking around. With round face and rosy cheeks, Dro had thrown his coat on one shoulder, walking briskly, with Vratsian trying to keep pace.

During World War II, the list of Hitler's hatreds was headed by the Jews, with Armenians, Slavs, and gypsies being a close second.

2

Who would have cared about the calamitous fate reserved for the Armenian prisoners of war and the Armenian communities in the occupied territories, as well as the security of all Armenians in the homeland, if Hitler's divisions were to have invaded the TransCaucasus? Which political party or association would have ventured to grapple with this complex and very dangerous task if not for Dro and his self-sacrificing, modest, and devoted associates?

I do not claim to have exhausted, with this book, the topic of Dro's heroic life. To the extent of my capacity, means, experience, and access to related bibliography, I gave what I could, to inform the reader as to how individuals with strong personalities, willpower, persuasion, and ideals, albeit with minimal education, can conquer great heights and reach exalted positions, become leaders, even army commanders for the sake of the homeland, for the salvation and rebirth of the endangered Armenian nation.

A. Ch.

# CHAPTER I

## THE YOUNG AND VALIANT DRO,
## THE NEMESIS OF THE COYOTES THIRSTING FOR
## THE BLOOD OF THE ARMENIAN NATION

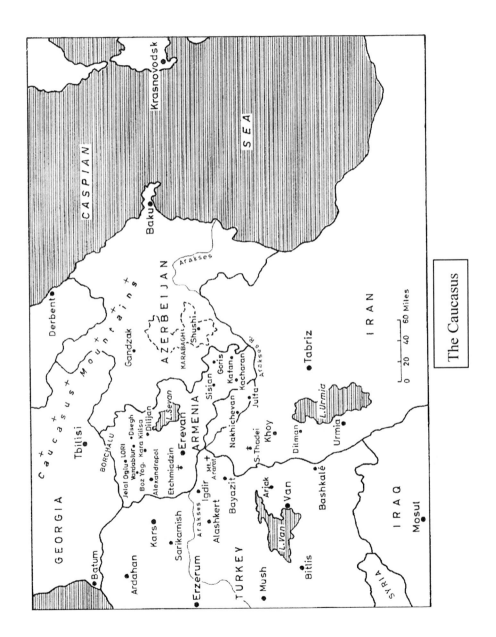

The Caucasus

## LATENCY AND ADOLESCENCE

Dro (Drastamat Kanayan) was born on May 31, 1884, during a storm and an earthquake in the Igdir Borough of Surmalu Province. Since he was born in a tempest, the boy would later be called "Tempestuous Dro."

Igdir, an Armenian-populated large country town, the central borough of Surmalu Province, was an important military center. Eight to ten thousand Russian forces were stationed there—infantry, Cossacks, border guards. Through commerce with them, the region's Armenian population had prospered.

Almost attached to Igdir was Ava Village, the birthplace of Avetis Aharonian, the renowned Armenian poet. After 1828, when the Russo-Turkish War ended with Russia's victory, Armenian refugees were brought and made to settle there, where the soil was suited to the cultivation of wheat, cotton, and vineyards. As a result of the Russian military presence, Igdir had also become a mercantile center.

The prosperous Armenians of Igdir did not spare any expense in recruiting good teachers to staff the borough's large co-ed school. Since the country town bordered Turkey, it was a way station for revolutionary intellectuals and warriors heading for Turkish-Armenia. Igdir was a cauldron of revolutionary ferment and militant acts. The people of Surmalu were known for their love of liberty, valor, hospitality, and folk songs. Komitas Vartabed collected many songs from the villages of Surmalu in his ethnomusicological field studies.[1]

As in many towns and villages of Armenia, the people of Igdir were also divided into factions that often argued and quarreled with each other.

Igdir's two most prominent partisan families were the Kanayans and the Avagians, who were consistently in opposition to each other.

The patriarch of Igdir's Kanayan family, Martiros, was an intelligent, entrepreneurial, prosperous, and

6

influential man who enjoyed his community's respect. He had vast holdings as a landowner, farmer, vintner, and merchant. He had acquaintances, friends, and enemies everywhere. His big house was full of life and blessings, and guests were never absent from his table.

Dro was born into this lively and prosperous home; he grew up in nature's bosom with his brothers and sisters, and especially with lads his age. Since his childhood he was notable as a leader, inclined to be a ruler and commander as an adolescent. He was temperamental yet also lively.

When Dro reached school age, his father registered him at Igdir's parish school, but soon it became clear that Martiros Kanayan's son was not interested in school or education. He liked to play with his friends and roam the streets, especially the barracks area. He was greatly fascinated by military drills.

When his father was convinced that the local school was not the place for his son, he took him to Yerevan's Gymnasium, a boarding school, thinking that perhaps this setting would help him to mature.

Yerevan's Gymnasium was not the place for Dro either. He was intelligent, had good memory, and was capable of being the first in his class, but he earned grades that just barely enabled him to get promoted to the next class. Whatever he heard from his teachers in the classroom was the extent of his education. Apart from this, he was not interested in reading and writing at home either. He took first place in play and mischief.

Yerevan's Gymnasium, like all the state schools of all the frontier provinces of the Russian Empire, was called upon to not only impart learning to the new generation, but also to pursue a policy of Russification. Moscow appointed Russian nationalist teachers who generally were contemptuous of the natives, whose language, church, and traditions they tried to Russify.

During Dro's school years, the principal at Yerevan's Gymnasium was Brazhnikov, who hated Armenians. Russophile sentiment and strict order dominated the school. The majority of the students were Armenians, the rest Tatars and Russians. All the subjects were taught in Russian, except for religion, which was taught in Armenian, through a poor priest. He was paid twenty-five rubles monthly, and to safeguard his job, he put up with the principal's whims without grumbling.

The Armenian nation, however, was not asleep. As the nineteenth century ended and the twentieth began, Armenia experienced a political awakening, and the liberation movement of Turkish-Armenia started. In the region of Erzrum, "a voice resounds from Erzrum's Armenian mountains" sang Armenian youth, the first song of the Armenian Revolution. Turkish-Armenia's provinces were bustling. The tragic conclusion of Sarkis Kukunian's raid, because of the Russian border guards' bloody Turkish-style atrocities, had filled Armenian hearts with wrath toward both Turkish and Russian tyrants. The revolutionaries, dedicated to the liberation of the Armenian nation, were pursued by both the Sultan and the Tsar with equal vigor. Armenian youth in the Caucasus were clamoring "Revenge! Revenge!" as they prepared to lend a hand to their Turkish-Armenian brethren.

Clandestine groups studied Armenia's language, history, and literature while struggling against Russification. In the schools, they sheared the hair of students speaking Russian. As for Armenian girls dancing with Russian officers, they smeared their white dresses with tar. Dro, naturally, was in the first rank of these revolutionaries in Yerevan's Gymnasium. This is how he reflected on his experiences during adolescence.

"We were adolescents. Our motto was to resist the regime and never to concede willingly. One of the main sources of revolutionary inspiration in those days was Andranik's heroic struggle. When Andranik, with a few hundred fedayeen, was resisting Islamic armies and Kurdish tribes in the name of the Armenian nation's honor and liberty, we committed ourselves to resisting the tsarist regime and spilling our blood in the name of Armenian rights. This exciting slogan was circulating mouth to mouth."[2]

One cannot wonder that in such times the Gymnasium could not seduce Dro. Books and studies were not for him, and his teachers complained about his laziness and mischief. They often called his father, admonishing him to counsel his son to read, to "become a man," but to no avail. The thunder of the guerillas' rifles could be heard from across the border. The students sang the exploits of Andranik and his comrades.

"Brave Andranik, with his comrades,
Wants war, awaits the Spring."

Dro decided to quit the Gymnasium and enter the military academy with the goal of becoming a revolutionary warrior. But to be accepted to the military academy required high grades. He assertively went to see the principal.

"Mr. Principal, I want to go to the military academy, but . . . my grades . . . could something be done . . . .?"

"My dear," rejoiced the principal, "I will change all your 3s to 5s, also the 0 for your manners to 5; just go . . . . I wish you success, that you become a general . . . ."

Diploma in hand, Dro departs from the fourth grade of Yerevan's Gymnasium.[3]


## REVOLUTIONARY ENDEAVORS

Dro did not join the military immediately. For a while he stayed in his hometown. It was a stormy, momentous period. Sassun (in Turkish Armenia) was in martial mobilization, where fedayeen and ammunition were aggregated under the command of brave Andranik. But on the Russian side of the border, on June 12, 1903, a tsarist decree was published regarding the appropriation of the lands and estates of the Armenian National Church. The Armenian Revolutionary Federation (Dashnak) revived the Self-Defense Central Committee and threatened any government officials or traitors who might be tempted to forcefully appropriate these holdings. Assassin groups were organized and a series of daring assassinations took place.

Could Dro sit back, content, when he was born for revolution and struggle? He dove into martial endeavors with his whole being; he joined an assassin group, took part in popular demonstrations against the government, and was beaten a number of times by the gendarmes.

"My mother," related Dro chuckling, "blessed the tsar; 'Blessed be Nicholas's throne. My son, who did not attend church, is now getting beaten for the church.' "[4]

The ARF pursued spies and traitors mercilessly. The Armenophobe prefect Boguslavski was in hot pursuit of Armenian revolutionaries. Tedjerebad Village's Chief Martiros had become a willing instrument in his hand. It was left to Dro, the dedicated dashnakist Gerdan, and another comrade to assassinate the collaborator.

A Russian officer named Sasha Zabolotko lived in Dro's home and taught Russian lessons to him. He was a close friend of the Kanayan family. Often other officers would congregate with him and have a good time.

One evening guests came over. Sasha asked Dro to go to the market for food. Dro had just returned home from shopping when he got word that Chief Martiros was heading to the public bath with two friends. Dro rushed out, fetched his comrades and, reaching the Chief, dropped him with one bullet. When he returned home, the officers were playing cards. Dro sat with them, watching the game.

Witnesses informed the police that Dro had killed someone. The police quickly surrounded the Kanayan household and wanted to arrest him. Sasha vouched for Dro, stating that he had been with them the whole time, but the police did not heed him and, arresting Dro, took him to the police station for interrogation. Dro refused to confess. They took him to the wounded Chief but Dro again refused to confess. They brought the Chief's companions, but they either did not recognize Dro or pretended not to recognize him. Dro was taken to prison. At dawn, the traitor Martiros died.

The following day the investigation was resumed. The

officers swore that Dro had been with them the whole day. After two days in prison, he was released.

Years later, Dro encountered Sasha in Tbilisi. The latter was now a brigadier general.

"Do you remember," Sasha asked, "when that useless Boguslavski tried to pin the Chief's assassination on you?"

"You know what, Sasha?" replied Dro. "Boguslavski was right. I did kill the Chief."

General Sasha Zabolotko stared at Dro's face, astonished.[5]

After this assassination, the ARF instructed Dro to leave Surmalu Province. But how could he leave, when he had fallen in love with one of the beauties of Igdir, a lass of the Kanayan family's archrival Avagian family. Under pressure, Dro left for Yerevan, and then Baku. There he enlisted in Akhulzinski's brigade, a military training unit for noncommissioned officers.

## THE BAKU BATTLE

(Note: "Turk," "Tatar," and "Azeri" are used interchangeably in the Caucasus.)

Sassun's second uprising took place in 1904, under the command of Andranik. A year later, in early February 1905, an incident happened that would serve as the immediate pretext for clashes between Armenians and Tatars in Baku.

When soldiers belonging to a Russian brigade were escorting the famous Tatar bandit chief, Ashurbekov, from the courthouse to the prison, he tried to escape. The soldiers started firing at the escapee, and, as it happened, it was an Armenian soldier's bullet that killed the prisoner. As news of the incident spread, the Tatars, enraged, decided to seek revenge by attacking Armenians.

On February 6, a large crowd of Armenians had gathered in the courtyard of the Armenian Church in Baku and the public square in front of it. Among them was the Armenian soldier who had killed Ashurbekov. A Tatar named Balayev approached him and fired, wounding him. The Turk ran from the scene but some Armenian young men raced after him and killed the Turk.

The same evening the Tatars wheeled Balayev's corpse around on a cart, inciting their community and roaring, "Revenge against the Armenians!" Before long, the Islamic mob started firing right and left, killing Armenian passersby. The following day the Tatars' massive assault against Baku's Armenian neighborhoods took place.

For the Armenian revolutionaries, the Baku massacres were sudden and unexpected. Armed Armenian young men capable of combat were widely spread out. The tsarist police had blockaded roads to prevent outside help from reaching the Armenians in the city. Furthermore, the ARF ordnance was stockpiled in Tatar neighborhoods.

The ARF, astonished by the suddenness of the massacres, was unprepared to confront the disaster. The Party's Baku committee was content with sending a threatening message to Prefect Nakashidze, saying, "Protect the people! Or else you will be held personally responsible." When the mob, bent on massacre, saw that the Armenians were shut in their houses, they started burning their homes. Wealthy Lalayan's entire family died in the arson; similarly, the head of the Adamian family with his wife and son. The Armenian landlord, who was armed, shot a couple of dozen Tatar marauders from his balcony, but this was an exceptional act; for a day and a half the enemy carried out its bloody carnage largely unhindered.[6]

During those days, Nikol Duman, who resided in the Balakhani region of Baku's outskirts, and who was a foreman at Arshak Ghukasian's oil wells, received an alarming telegram from ARF Committee member Abraham Gulkhandanian, regarding the explosive situation in Baku.

Duman reached Baku the second day of the massacres and, as instructed by the Party, immediately got busy organizing the Baku Armenians' self-defense. The dauntless guerilla chief, taking along four armed men, succeeded in reaching the ordnance stockpile located on the edge of a Tatar neighborhood from where he fetched ten to twelve rifles. In addition, a few Armenian soldiers in the Russian army delivered guns and ammunition from the state barracks to Duman's men. This laid the foundation for the Armenian self-defense.[7]

On February 7, the Turk-Tatar mob rushed the Armenian neighborhoods, roaring "Orders from above: three full days to massacre and loot the Armenians without punishment!" Duman, with his small band, emerged from his hiding place and, with decisive strikes, halted the agitated mob's advance. Inspired by Duman's successes, many young Armenians gathered under the flag of the guerilla chief. Taking the initiative, Duman's experienced and bold fighters, with excellent aim, succeeded in mowing down many of the chaotic Tatar mob, spreading terror and panic among them. Soon the Armenian neighborhoods were cleared of Tatar marauders.[8]

Unable to penetrate the Armenian neighborhoods, the Tatars tried to vent their wrath on Armenians living in Tatar neighborhoods. Here also Duman performed miracles, extricating the majority of Armenian families from these areas.

In one incident, a man emerged, pale, panting, and terror-stricken, saying that his arson-stricken house was surrounded by Tatars, and that his children had ascended to the roof and would soon get burned. A band of armed Armenians rushed to help and, reaching the house, witnessed the terrible scene. The Armenian fighters' rifles thundered. The Turks started running and within a few minutes the neighborhood was deserted. The Armenian lads gathered their kinsmen in the neighborhood and relocated them to a safer part of town.[9]

The counter-strike organized by Nikol Duman was effective and astonishing. The enemy mob was retreating everywhere, gathering approximately a hundred of its dead and many more wounded. The Tatars raised the white flag and appealed for *bareshek* (reconciliation). The Armenians gladly responded to these appeals. During these clashes that lasted three days, the Armenian casualties were 205 dead and 121 wounded, and the Turkish casualties were

111 dead and 128 wounded.[10]

## GENERAL NAKASHIDZE'S ASSASSINATION

The Armenians suffered more casualties in the battle of Baku than they would have otherwise had, because Nikol Duman was able to reach Baku only the second day of the clashes and start the counter-strike.

It was evident to all that the one responsible for the atrocities and bloodshed in Baku was the city's military prefect, General Nakashidze. Baku's former mayor, Novikov, sent the following open letter to Nakashidze:

"All of Russia and the world were shaken, learning of the February 6 atrocities that took place in Baku . . . . Whoever recognizes the author is obliged to point him out publicly . . . . I recognize the culpable party and consider it my holy duty to name him. You are the author of the massacre . . . .

"You are worse than Cain—Cain only killed one brother, you dipped your hands in the blood of hundreds of innocent brothers.

"You are worse than Judas because Judas, after conspiring his terrible act, felt remorse and hanged himself, whereas you find it conceivable to live.

"You dishonored the fabulous Georgia, which considered you its offspring. You dishonored Russia. . . . May your name be forever scorned!"[11]

The ARF Voskanabad Central Committee decided to punish Nakashidze. The same decision regarding Nakashidze was made by Russia's Social Revolutionary Party, which struggled for the overthrow of the tsar's tyranny. After much delay, the Social Revolutionaries' assassination attempt was unsuccessful. The task was left to the ARF. Dro requested that he be entrusted with the mission, and the Central Committee vested Dro with implementation of the decision, having as assistant Kro of Gandzak.

It turned out that every day, at a certain time,

14

Nakashidze would go to his workplace by carriage, passing the Parapet Central Square. But the Central Committee of Baku hesitated trusting Dro with the death penalty, because Nakashidze's assassination was a major responsibility and an exceedingly dangerous task. The issue was resolved by Nikol Duman, hearing of Dro's entreaties and his pleas to have the task assigned to him. Duman finally conceded, exclaiming, "Alright, go! The Lord be with you." He convinced the other members of the Central Committee to assign the task to Dro. General oversight of the implementation of the death penalty was assumed by the Central Committee official, Abraham Gulkhandanian.

It was decided to use a grenade, although Dro would have preferred a revolver. It was said that the impression left by a grenade would be more shocking.

The grenade would be stored at a comrade's shop near Parapet Square. Assistant Kro would stand watch at the corner of the street leading to the square waiting for the carriage, while Dro would put the grenade in a bag of cherries, as if he were just walking on the sidewalk, eating. When the carriage approached the square, upon a signal from Kro, Dro would throw the grenade into the carriage.

The planned scenario, however, did not correspond to what actually occurred. At the predetermined hour Dro entered his comrade's shop, but Kro was not there. He waited; Kro did not come. He could not wait any longer. He put the pin on the grenade, placed the grenade in a paper bag, and came out. Kro was not at the street corner. Gulkhandanian appeared for an instant and then disappeared. Another complication was that Dro was suffering from dysentery. He was worried he might get abdominal cramps. He moved forward slowly, limping as if his leg was hurt and he had trouble walking. At the corner of the square was a Turkish fruit seller. He had placed a large basket of cherries on the sidewalk. Dro approached and tasted them. They were large and juicy. He told the Turk to weigh some cherries for him, while he ate a few. He glanced sideways furtively. Kro was not around.

"Suddenly, related Dro, from the top of the wide

15

boulevard was heard a loud whistle and crackle as the carriage appeared surrounded by mounted soldiers racing towards Parapet Square. It was Nakashidze. My heart pounded forcefully. The carriage got closer . . . . 'O Saint George of Putk,' I exclaimed, lunged from my spot and threw the grenade with force at the carriage . . . . A terrible explosion was heard. Smoke and dust rose. Moans and screams. People were running in every direction terrified. Taking advantage of the commotion, I too blended in the din and safely disappeared. For a moment I wanted to approach the destroyed carriage to check and see that the monster was killed, but I changed my mind. I did not find out just then what had happened . . . ."[12]

The inevitable took place on the afternoon of May 11, around 3:00 p.m. Nakashidze's crushed and bloodied corpse was thrown on the ground. The carriage was broken into two pieces. The Tatar coachman soon died of his severe injuries. The prefect's valet and the fruit seller who sold cherries to Dro also died.

Dro hid for a few days at a comrade's house, then went to Tbilisi, but he did not stay there long either. He passed on to Yerevan, where the city's self-defense in the context of the Armeno-Tatar war was assigned to *Dashnak* Khecho, pending the arrival of Nikol Duman.

During the period of the occupation of the Armenian Church estates by Tsar Nicholas II's edict and the Armeno-Tatar War, 1904–1905, many assassinations took place in the Caucasus. *Dashnak* assassins' vengeful bullets killed the man known as the Massacrer of Olti, Brigadier Brikov; the vice-prefect of Gandzag, Andreyev; provincial governors Boguslavski, Shmerlind, and Pavlov; the police chief Sakharov; and many others. However, none of these left as shocking an impression as the assassination of Nakashidze in broad daylight in a busy central square.

## BRIGADIER BRIKOV'S INHUMAN TREATMENT OF ARMENIAN FEDAYEEN

Some readers may wonder what the tsarist state officials had done to the Armenians to deserve the death penalty. As an example, I will briefly note the case of Brigadier Brikov, focusing on his actions more than a year prior to the assassination of Nakashidze.

During the night of July 15, 1904, a 61-member band of ARF fedayeen crossed the Russo-Turkish border to lend a hand to Sassun, which was in a crisis. A life-and-death struggle was in progress, with the Armenians under the command of fedayeen chieftain Andranik. He was said to be "like an eagle soaring" from one Sassun mountain to another against the Turkish army and thousands of Kurdish bandits.

It was the second uprising of Sassun. Why "uprising"? Because the knife had reached the bone—the government demanded taxes for the prior seven years from the poor peasants. Using that pretext, the Turkish army had surrounded the province of Sassun, and, with the help of thousands of Kurds who had assembled to massacre and loot, had resolved to destroy the "eagles' nests" of Sassun. . . . Thus, the people of Sassun had no choice but to die fighting, rather than be slaughtered like sheep.

The band of 61 ARF fedayeen included young intellectuals, two doctors, students, and Father Ghazar of Ghushjegh Village, a priest in his fifties. This cleric had ardently pleaded with Torkom (Tuman Tumiants) to accept him into the band also, saying, "I have vowed in my soul to go and sacrifice myself for the redemption of my nation."

After crossing the border by night and barely advancing a few kilometers, the fedayeen became engaged in fighting with Turkish soldiers. Receiving reinforcements, the enemy started pressing the Armenians, who continued to fight for half a day against at least 300 Turks, suffering only two wounded.

Suddenly, in the most heated period of the battle, the Armenians were showered with bullets from behind. They came from Russian Cossacks, who were attacking the Armenians mercilessly. Trapped by the fire of enemy units from the front and the back, the Armenians had more than ten casualties within a half hour. The whole band was in danger of being annihilated. Surrounded on all sides, there was no escape route left.

The Armenians naïvely assumed that the Russian forces were mistakenly subjecting them to friendly fire. A sergeant in the band, Levon Kalantarian, went to the Russians to explain their goal of rushing aid to Sassun. The Russians arrested the delegate and continued firing at the Armenians.

A second delegate, Russian army officer Anushavan Dilanian, presented himself to the Russian commander and tried to explain:

"We are not against the Russians; as you saw, we did not aim a single bullet at you; our struggle is only against the Turks; thus, we request that you cease fire."

The Russian officer responded, "You are revolutionaries and bandits and we will mercilessly massacre you all."[13]

The Turks, emboldened by the Russians' favorable position, began to press the Armenians further. Father Ghazar, displaying a piece of white fabric and holding aloft his cross, headed toward the Russians.

The "Christians' " bullets, however, felled both the priest and the cross; the poor cleric was the recipient of contempt, insults, and curses.

The fedayeen's dead soon numbered twenty-seven, plus six wounded. The Russians nabbed fourteen, in addition to those sent to negotiate. Twelve fedayeen succeeded in finding refuge in nearby forests.

The band that was formed in response to Hrair-*Dzhoghk's* appeals and had rushed to the aid of Sassun was cruelly decimated. This was only the first act of the tragedy. The second was soon to begin.

The commander of the Russian border guards in the Olti region, Brigadier Brikov, ordered the Cossacks to dispatch with their swords the six wounded first, and then the fourteen prisoners. The order was carried out.

Most disturbing, however, was that the slaying of the Armenian wounded and prisoners was carried out in the presence of Turkish officers who had come to witness the heart-rending execution at the invitation of Brigadier Brikov.[14]

After hearing the story, our esteemed readers can understand why Dro and his comrades most readily expressed a willingness to slay the "Godly" tsar's functionaries—governors, prefects, generals, etc.


## BRIKOV IS SENTENCED TO DEATH

The ARF Kars Central Committee sentenced Brigadier Brikov to death. To carry out the just assassination, there was no dearth of self-sacrificing fighters in the revolutionary organization; however, a non-partisan young man named Hamo Djanpolatian, who, previously had neither carried out assassinations nor revolutionary activities, nominated himself for the role. Until then this nineteen-year-old, scion of wealthy parents, well dressed and with a groomed, newly grown mustache, was wasting his father's money in the company of girls.

Hamo had pleaded for months to the Kars Committee to be sent to the homeland to fight and sacrifice himself for the liberation of his Turkish-Armenian brothers and sisters. But his supplications were to no avail, because the Central Committee doubted him due to his inexperience.

Around that time, on behalf of Tbilisi's ARF Eastern Bureau, Sako of Sevkar came to Kars to arrange the assassination of Brikov.

Hearing about Sako of Sevkar, Hamo rushed to him, begging and pleading to be entrusted with the duty of carrying out Brikov's assassination.

Sako instinctively understood that this budding young man was sincere in his wish, and so, as fully authorized by the Bureau, decided to assign the task to him despite his youth and inexperience.

Hamo Djanpolatian, with expertise unexpected from him, explored and examined Brikov's movements in terms of time and place.

The very evening of the massacre, Brikov, self-confident and with calm conscience, had drunk cognac with his assistants and Turkish officers and got inebriated. To take the revelry to its peak, Brikov had collected the corpses of the fedayeen fallen on Russian soil and was photographed standing behind them with Turkish officers, so as to send historic photos of his "heroism" to Kars, Tbilisi, and Petersburg.

Before long, Brikov began to realize that Armenian fedayeen could be vengeful. Thus, he limited his promenades to nearby places only and did not venture far from his workplace and home and the nearby club, which he frequented to play cards or to drink. He instituted strict surveillance of all roads leading to that small area.

But Hamo, proving shrewder, thwarted the sentries' wary surveillance. Wearing a wretched painter's clothes, he started circulating house to house looking for work, "pitiful in appearance, his hair disheveled, his face unwashed. His hat, jacket, pants and shoes worn out, patched up, stained with paint and soot."[15]

This ruse allowed "painter" Hamo to verify the hours when Brikov would leave his house heading to the club. And thus one evening, on the way to the club, Hamo shot the Brigadier with a hunting rifle. The bullet met its target directly and Brikov fell lifeless to the ground. Hamo did not flee. Instead, he ran to the corpse, put a few more bullets into its chest with his revolver, and then fled to the nearby woods.

Soldiers, guards, gendarmes, all were in a frenzy, but failed to find any trace of the assassin.

The ferocious brigadier was killed on August 31, 1904, precisely one-and-a-half months after the massacre of the fedayeen.[16]

## ARF'S APPEAL TO THE ARMENIAN PEOPLE
## AND THE ULTIMATUM TO THE RUSSIAN
## STATE OFFICIALDOM

On May 11, 1905, the day of Nakashidze's assassination by Dro, the ARF Voskanabad Central Committee addressed the following appeal to the Armenian people:

"The bomb spoke.

"It was the thunderous voice of the enraged Armenian people's revenge. The monster that drained our heart's blood is a pitiful corpse now. Let the souls of our loved ones martyred on February 6–9 rest in peace now.

"The bomb has many more judgments yet. Woe to those who will prey on the Armenian people from now on.

"Down with tyranny!

"Long live the fraternity of the peoples of the Caucasus!

"Long live the free Federation government.

"May 11,1905" [17]

The following day, May 12, the Central Committee addressed the following appeal to the community:

"Citizens, on Wednesday May 11, at 3:00 PM, on Parapet Square in the center of the city, the governor of Baku, Prince Nakashidze, was subjected to the death penalty.

"The Armenian Revolutionary Federation had condemned him to death as the author and planner of the February 6–9 bloody days. This sentence was conveyed to the condemned at the time. This sentence was also delivered by the other revolutionary organizations active in Baku, without distinction of ideology and party. The sentence was carried out by the Federation, which in this case is the preponderant claimant of the communal revenge.

"Let the punishment suffered by Prince Nakashidze

21

confuse no one. That is a just payment for a heinous crime—to pit neighbor against neighbor and to organize massive carnage, with the aim of terrorizing the peaceful people. Prince Nakashidze was a murderer and traitor. He betrayed the city entrusted to his security to bandits and plunderers, and put lethal weapons in the hands of murderers. The convict Nakashidze was obliged to conclude his nefarious life with an ignoble death. That was demanded by the communal disturbed conscience, and the ARF expressed that.

"We invite you, citizens, to peace and tranquility. Don't lose your calm. Prince Nakashidze was punished as a criminal whose brow was already branded with communal contempt and who was condemned by public judgment.

"Let not the bomb that exploded on Parapet inspire you with fear about tomorrow. That bomb was directed against a rascal, who was sowing hatred and discord in the populace, who was your and our enemy, who slaughtered your offspring, fathers, mothers, brothers and sisters."[18]

The ARF newspaper *Droshak* (Flag) headlined in Geneva:

"By the decree of the ARF Caucasus Bureau's Central Committee, the Governor of Baku, Prince Nakashidze, the main author of the February massacre, was assassinated with a bomb on May 11. The Governor was killed on the spot. The assassin is free."[19]

Simultaneously, the ARF's Caucasus Bureau issued the following decree-warning to the populace and Caucasus officialdom:

"To the Caucasus Administration of the Russian Government:

"The Armenian Revolutionary Federation herewith declares to all policemen, chiefs of police, prefects, gendarmes and detectives, that from now on each one of them will be annihilated ruthlessly if they dare to confiscate arms from the Armenians, conduct investigations, or imprison them for that purpose. Before embarking on such action, let each one of them remember the Baku Governor Nakashidze, the Gandzak Vice-Governor Andreyev; the prefects Boguslavski, Shmerling and Pavlov; the chief of police Sahakov; officers Nashchanski, Djavakhov, Shumakevish, and Ter-Sahakov; policeman Serko; doorkeeper Sheko; and many others who, by the ARF's judgment, were sentenced to death. A gift of twenty-five rubles by the viceroy or the revolutionary's bullet—that is your choice. The viceroy promises to compensate the families of those who became casualties this way. That lightens our work because only the helpless condition of the innocent families of the executed could have weakened the resolve of the revolutionary's arm; now that obstacle is also removed.

ARF's Caucasus Bureau Central Committee."[20]


## ARMENO-TATAR WAR

In early February 1905, after the three-day battles in Baku, reconciliation had taken place between the Armenians and the Azeris.

Reconciliation, however, was merely a cease-fire for the Azeris thirsting for Armenian blood.

Nikol Duman did not trust the Tatars' sincerity. He knew that the tsarist government would start similar fires in other regions. To confront the coming blows, the ARF fielded its most famous fedayeen and captains, and instructed them to congregate in Yerevan.[21]

The Armeno-Tatar war, altogether eight battles— Baku, Nakhidjevan, Yerevan, Zangezur, Karabagh (Shushi and Askeran), Gandzak and Tbilisi—all concluded with Armenian victories, described in my book titled *Revolutionary Figures,* in Chapter Seven. Duman sent those fighters and captains with many years' experience in pairs to different regions, to organize the local self-defense.

Here I will address only Dro's role in the heroic battles of the Armeno-Tatar war that lasted a year and a half, including the fighting in Baku.

23

## DRO, THE FUGITIVE

After the killing of Nakashidze, Dro hid a few days at a friend's house, where he suffered from cramps due to dysentery. A few times a day Dr. Ter-Tovmasian visited him, but he did not see any benefit from the doctor's treatment.[22]

The police were looking for Nakashidze's assassin everywhere. To remain in Baku was dangerous for Dro. The Central Committee decided that he should be transferred elsewhere immediately.

Dro did not intend to leave Baku. The labor organizations of the oilfields were pregnant with revolutionary ferment against the tsar. Dro wanted to take part in the pan-Russian general revolution. He was excited by Russian terrorists killing Russian state officials, particularly by the heroic actions of Kalyayev. In the face of the persistence of the Central Committee, Dro agreed to depart for Tbilisi, with Kro of Gandzak, who had not been at the assigned place when Nakashidze was assassinated. The Central Committee wanted to punish Kro, but the Committee yielded and Dro went on to Tbilisi with Kro.[23]

In Tbilisi Dro reported to the Bureau's Deputy Dr. Ter-Davidian and Director of Ordnance Sargis Manassian, who presented him with a new Mauser revolver on behalf of the Party.[24] After staying in Tbilisi for a few days, Dro went on to Yerevan where he was welcomed with great joy by *Dashnak* Khecho.

Yerevan's Turks (Azeris) had attacked the Armenians unexpectedly and killed twenty to twenty-five people. The city's Central Committee, lacking sufficient arms, had panicked and instructed Khecho to be wary and avoid fighting.

The Central Committee's prudent policy, however, would embolden the Turks. Dro consulted with Khecho and Mkrdich; the outcome was their firing at the Turks from two directions and delivering a stunning counter-strike to them.

Soon, Nikol Duman arrived in Yerevan. Dro requested from Duman to be allowed to stay in Yerevan and conduct operations under his command, but Duman declined and sent Dro to Kodaïk to organize the self-defense of the region. Dro was not pleased, but could not do anything about it. He conceded.[25]

In late August, Duman called Dro to a meeting and revealed that the latter was now assigned to be the captain of a better trained and more seasoned band of guerillas, and was to be sent to Nakhidjevan to organize self-defense.

Before moving on to Nakhidjevan, Dro went to Igdir. He stayed with his parents for a few days, visited family and friends and, of course, his beloved. He and his friends were successful in putting out the old clannish Avagian-Kanayan feud and effecting a reconciliation. Dro was already a hero for the people of Igdir and it was an honor for the Avagians to have a hero as their bridegroom. Dro's father was also noticeably changed and inclined to reconcile. Dro left his hometown, having decided to form a family with the Avagians' daughter.[26]

Dro, with his band, went through Daralagiaz to mountainous Nakhidjevan, and chose as his headquarters Nors Village. The condition of the Nakhidjevan Armenians was very poor. The majority of Armenian villages were looted and their dwellings ruined. Although the villagers had returned to their half-destroyed homes, eking out a living had become harder.[27]

The Turks tried to occupy Nors. The Armenians displayed a fierce resistance, and then Dro's band, with a forceful assault, pushed back the enemy forces. The villagers pillaged the Turks' spoils.

The brilliant victory at Nors, which was Dro's bands' baptism of fire, greatly increased the hero's authority.

After the Nors battle, *Dashnak* Khecho, Kolod Sargis (Odabashian), and *Keri* came to see Dro. Duman had assigned *Keri* as general commander for the regions of Daralagiaz, mountainous Nakhidjevan, and Zangezur. Dro immediately agreed to serve under *Keri's* command and transferred authority to him promptly. For a whole year after that, Dro and his band served under *Keri's* command.

They engaged in many battles and the enemy, exhausted, was forced to seek a truce.[28]

Taking advantage of a brief period of peace, Dro returned to Igdir, his hometown, and married his beloved blonde and blue-eyed Nvart Avagian. As noted earlier, the Kanayans and Avagians were Igdir's two rich but feuding families. With this wedding the long-standing enmity between the two families came to an end.

Following the wedding ceremony the reception was barely finished when Dro received a letter and instructions from Duman to return immediately to the front, which he did, leaving his bride with his parents.

From this marriage Dro had a son, Liutik (Ludwig). After the birth of her firstborn, Nvart contracted tuberculosis and died.[29]


## ALIKHANOV'S ASSASSINATION

When Dro was in Zangezur, echoes of revolutionary storms in Russia were reaching the Zangezur revolutionaries—Dro, Martiros Charukhjian, Brikov's assassin Hamo Djanpolatian, and others. Dro especially thought that he was wasting time fighting the Tatars of Nakhidjevan and Zangezur. He dreamed of throwing himself into the Russian revolutionary tempests in order to continue the work of the bold assassins Sazanov and Kalyayev. He repeatedly tried to convince Duman to release him, but his commander remained unmoved and did not let him go until the Armeno-Tatar War was over.[30]

This time the ARF decided to assassinate the Russian army General Alikhanov Avarski, a Tatar from Nakhidjevan. He was entrusted with the repression of peasant movements in the Guria region of Georgia. With brutal measures and causing many deaths, he had submerged in blood the peasants in the region. The Georgians tried to assassinate him but failed. Consequently he was very wary and well protected.

Alikhanov was also the organizer of the Nakhidjevan Tatars' anti-Armenian assaults. The task of "punishing" Alikhanov was entrusted to Dro and his dear friend, Martiros Charukhjian.

Alikhanov had settled in Alexandropol, as commander of the city's garrison.

The poet Avetik Isahakian also lived in Alexandropol; he was a member of the region's ARF Central Committee. Dro and Martiros arrived at the poet's residence. When Isahakian saw the Armenian assassins, he was tongue-tied.

" 'What do you want from me? Why did you come here?' he asked when we entered the room.

"We delivered to him the letter with the red seal of the Voskanabad Central Committee, which instructed him to provide us with every assistance, and related the purpose of our arrival in Alexandropol.

"Avo exclaimed, terrified, 'I cannot do anything for you — get out of here —quickly!' "[31]

When they left, Martiros said to Dro, "I knew Avo was timid."

It was late in the evening. They stood a moment on the sidewalk. Where to go? They could attract the attention of the police.

Suddenly they encountered a young man with his shirt loosened, singing a song, apparently a little inebriated. Dro recognized him. He had been expelled from the Party.

The drunkard halted, confused, silent for a moment, approached, and . . . smiled.

"Yo!  I would die for you. . . . Is that you? It's me . . . my dear; what are you doing here?"

Dro explained, "We are going on a pilgrimage to Ani, we don't have a place to spend the night. . . ."

"Yo! My dears, here is my home; be our guests."

In any event, they had no other option. They picked up their luggage and followed him.

When they entered his house, the "Ani pilgrims" were received by the older brother—Mikidan, a married father of children, a liquor merchant, and a joyful, gregarious man.

The Gumri (Alexandropol) native's feast was laid out on the table. The *raki* bottle and glasses were set, and soon they were engaged in conversation.

It turned out that the two brothers were staunch Dashnakists, but had been expelled from the ranks because of their undisciplined lifestyle. Mikidan did not know any other life. The tavern was his club.

For a time the "Ani pilgrims" worried that they were not in the right place and might jeopardize their mission, especially since the younger brother kept emptying glasses to the health of the "Ani pilgrims."

The older brother, guessing the guests' state of mind, sought to dispel their doubts.

Close to midnight there was a commotion outside. People were running fast; whistles, din. The younger brother ran outside.

Martiros jumped from his place and suggested to Dro that they leave.

The older brother became emotional; his wife started to cry. The younger brother came back.

"Leave? Impossible! The streets are filled with policemen. Don't be afraid. Over our dead bodies can the policemen enter."

They stayed, under the brothers' watch.

Early the following morning, Dro and Martiros wanted to leave, but the brothers would not let them. Maybe they understood the identity of their guests. . . .

First, their hosts went outside to assess the situation.

Before long, the older brother returned and related that an incident had taken place during the night and the police were still on the streets.

Dro and Martiros agreed to stay, and instructed the two brothers to conduct certain investigations in the city. They headed out happily.

Martiros, angrily, "What if they betray us; if we are arrested, how will we face Duman?"

Dro chuckled at Martiros's anxieties.

After noon, the brothers returned, merrily relaying

28

their findings to their guests. The previous night's incident involved the police pursuing robbers who disappeared, defending themselves with their revolvers. General Alikhanov, extremely wary, suspecting a conspiracy against him, had placed troops on the streets.

Now the streets were cleared, and the police had returned to their homes. The police that frequented the tavern had said that Alikhanov was preparing to go to Kars.

Dro and Martiros sat down for lunch—full glasses and toasts followed. After lunch, they left a basket full of apples with their hosts and stepped out for some fresh air...

Separating from each other, the two "pilgrims" took different routes and toured the city's neighborhoods, including the barracks region. They investigated the roads Alikhanov would take and gathered information in taverns.

Heeding their experience with the poet Avo, they did not approach any friends. By chance Dro encountered the pedagogue director Rashmajian, who worked at the Armenian school. Rashmajian took him home and wanted him to stay there. The director was an unassuming, well-liked man, and a party member. Dro remembered him with admiration.

Before long Martiros arrived. It was revealed that Alikhanov would soon leave for Kars. They had to hurry.

After a brief consultation, they decided to get busy forthwith. Martiros insisted that it was his turn and this time he would throw the bomb at the carriage, to which Dro agreed. After the bombing they intended to add to the chaos by firing their revolvers, hoping to lose their tracks in the commotion.

They went to the brothers' house, fetched their apples, and, after saying goodbye, left.

Alikhanov's carriage appeared, surrounded by soldiers. The General was sitting in the carriage and looking around with searching eyes.

Suddenly, Martiros darted from the shadows and, saying, "Take this!" flung the bomb at Alikhanov's head. A horrific explosion. The carriage and everyone inside were torn apart. Dro's Mauser pistol thundered. Taking advantage of the general commotion, the assassins disappeared.[32]

By coincidence Dro landed at Rashmajian's house. After a brief rest he prepared to leave, to avoid endangering the family with several children. Rashmajian stood by the door and blocked his way.

Dro pleaded that he had a secure place to go to but his host remained unmoved.

Dro spent the night at Rashmajian's house. The following day local comrades spirited him safely out of the city. Martiros had already departed from Alexandropol.

The assassination of Alikhanov left a stunning impression in the Caucasus, and confusion in government circles. Everyone thought it was the work of the Georgians as revenge for the massacre of Guria's peasants. Georgians were arrested in Alexandropol, and those employed at train stations were led to jail. The Georgians did not deny their alleged complicity and even boasted that they had avenged Guria.

Of course, eventually the truth was revealed that General Alikhanov's assassination was the work of ARF warriors. Even the names of the assassins were revealed— Martiros and Dro.[33]


## ON A MYSTERIOUS MISSION

With Alikhanov's assassination began the persecution of the Armenian Revolutionary Federation, and as a result many members were led to prison.

Luckily the Young Turk overthrow of the Ottoman government took place next, in the year 1908. Many revolutionaries crossed to the Turkish side of the border or went south to Persia, where an armed struggle against the tyranny of the Shah had begun.

Dro's close friend, Martiros Charukhjian, went to Persia with Duman and Rostom and was martyred during a battle.[34]

30

Dro went from Alexandropol to Baku, where an ARF conference was held in the summer of 1908. Those of the Party's dignitaries who remained free also had arrived in Baku. Simon Vratsian had come to the conference as the delegate of the students in St. Petersburg. After the conference, when the cabinet was busy formulating statements and manifestos, the police arrived to conduct a search. Holding the pile of documents, Vratsian fled. His comrades got him in a carriage and delivered him safely to Dr. Zavrian at the hospital. The doctor introduced him to a young man, Dro, who turned out to be "Seth's wife's brother."[35]

Vratsian recalled that toward the end of 1905, when he was in Yerevan, his compatriot Seth Harutiunian, Gevorkian Academy's Armenian language teacher, had married the sister of a young man named Dro. Vratsian often visited Seth at his home. One Sunday, at dinner time, a boisterous young man laden with packages arrived, played with his sister's children, got satiated going in and out of the kitchen before dinner and, without paying attention to or conversing with anyone, or sitting at the dinner table, left. Vratsian later found out that the young man was Seth Harutiunian's wife's brother, Dro.[36]

The meeting at the Baku hospital led to a closeness between Vratsian and Dro that was to last until the end.

Vratsian learned from Dr. Zavrian that the young man was General Nakashidze's assassin.

Vratsian took refuge in the hospital for a few days. He would meet with Dro every day and the two would dine with the doctor.

By the Party's instructions, Vratsian had to move to Yerevan, where there was a need for activist cadres. On his way there he visited Tbilisi, where the Party was in an acute crisis and it was difficult to assemble even a few young men.

Vratsian was headed to the train station to go to Yerevan, when he ran into Dro at the Vorontsov Bridge.

"You're here?"

"Yes, here."

"Where to?"

"Yerevan."

"Me too. Yerevan. Let's go together. Do you have cash with you?"

Vratsian had ten rubles with him and the train ticket.

Dro also had a train ticket, but his pockets were empty.

"Since you have money, let's go eat."[37]

They entered a restaurant by the riverside. They had barely settled when the waiters, who knew him, rushed to Dro. Soon the table was filled with food and drink.

After the meal, when they paid the bill, a few kopeks were left from Vratsian's ten rubles. A few more kopeks were found in Dro's pockets. Vratsian took charge of all of it, so they would not go hungry on their way.

They began their journey. Vratsian wanted to know Dro's aim in going to Yerevan. He was going as a Party organizer; what did Dro have to do in Yerevan? Dro joked around or was evasive in response to each of Vratsian's queries.

They finally arrived in Yerevan, both of them broke.

"Let's go to Amirov's," suggested Dro.

Gevorg Amirov, a young merchant, was a renowned figure in Yerevan and a friend of the ARF. At his place they could rest, eat a meal or get a loan.

When they got there, they found the store closed and all the windows in the building shuttered. Not a sign of life.

A little beyond was the house of Ardush Avedov, also an ARF friend.

" 'Let's go to Ardush's,' suggested Dro.

"They went. Once, twice, three times they rang the doorbell. The sleepy servant opened the door.

" 'The master is not at home!' he declared with contempt.

" 'Where is the master?'

" 'How would I know? . . . Could be playing cards at the club, having a drink at the café . . . . Who knows what

32

the master is up to?'

"Ardush was not at the club playing cards. They found him at the Zanta Brewery. He was having a drink.

"Ardush was Dro's close friend. He welcomed them with open arms.

"He set up a feast right by the Zankou riverside. He played the host, fed them, and told them amusing stories. He and Dro exchanged a few words discreetly. A little later, 'our lads' appeared, a few young adolescents, with Vacho's leadership.

"Dro briefly met with them in private. Then Vacho remained with them; the others left.

"When the feast was winding down, Ardush asked Dro, 'Do you need any money?'

"Of course they did. He pulled a twenty-five-ruble bill from his pocket and gave it to Vratsian.

" 'Do not give it to Dro,' he joked, 'or else nothing will be left tomorrow.'

"Their residence was reserved at Vacho's."[38]

Vacho (Vachakan Melikian) was a young member of the ARF, a scion of a loyal Dashnak family. With his brother and sister he continued the work of more senior imprisoned comrades. He was a member of a martial team. Later he was incarcerated and died in prison.

Dro and Vratsian settled down at Vachakan's home. Vratsian commenced his organizational work. Dro frequently vanished without saying where he was going. At home, he and Vacho seemed engaged in some secretive planning. Vacho's older brother, who had an independent streak, would mock their "secretive whispers. . . ."

One day, Dro said he was going to Igdir to visit his parents.

Vratsian later heard that Dro, rather than going to Igdir, had immediately returned to Yerevan. A few days later the following shocking news was received from Yerevan:

In broad daylight, in the city center in front of the Shahnazarov pharmacy, Ter Sahakov, the chief of police, was felled on the sidewalk. No trace of the assassin was found.

The death sentences of Ter Sahakov, and, before him, the Gendarmerie Colonel Burgatski, carried out by ARF assassins were received with enthusiasm and satisfaction by the Armenians of the Ararat Plain. The people's hatred toward the Armenophobe tsarist functionaries had mounted, especially against Ter Sahakov, who had become the loyal dog of Governor Tizenhauzen, and who had declared that with his efforts, there were no revolutionaries left in Yerevan.[39]

## OIL MERCHANT

Dro secretly crossed the Russian-Turkish border and settled in Old Payazit. With the assistance of his father and his friends, he undertook the wholesale trade of petrol, sugar, and cattle. Using the name Suren Effendi, he soon became a famous merchant and established branches of his business all the way to Van and Karin. Around him gathered fugitive revolutionaries from the Caucasus and Siberia as managers, such as Vahan Minakhorian and others. He was involved also in smuggling weapons to the homeland.

He became renowned and established friendly ties with Kurdish tribes, Turkish officials, and military officers. He captured their hearts with his sweet personality and especially his generous hospitality. His home and heart were open to all.

In becoming a renowned merchant he did not forget his partisan and revolutionary duties. He was in contact with Aram and Ishkhan in Van, with Rostom and Dr. J. Ter-Davidian in Erzrum; and he, himself, was director of arms transport.

Dro was in contact with Russian revolutionaries. He assisted the Socialist Revolutionaries by transporting literature to Russia.

In 1910–1911, when Vratsian was a teacher in Karin and the editor of *Haradj* (Forward) they frequently received bundles of Russian books and letters from Dro. His letters were nearly illegible. Vratsian would assist Rostom in deciphering them and Rostom sometimes would say with a smirk, "Let's telegraph Dro, to come and read his letter in person."

Dr. Ter-Davidian would object, "It's useless. Even he could not read his writing . . . ."

As a rich merchant and a modest and friendly man, Dro's influence and charm was great among the region's Armenian and Kurdish peoples. The Armenian peasants particularly adored "Comrade Dro." He spared neither effort nor means to promote Armenian books and to encourage cultural enterprises.

Actor Hovannes Zarifian related that he organized the first Armenian play in Old Payazit, at Dro's house and with the host's material and moral support. He said, "Dro should be considered the founder of Old Payazit's Armenian theater. . . ."

Besides educational and cultural enterprises, Dro's foremost work outside of his commerce was the transport of armaments and arming of the people.

("Arming the people." In this point of character and political belief, how close was Dro to Andranik! The Great Hero's heart would bleed if he went to a village and saw that the youth were unfamiliar with arms and martial training.)

During the Armeno-Tatar war, the ARF's Caucasus warehouses had stored large quantities of arms and ammunition, which were not needed now and could be confiscated by the tsarist government. The ARF decided to transport these arms and armaments to Western Armenia by various routes. One of the routes was the Surmalou-Payazit road under Dro's watch. Dro had established various stations and representatives; and the transport of arms and armaments toward Vaspurakan, Daron-Duruberan, and Upper Haik took place from station to station.

This network for arms smuggling was Dro's enterprise, and the intrepid warrior periodically would send reports to Karin, the Armenia Bureau section, through

Rostom. His revolutionary enterprise was highly appreciated by Rostom.

Rostom instinctively appraised individuals at first glance. Every man was important for him if he was capable of accomplishing a given task. But there were individuals toward whom he had love and affection. Among them were *Keri,* Dr. Ter-Davidian, Hunan Davitian, Aram, Armen Karo, Dro, and others. Rostom had unlimited love and trust toward Dro.[40]

# NOTES

1. Simon Vratsian, *Along Life's Pathways: Events, Personalities, Experiences,* Vol 4, Beirut, 1965, p 122.
2. Ibid, pp 125–126.
3. Ibid, p 126.
4. Ibid, p 127.
5. Ibid, pp 127–129.
6. Michael Varandian, *A. R. Federation History,* Vol 1, Paris, 1932, pp 362–363.
7. Ibid, pp 364–365.
8. Ibid, pp 365–366.
9. Ibid, p 366.
10. Ibid, p 367.
11. Ibid, p 368.
12. Vratsian, *Along Life's Pathways,* Vol 4, p 134.
13. *Hairenik* (Homeland) Monthly, July 1959, #7, p 75.
14. Ibid, p 76.
15. Ibid, p 78.
16. Ibid, p 78.
17. Vratsian, *Along Life's Pathways,* Vol 4, pp 134–135.
18. Ibid, pp 135–136.
19. Ibid, p 136.
20. Ibid, p 136.
21. Andranik Chalabian, *Revolutionary Figures,* Ch 7, pp 371–431 (re Nikol Duman).
22. Vratsian, *Along Life's Pathways,* Vol 4, p 137.
23. Ibid, p 137.
24. Ibid, p 137.
25. Ibid, p 140.
26. Ibid, pp 141–142.
27. Ibid, p 142.
28. Ibid, pp 143–144.
29. Ibid, pp 144–147.
30. Ibid, pp 148–149.
31. Ibid, pp 149–151.
32. Ibid, pp 151–155.

33. Ibid, pp 155–156.
34. Ibid, p 157.
35. Ibid, p 158.
36. Ibid, p 157.
37. Ibid, p 158.
38. Ibid, pp 158–160
39. Ibid, pp 160–161.
40. Ibid, pp 161–163.

# CHAPTER II

## DRO PLAYS AN ACTIVE ROLE IN ARMENIAN LIFE AS MILITARY COMMANDER

Dro, commander of the Second Regiment

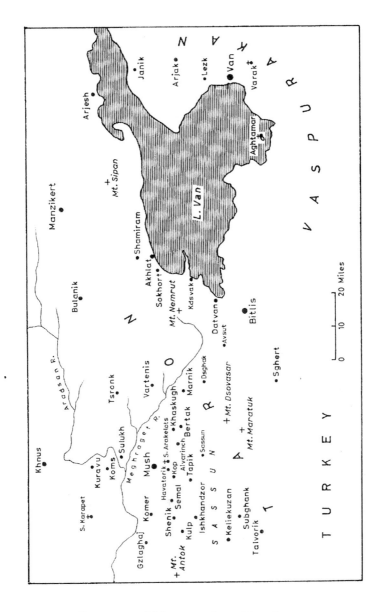

Taron and Vaspurakan Provinces

41

## THE FIRST WORLD WAR AND THE ARMENIAN VOLUNTEER MOVEMENT

On July 28, 1914, the First World War began with explosive fury. Andranik, who was living in Varna, Bulgaria, immediately sent word to Istanbul that all the intellectuals and revolutionaries leave the city and escape![1] The Istanbul prosperous elite did not listen to Andranik. "[L]ionesque men were led like sheep to the slaughterhouse" would write the hero later in his memoirs published in *Hairenik* (Homeland) magazine.[2]

A few days after the war had begun, Andranik himself boarded the last Russian ship, leaving Varna for Odessa, and on August 12, reached Tbilisi via Yalta.

It was August 1914. Europe was already at war. The majority of ARF's 8th General Assembly delegates had left Karin. The remainder, led by Rostom and Vramian, were negotiating with *Ittihad* (the ruling Young Turk organization) representatives, Nacci Bey and Behaeddin Shakir, who before long would be the organizers of the massacres of the Armenians.

Dark news was emerging from the Armenian provinces that Turkey would plunge into the war, which could have dire consequences for the Armenian people.

For Old Bayazid's oil merchant, Suren Efendi, the danger was obvious, because he could see that his friends among district officials and officers were looking at him with suspicion and distrust. He noticed also that his every move was being monitored covertly. A Turkish officer who owed him a big favor, as he had rescued this man's wife from certain death, had informed Dro that a secret telegram had been received from Istanbul ordering Dro's strict surveillance, of course with the goal of arresting him later. The officer had advised him to look out for himself.

Foreseeing such danger, Dro had already transferred his family to the Caucasus.

Dro immediately sent word to his Kurdish friends in Chingli to wait for him on the Payazit-Chingli road.

The next morning, as usual, Dro mounted his horse

and left his house. As he passed by the government building and the barracks, the officials and officers stood and greeted him without animosity. They joked around, and Dro humored them that upon his return he would take them out to breakfast.

Dro quietly slipped out of the city. He looked around. He did not see anyone following. He descended the valley. It was deserted. Nature was joyful, but an uncertain ache was gnawing at his chest, as if he were taking part in a funeral.

It was not the material loss that was hurting him: not his earnings of years, his warehouses full of supplies, his flocks of animals, large sums of accounts receivables from merchants, his estate, and substantial family wealth. After riding some distance away from the city and casting a sharp glance all around, he spurred his horse and dashed forward. Near a spring, the Kurds were waiting for him with bread and barbecue.

After a brief rest, Dro continued on his way surrounded by Kurds. They reached the Bartoghian highlands and the Gailadua Lake, a place which was inaccessible to the conspiring Turk. Before long, Dro reached Igdir, surrounded by kin.


## THE ORGANIZATION OF VOLUNTEER REGIMENTS

Dro did not stay long in Igdir. He hurried to Tbilisi, where the Armenian volunteer movement was in a preparatory stage. The Armenian National Bureau, which was formed for the pursuit of the Armenian Cause as Boghos Noubar's assistant body, was now in negotiations with the viceroy of the Caucasus and the military general staff. Andranik and Hamazasb were already in Tbilisi, while *Keri* would arrive from Persia. They were awaiting Sebouh and Vartan. Dro joined the group.

Simon Vratsian also arrived in Tbilisi and reported on the resolutions adopted at the ARF General Assembly that took place in Erzrum.

Dro asked about Rostom's opinion on the Armenian

volunteer movement. Vratsian responded that Rostom was against the Armenian volunteer movement.

Dro was silent for a moment and then said, in Russian:

"*Bez durakov, di chdo dumayesh*"—without foolishness, what do you think?

"I am against forming Caucasian volunteer regiments. They will exploit and then abandon us . . . ," replied Vratsian.

"You don't understand anything," Dro said angrily. "It is already decided that by the New Year we will be in Erzrum."

What was Andranik's position regarding the Armenian volunteer movement?

"Andranik thought that Russia, which had mobilized 20 million soldiers, did not have the capacity to train all its soldiers and consequently did not need a few thousand Armenian volunteers. Besides, the volunteer movement could serve as a pretext for the Turks to massacre the Armenians. Nevertheless, when the National Bureau decided to organize Armenian volunteer brigades, Andranik accommodated."[3]

The volunteer regiments were formed. Andranik assumed the command of the First Regiment, and Dro the Second.

On the occasion of Dro's going to the front, a dinner was held at the Anona Restaurant. Those present included Hovannes Tumanian, Khachik Garjikian, Dr. Hakob Zavriev, Nikol Aghbalian, and Hovsep Arghutian. The latter, citing Nerses Ashdaraketsi as an example, gave a very Russophilic speech.

"As the last to speak, Dro said, 'I am a soldier. I do not understand politics.'

"Continuing in Russian, he said, 'This will be the last and decisive battle . . . either freedom or death. . . . I also feel that who knows how many of us will not return from the battlefield. . . . Big enterprises demand big sacrifices. . .

. Guys, until I see you again. . . .'

"Everyone was stirred. Toumanian stood up, his handsome head up on his long neck, and replied 'Dear Dro, this is your Armenian nation speaking through you . . . . God bless you, you spoke so well. Big enterprises demand big sacrifices. . . . Let me kiss your hero's brow. . . .'

"And he kissed him.

"The next evening Dro departed to Yerevan to assume command of his regiment."[4]

— — — —

On October 21, 1914, the Russo-Turkish war began. We have gathered the following statistics from different sources about the Armenian volunteer regiments:

—In the initial phase (the fall of 1914) there were 3,082 volunteers. By the fall of 1915, this number rose to 5,000.[5]

—A Regiment, 1200 troops under the command of Andranik, went to the Turkish-Persian border, on November 3, 1914.

—B Regiment, 500 troops under the command of Dro, went toward Igdir, on October 24, 1914.

—C Regiment, 500 troops under the command of Hamazasp, set out toward Sareghamish, on November 1, 1914.

—D Regiment, 500 troops under the command of *Keri* of Karin, set out toward Karin, on November 6, 1914.[6]

—E Regiment, under the command of Vartan, set out toward Van.

—F Regiment, under the command of Krikor Avsharian, headed toward the Bassen plain.

—G Regiment, under the command of Ishkhan Arghutian, as a reserve force, set out toward Van.[7]

"Along the entire front, from Olti to Salmast, the four Armenian regiments were arranged as vanguards. Dro was on the Van frontline. According to Vratsian, his regiment comprised of around 400 volunteers, stood out with its elite officer corps, provisions, and general organization. His

45

assistants were Armen Karo and Dashnak Khecho."[8]

## DRO IS SEVERELY WOUNDED

Before reaching Abagha, Dro's regiment encountered fierce enemy resistance. As they approached Abagha, the volunteers were subjected to a furious onslaught by Kurdish brigands. After a heated clash, the enemy fled; the battle was over. At a forward position, Dro was issuing orders. Suddenly, from behind some rocks, a treacherous bullet struck Dro in his chest.[9]

The command of the regiment passed to Armen Karo. Wounded, Dro was taken to Igdir and from there to Tbilisi, the Aramian Hospital where he underwent surgery. But the bullet remained in his lung for the rest of his life.

Dro's survival seemed like a miracle. To travel in such a condition from Giavre Shami through the Armenian plateau's snow storms, over rocky, uneven mountainous paths to reach Tbilisi would require an iron physique.

During surgery at the hospital, Vratsian and Khachadur Karjikian were in the waiting room, anticipating news about the surgery's outcome. After a long wait, when the wounded man was brought out covered with a white sheet, the doctor greeted Dro's friends with a wave of his hand and passed without saying anything. The nurses, similarly, passed like shadows, their faces pale. "It's over," whispered Khachik . . . .

The next day, Vratsian hurried to the hospital at the appointed hour. Sister Ashkhen joyfully held Vratsian's arm and escorted him to the patient's room. Dro smiled weakly and closed his eyes. The danger had passed. The doctors were surprised at how he survived after having lost so much blood.

Henceforth, day by day, Dro's health and spirits improved. Not until early December was he, though still in bed, able to move and talk.

In the early days of December 1914, when Tsar Nicolas II was in Tbilisi visiting military hospitals, he also visited Dro, accompanied by Mayor Alexander Khadisian, doctors, and nurses.

Khadisian informed the Tsar about Dro, the circumstances under which he was wounded, etc. The Tsar congratulated Dro, thanked him for his military service, decorated him with the "Georgian Valor Cross Medal," and asked:

" 'Where did you learn the military art?'

" 'In the revolution, your Highness,' boldly responded Dro. 'In the revolution.' In Russian, *'vrevolutsii'* sounds more forceful. The tsar, who by nature was a timid man who hated the revolutionaries, was shaken and wanted to leave the room. Khadisian hurried to calm him, noting that the reference was to the revolution of Turkey's Armenians . . . .

"The next day all of Tbilisi was talking with admiration about Dro's encounter with the tsar."[10]

Dro's recuperation lasted for months. By the spring of 1915 he was on his feet again. From Tbilisi they returned him to the front with joy and passion.

## ANDRANIK AND DRO SET OUT TOWARD MUSH AND SASSUN

Commander Andranik presented a petition to General Turukhin, saying, "At this time my country is subjected to fire, destruction and massacre; allow me to go to Mush and Sassun."

The petition was relayed to the division's General Commander Okanovski. He allowed Andranik to move in the direction he wanted, and ordered Colonel Vasiliev to follow him with his troops and ordnance and submit to Andranik's command. The Armenian commander also took Dro and his regiment with him.

On July 13, 1915, Andranik had barely reached Sokhord village, the birthplace of his revolutionary life's great mentor, the martyr Serob *Aghbiur* (Fountain), when two Cossack horsemen reached him from the rear, sweating and out of breath, bringing a letter from Turukhin. Colonel Vasiliev read the letter and Andranik's translator-bodyguard translated it.

The substance of the letter was that the Russian troops were retreating on all fronts, and thus Andranik must return to Kamurdj to meet with General Nazarbekov.

Andranik and Dro promptly gathered their troops and set out toward Kamurdj. In Arjesh Andranik got into an argument with a Russian general, to whom, among other things, he said the following:

"This retreat is a complete subterfuge. You want Armenia to remain without Armenians. Nature has provided gigantic mountains, fortresses, ramparts; why don't you stay put somewhere and hold a position? Instead you retreat, ignominiously, 200 verst [.663 mile] without looking back. Let the enemy come, let us measure up to them; if they are stronger, then we retreat."[11]

During the argument the general threatened to subject Andranik to court martial.

Why were the Russian forces retreating?

In the Russian Caucasus army there was an agent named Tigran Tevoyants, whose job was to spy on the Turkish forces. Tevoyants had informed General Commander Okanovski that "The Turks are coming on us with 11 divisions."[12]

Upon this sham and fake news (the nature of which Andranik had guessed . . .) the Caucasus front's 4th army with its 64,000 soldiers and seven generals (Apatsiev, Varapanov, Stuyanov, Nazarbekov, Turukhin, Sharpantiev, and Nikolayev) began a panic-stricken retreat without checking to verify the news. The chaos was so great that the army's General Commander Okanovski got "lost" for three days.[13]

Aram was decisively against retreating from Van. His rationale was the following:

"For a whole month we resisted the Turkish army and the Turkish and Kurdish armed mob, having approximately a thousand firearms, of which 400 were pistols, some of the rest were hunting rifles, and only about 500 proper military firearms. We had as well a very limited supply of ammunition. Now for Van's defense we can have our volunteers' four regiments . . . .

"From the youth of Van, Moks and Shadakh we could possibly arm another one or two thousand.

— — — — —

"Until the Russians' return we can defend the Armenian people whereas our troops' leaving and the exile of the Armenians could break the people's back."[14]

Aram's viewpoint was defended by all the commanders of the Armenian volunteer regiments and the representatives of the National Bureau, but the Russian command was steadfast in holding to its plan for retreat, the main objective of which was to empty the Armenian provinces of Armenians, as Andranik had guessed at the beginning of the retreat . . . .

## THE ARMENIAN PEOPLE OF VAN-VASBURAKAN BEGINS THE PATH TO EXILE

Behind the Russian armies' chaotic retreat followed also the retreat of the Armenian inhabitants of Van-Vasburakan under heart-wrenching conditions. Vasburakan's people had to cross the Berkri gorge within three days.

The retreat from Vasburakan was a complete disaster. Everyone, young and old, abandoned their ancestral home and estate and took the path of emigration.

The spiritually broken and physically worn-out crowd of 150,000, under the searing rays of the sun, through the suffocating dust of the roads, terrified of the danger of being massacred by the Turk and Kurd, hungry and thirsty, flagging and suffering epidemics, finally caught its breath on the Araratian Plain, a third of the emigrants having died along the way.[15]

As a result of Tigran Tevoyants's false information, Armenian exiles would come not only from Vasburakan but also from Bassen, Erzrum, Mush, Bitlis, Akhlat, and Bashkale and fill the streets of Yerevan and Edjmiadsin, bringing the number of refugees to 350,000.[16]

## RUSSIAN FORCES AND ARMENIAN VOLUNTEER REGIMENTS RETURN TO THE FRONT

The National Bureau appealed to the Russian government to have the volunteer regiments united on one front under the name "Araratian Corps" under the command of Vartan of Khanassor, as the forward element of the Russian forces preparing to advance on Van.

In April 1915, all the volunteer regiments were reformed. The First Regiment under Andranik's command, around 1,000 troops, would move from Salmast toward Van.

The Second, Third, and Fourth Regiments, Hamazasb, *Keri* and the cavalry, *Dashnak* Khecho under the general command of Vartan, would form the forward position of General Nikolayev on the Yerevan-Van line.

Andranik and his group approached the Kurubash Village near Van. Van Armenians welcomed them and organized a feast in honor of Andranik. After the toasts and speeches, the hero spoke:

"From you, people of Van, I demand 2,000 soldiers to be our rear-guard, when we advance toward Mush. Until we occupy Bitlis and Mush, Van will never be secure. In this province there are approximately 10,000 armed regular and nonregular riflemen. If you do not give me 2,000 volunteers and fulfill your duties, you know, although Van Lake is small, its waves are sufficiently strong. They will come and cover your city and you will all drown . . . . Do not say that Van is liberated and let the Bitlisian worry about Bitlis, the

Mushian about Mush, the Kharbertian about Kharbert. We must work and act together."[17]

Adnranik appealed in writing to Aram Pasha, emphasizing the Van Armenians' duty. Aram read Andranik's letter in public, but the Van Armenians did not volunteer a single soldier to Andranik. Also, those volunteers serving in Andranik's army who were natives of Van, upon arriving at Van, immediately escaped at night into their hometown.[18]

When the volunteers finally entered Van, Dro was one of the first. Upon his arrival, he hurried to visit with and console the family of Ishkhan, who had been stealthily killed by the Turks. During the years of his mercantile business in Old Payazid, Dro had established close friendships with Van's Party activists and particularly with Ishkhan, the leader and organizer of Lernabar's martial forces.

Aram Tabaghian, witnessing Dro's meeting with Ishkhan's wife, Siranoush, and recalling that emotional scene, would write:

"May 3, 1915, was the first day of victory in Van's heroic battle. I was at the house of my uncle's daughter, the martyr Ishkhan's grief-stricken widow, when suddenly at the door appeared a barely 30-year-old young man, dark complexioned, in Circassian uniform. Stretching his hands to Siranoush, he said in an anguished voice,
" 'Oh my unlucky sister . . . .'
"Siranoush, crying, speaking to the visitor, asked,
" 'Suren Efendi (Dro's aka), where is he? Where is your dear friend, my special *Ishkhan* [Prince] . . .?'
"To lighten the sad and oppressive atmosphere, Dro started telling how his regiment had arrived in Van.
"Upon Dro's direct initiative, Armenian soldiers went to the Hirj village and discovered *Ishkhan's* and his comrades' corpses and, after transferring them to Van, interred them in the city's cemetery."[19]

51

After the liberation of Van, the forces of Andranik, Dro, *Keri,* and Hamazasab won brilliant victories in the battles of Shadakh, Moks, Sorb, and Datuan.

Describing Dro's military skills, Dr. Yervant Khatanasian wrote:

"I have witnessed from Sorb to Datuan and Grgur the battles fought by the volunteers' four regiments. With deep emotion I saw how, after the victory at Sorb, Andranik hugged Dro like bind-weed, kissed him and, addressing his long-time friend, unmatched fedayee *Keri,* he said, 'Dro is *Aslan!* (lion) *Aslan'!"*

Andranik pronounced Dro's name as *"Dero,"* but in that accent converged admiration, affection, pleasure, and pride.[20]

The Russian army, under the command of General Turukhin, advanced through the lake's southern coast toward Vostan, Aghtamar, until Urtab.

## SIMON VRATSIAN AND NIKOL AGHBALIAN VISIT THE ARMENIAN VOLUNTEER REGIMENTS

In July 1915, Vratsian and Nikol Aghbalian visited the assembly point of the volunteer regiments at Aghtamar; General Turukhin's general staff was there, as was the command corps of the Armenian volunteer regiments: Andranik, Vartan, *Keri,* Hamazasb, Dro, Khecho. A military conference was to take place, but from the front-line came news that the enemy had attacked and threatened to occupy forward positions.

Dro rushed from his position and forged ahead. The others followed behind him. After a fierce clash, the Turks retreated. Instead of Aghtamar, the conference took place at *Khndzorik* (little apple) Village, on the lakeshore.

Vratsian and Aghbalian, on behalf of the National Bureau, suggested to the commanders of the volunteer regiments that they accelerate their expedition toward Mush, in order to reach out and help Taron Province's Armenian populace.[21]

Almost all of them hesitated, particularly Andranik, who considered it foolishness to race to Mush with only the volunteers. On the other hand, Dro outlined the following plan:

Appeal to General Turukhin and request authorization to assemble all the Armenian volunteer regiments under one command, such as Andranik's. Appeal to Turukhin to attach 200 Cossacks and an artillery battery to the Armenian legion which was to move forward toward Taron. Dro was convinced that the volunteers could successfully reach Taron and save the region's Armenians.[22]

The plan was bold; in the event of failure the volunteers would be sacrificed, yet in the event of success the result would be the salvation of Taron's Armenians, who were engaged in a desperate struggle against the enemy.

Andranik objected and called the National Bureau suggestion "academic." He was upset and did not forgive the National Bureau for appointing Vartan of Khanasor, instead of himself, as Commander of the Araratian legion.[23]

Dro was fond of Andranik. He would have preferred that Andranik were the commander of the Araratian legion rather than Vartan. As to the other commanders, only *Keri* and Khecho agreed with Dro. When Andranik concluded his counterpoint to Dro, *Keri* raised his head and said, "I am with you, Dro."

Khecho added, "Me too."

The rest remained silent; the decision was postponed to the next day.

Soon the Turkish offensive began. Khecho was killed at the Rahvay battle. Dro again insisted on his plan, but this time Andranik's counterpoints seemed more valid and the obstacles that he pointed out clearer. He decisively refused to take part in such a "foolish" plan and departed from Igdir. While the conference was considering implementation of Dro's plan, it was revealed that it was already too late. Ruben and *Koms* (Count), with the help of a band of armed fighters, were able to cross from Sassun to the Russian side and bring with them the sad news of the annihilation of Taron's Armenian population.[24]

In the summer of 1915, after the Kurds massacred Taron's Armenians, Dro with his detachment came to Zilan, where the Kurds had also wreaked havoc on the Armenians. Dro occupied Zilan, punished the Kurds, and drove their flocks of cattle and sheep toward the Caucasus to distribute to the Armenian refugees.

After the attack on Zilan, when the regiment withdrew to the rear to rest and regroup, Dro got married a second time in Yerevan, to Galust Aloyan's niece, Arpenik. Dro had two sons with Arpenik.[25]

Here in parentheses I want to refer to the escape of Ruben and *Koms* from Sassun, a story which has two versions.

The first: In the summer of 1915, after fighting for 15 days against the Turks in the city of Mush, Haji Hakob Kotoyan succeeded in occupying a number of good positions. He sent word to Ruben and *Koms* (Vahan Papazian) in Sassun to come to his aid; together they could occupy the city and confiscate the Turkish military supplies.

Ruben declined that help to Haji Kotoyan. Before long, Haji was martyred along with his twelve-year-old son.

When the massacre of Taron started in the summer of 1915, Sassun's "barons," Ruben and *Koms* started preparations to escape to the Caucasus in order to save their skin. Guarded by 33 fighters, they headed to the Russian border by secret paths. Ruben refused to take along the martyr Haji Kotoyan's cousin, Arakel, even though he, Ruben, had stayed for months at the Kotoyans' home . . . .

When Ruben reached Igdir, his friends organized a feast in honor of their survivor friend. Toasts and speeches followed each other. When it was Rostom's turn, he said, "I cannot empty a glass to the health of a deserter revolutionary, except when he falls with his people. Ruben, why did you come? Where is the Armenian population of Taron and Sassun whose safety was entrusted to you...?"[26]

It is true that when a ship sinks, the captain of the

ship sinks with it; but in this case, we all should be glad that Ruben escaped from Sassun to the Caucasus, because, had he stayed there and got martyred with his people, today we would not have his valuable 7-volume memoirs.

To allay the people's wrath against the deserter Ruben, the ARF temporarily sent him to the Meghri (Goghtan district) region, but before long he was invited to Yerevan and became the Republic of Armenia's minister of war.[27]

This story's second version presents Ruben's escape from Sassun-Taron in more positive terms, as related by Captain Mushegh Avetisian of Sassun.

After the martyrdom of Gevorg *Chavush*, in 1907, Ruben assumed the leadership of Sassun's revolutionary organization.

In the summer of 1915, during the Armenian Genocide, Vaspurakan also waged battles of self-defense against the enemy. A month later the Russian army and the Armenian volunteer regiments arrived and the population of Vaspurakan was saved temporarily.

The Armenians of Sassun and Taron held out for seven long months against a hundred thousand Turk and Kurd enemies, with their eyes on the horizon, anticipating that any day the Russian forces and Armenian volunteer regiments would arrive. But instead of assistance, they received news that the Russian armies were retreating without looking back to check whether the intelligence on which they acted was correct or false—whether the Turks, indeed, had enough forces to overwhelm them. Time would tell that the Turks did not have that strength and that the Russians' aim was to decimate the population of Armenia, which they succeeded in doing. In other words, the old tsarist scheme of "Armenia without Armenians" was accomplished.

Only after struggling for seven months, when their ammunition was exhausted, the chiefs of Sassun, with Ruben's leadership, held a conference at Antok Mountain and decided that all individuals, families, or groups had to fend for themselves.

Ruben and *Koms,* accompanied by 33 fighters and led by two old and experienced guides, managed to reach Igdir via Manazkert.[28]

## ANDRANIK, DRO, *KERI,* AND HAMAZASB
## TOGETHER ON THE DATUAN LAKESHORE
(From the memoirs of Captain Martiros Abrahamian)

(Note.—Captain Martiros from Tehran was one of the ARF's veteran fighters and he was one of the best captains in Dro's volunteer regiment; during military operations at Datuan he held forward positions. The Dashnakist captain was full of praise for Andranik Pasha's "intuitive" military talent.)

"[Captains Sujian and Martiros] at one time got together between our battalions and started conferring about the situation, when we noticed Andranik, Dro, Keri and Hamazasb sitting under the walnut trees on the Datuan lakeshore. A little later Andranik got up and headed toward us. Because of our higher locations it was possible to see all the way to Grgur's slopes from there. Pasha was a few steps from us; with binoculars held to his eyes, he was carefully checking the slopes of the mountains across from us and the road stretching to Bitlis.

"After looking for a few moments, he turned to us and pointed to the road to Bitlis, saying, 'Guys! Had you noticed forces coming from Bitlis or not?'

"Our binoculars immediately turned to where Pasha had indicated. Indeed Turkish cavalry came near Datuan, then veered toward one of Grgur's valleys and vanished from sight.

" 'Do you understand what is happening?' he asked again.

" 'No, Pasha,' we answered.

# ARMENIAN FEDAYEE

*KERI*

(Arshak Galfayan)
1858–1916

"Andranik, with his wit and eagle's gaze, had guessed the enemy's intention. He had frequently displayed his skills in such circumstances. With his inborn sense of strategy and experienced intuition he was capable of instantaneously seeing and feeling the battlefield's positive and negative sides and possibilities, without missing the enemy's slightest movement. With opportune martial initiatives he was able to grab positions that offered advantages and imposed on the enemy untenable circumstances, securing full victory for himself and leaving the enemy in a state of shock and surprise mixed with stupefaction.

"After our negative reply, lowering the binoculars from his eyes, he said, 'The Tajiks [referring to Moslem Turkish and Kurdish forces] are preparing to retreat. That cavalry force that you saw has come to secure the rear of the enemy across from us preparing to retreat. Guys! Be ready to launch an attack by the time I get our cavalry in order.'

"He had barely finished speaking when he quickly, almost running, went to his horsemen. We were already prepared to attack when Dro came up near us and said:

" 'Guys, attack!' "[29]

Artashes Sujian's battalion began its attack on the lakeshore, whereas Martiros Abrahamian's battalion attacked the enemy fortified in the heights across. With the Armenian volunteers' coordinated onslaught, the Turks simultaneously poured out from all their positions and began their chaotic retreat. Mardiros Abrahamian describes the frightful battle:

"To strike terror in the heart of the retreating, panic-stricken enemy, our mounted volunteers led by Dashnak Khecho swiftly moved forward. With hurrahs, glued to their saddles, and melded with their mounts, like a rapid and raging river they were fast approaching the enemy infantry running a few dozen feet ahead of them.

"After a last-minute adjustment of the hilts of their

swords in their fists, the carnage began. The first victims, drenched in their blood, fell to the ground with cries of agony. Suddenly from the right flank of our lads an Islamic cavalry unit rushed to the rescue. They approached our men quickly and mixed with them.

"In this close combat it was not possible to use weapons other than swords and revolvers. With the impetuous force of strong arms, the raised swords landed on the enemy, cutting someone's arm, cracking another's skull. Here or there someone's blade had broken from a forceful strike, and the next blow would put an end to another life, the dying man falling under the hooves of the horses.

"The neighing of the horses, the din of the fighters, the agonizing cries of the wounded rising from under the hooves, the last moans of the dying mixed with the metallic clang of the swords and the firing of the revolvers and the thud of the horses' hooves—these turned the battlefield to such chaos that no one could think of anything but to strike, let alone notice the fall of the peerless warrior, the *Fedayee* [in the revolutionary organization the widely recognized, and loved by all, *Dashnak* Khecho.]"[30]

Karo Sassuni mourns the death of the devoted revolutionary hero in these words:

"Khecho had fallen with his sword in hand, his fingers tight, fulminating wrath frozen in his expression. Forged and hewed in numerous battles, that revolutionary had so many times laughed in the face of death. Many times death had reached for Khecho with its bloody paw and opened its jaws to swallow him, but Khecho had always managed to evade it, to fight another day, in another battle.

"Khecho had fetched a high price for his life—around him were strewn ten soldiers' corpses.

"My pen is not up to the task of portraying Khecho, as well as his peers, in their full stature. Thumb through the bloody pages of our history and see them in their enormity, to picture the odyssey and heroic end of each one of them. Glory be to them!"[31]

Martiros Abrahamian continues his description of the battle of Datuan:

"Gradually the enemy was swarming, on the verge of engulfing our men, when we were ordered to retreat. The Tajiks were not emboldened by our pulling back, but were content to have thrown back our horsemen, thus securing the retreat of their infantry towards Bitlis.

"I pursued the enemy infantry as far as the caravanserai at the mouth of the Bitlis valley, taking as loot two mules. I was intent on advancing with the same impetus when I received a note from Dro. 'Retreat immediately, the enemy is behind you, you could be captured.'

"And in fact the Tajik forces on my right and left sides, thinking my battalion to be one of theirs, had not paid attention to me when I was advancing, but when I began to retreat, they noticed and realized I was the enemy. An untenable situation ensued for my battalion. They put us under fire from all directions, threatening to annihilate us entirely. Fighting and retreating, we barely managed to escape from them and reach our side."[32]

Armenian volunteer forces stayed seven more days in Datuan, scouting the enemy's movements.

On Transfiguration Day, when they were still in Datuan, they received a letter from Sassun signed by Ruben and Vahan Papazian, whose content, as recalled by Martiros Abrahamian, was approximately as follows:

"Why are you taking so long? The people of Mush were massacred; only a portion managed to escape to us, in Sassun, with some others having gone into hiding in different places. The Armenian villages have been filled with aliens, refugees who are Kurds.

"There are no Islamic forces on the Mush plain. Do not delay, attack from the direction of Nemrut; we from our side will fight and try to reach you, to be able to rescue our 40,000 people in this region. These have taken refuge with us from Tiarbekir and Mush and are homeless. Hurry up as our food and ammunition is running out! For heaven's sake, hurry up if you do not want the people to die of starvation" . . . etc.[33]

Andranik, Dro, *Keri,* and Hamazasp hurried to General Turukhin to request an order to reach out to the people of Sassun and the refugees who had sought shelter there, pointing out Ruben's letter filled with supplications.

General Turukhin issued the command. However, in the meantime, as was noted earlier, on the basis of false intelligence provided by a certain Devoyan (or Devoyants), the Russian army began to retreat along the entire front-line and the Armenian volunteers were unable to rush to the rescue of the unfortunate people of Sassun.[34]

Karo Sassuni rightfully reflects upon the retreat of the Russian forces from the Caucasus front:

"From that moment on, unfortunately, neither Andranik, nor Dro, nor *Keri,* nor the volunteers hailing from Taron, mutinied against this order of retreat nor did they invade the plain of Mush. This fact, however it may be rationalized or explained, remains condemnable, because the Armenian volunteer regiments' creation was solely based on the mission of rescuing the people of the Armenian provinces (of the Ottoman Empire). At that time it could have been possible to rescue around 60,000 Armenians from Taron. Alas . . . but the volunteer regiments failed to carry out this sacred duty.

"This is, we think, history's verdict."[35]

## ANDRANIK'S AND DRO'S SUCCESSFUL MILITARY OPERATIONS

Toward the end of 1915, with unexpected and intermittent attacks, Kurdish bandits and cavalry had created a dangerous situation behind the frontline, undermining communication lines among the Russian forces. To clean up rear areas and to reestablish communication lines, the Russian command instructed Andranik and Dro, with their First and Second Regiments, to throw back the Kurds and to open up communications between the frontline and the rear.

In early January, Dro's regiment, smashing the Kurdish armed forces, joined up with Andranik's regiment in the vicinity of the Aghi-Giaduk mountain pass. In the severe winter weather, the Armenian First and Second Regiments admirably carried out the mission entrusted to them. The lines of communication among the Russian forces were reestablished.

In early February 1916, the offensive military operations initiated by the Russian forces were successfully concluded.

On the fifth of the same month Mush was occupied. The Second Regiment under Dro's command entered the city. Two days later Dro ascended to Sassun and from there went to the Holy Apostles' Monastery.

Dro had finally reached Taron and Sassun, the homeland of those legendary fedayeen: Andranik, Serob *Aghbiur* (Fountain), Gevorg *Chavush* (Policeman), Hrair-*Dzhoghk* (Hell), Murad of Sebastia, and others, about whom the people had woven stories and songs, glorifying the memory of these unmatched heroes.

The rebel braves of these mountains who had inspired Dro's adolescent dreams were no longer there. Conditions in the ancient homeland of the Armenians were horrible. The dwellings and villages of Sassun's braves were turned to heaps of ashes by the Turks and Kurds.

After occupying Mush, Dro became ill and relocated to the rear of the frontline. The command of the Second Regiment was transferred to Colonel Ekor Ter Avedisian.

During Dro's absence, the Second Regiment took part in the battles to clear the Turks and Kurds out of the Taron and Sassun regions, and then it moved on to the Baghesh front.

(The occupation of Baghesh [Pitlis] by General Andranik is detailed on pages 344–349 of my historical volume, *General Andranik and the Armenian Revolutionary Movement.*)

On April 3 Dro, recuperated, returned to his regiment. A day later he led his lieutenants to battle. He was already informed that the Russian command had decided to demobilize the Armenian volunteer regiments. Dro's lieutenants, upon hearing this news, decided not to take part in the ongoing battle, but ". . . Dro proposed that they engage in this last battle and then bid each other farewell with honor."[36]

For the last time on the soil of Western Armenia, Dro led his volunteers in warfare, battling the Turkish forces massed in the Kazmagiaduk settlement. The volunteers' first strike proving unstoppable, the Turkish detachment began retreating with great losses. Soon though, new Turkish brigades reached the battlefield and, joining with the retreating Turkish forces, attacked the Armenian forces. Bullets fired by the Turks wounded the commander of the second brigade, Martiros of Bashgarn. Ivanov, the commander of the Russian brigade serving in the Armenian legion, was killed. The Russian soldiers, witnessing their commander's fall, began to flee. Soldiers under the command of wounded Martiros followed the Russian soldiers. Dro reached them. The Armenian soldiers who had begun to flee stopped upon seeing their commander.

Dro regrouped his forces, picked up machine guns left behind by the Russians, and led an orderly retreat to the Zandog heights, where he fortified his positions. Dro handed command of his detachment to Brigadier Zamardzev and with a group of comrades in arms headed toward Yerevan.[37]

Deeply disillusioned with the tsarist policies, he repeatedly declined to wear the epaulets of a Russian commander which were offered to him many times, and he refused to serve in the Russian army.


## END OF ARMENIAN VOLUNTEER REGIMENTS

In the summer of 1916, with the occupation of the Armenian provinces, the recall of Viceroy Vorontsov-

Dashkov, and the appointment of new Viceroy Nikolai-Nikolayevich, the work of the Armenian volunteer regiments came to an end.

By the decree of the Viceroy, the Armenian volunteer regiments were demobilized. In their stead were formed Armenian musketeer companies. Dro was given an offer to join a musketeer regiment with the rank of an officer. He refused. Instead of getting autonomy, the Armenian provinces would be joined to Russia.

The Armenian volunteers and their commanders, for the sake of Armenia's liberation, had tied so many hopes and golden dreams to the victorious marches of Russian armies towards historic Armenia. . . .

For centuries the Armenian peasant dreamt, "The Russian uncle will come. . . ."

— — — — —

Armen Karo, sorely disappointed with the anti-Armenian policy of Tsar Nicholas II, retreated to his brother-in-law's farm, in Gandzak, buried in sad ruminations.

As for Dro, his disappointment and discouragement surrendered him to wine and gambling, in Yerevan, Tbilisi, or Igdir. He would spend whole nights around the card table or partying to forget the mistake of the Armenians' naïve politicians in giving 5,000 volunteers to the tsar's armies.

One evening, in Yerevan, Dro caught up with Vratsian and said,

"Let us go to Igdir."

"To do what?"

"Nothing."

They went to Igdir.

At his father's house, after barely eating something, Dro stood up and said, "Let us go."

They went. An unfamiliar large house, in an expansive vineyard. From the windows one could observe a large crowd, around tables, having a feast.

Soon after dinner, green card tables were laid out. Dro sat at the head of a table, with Vratsian next to him. He chain-smoked and drank cognac.

Hours passed and it was already dawn. The hostess announced that "dinner" (we would have said "breakfast") was ready. The gamblers were noisily counting their gains or losses. Dro had won 3,600 rubles—a jackpot in those days.

He divided the bills three ways.

"This one to you, for the Red Cross," handing it over to the hostess.

"This one to you, for the Organization," handing it over to *Topal* (Lame) Yegho.

"This one to you," turning to Vratsian. "Give it to Rostom, he knows how to use it."

After distributing the money, he folded his arms on his chest and said, "This is the last. From now on I will not pick up cards."

From then on, and for a long time afterward, he avoided cards, moderated his smoking and drinking, and got to work.[38]

Thanks to his extensive contacts, Dro received the contract for building a military road on the Kaghzuan-Koghb line, and commenced working to earn money. He put to work many of the lads in his regiment. By engaging in honest employment, these fighters remained free of the moral flaws to which demobilized troops are vulnerable.

For more than a year he was engaged in this contractual work. Sometimes he would appear briefly in Tbilisi and disappear again. Those were bad times. Horrific news would arrive from the Turkish side of the border. Instead of true autonomy, the tsar was promising "ecclesiastical autonomy" to the Armenians. Viceroy Nicholas Nicholayevich, like his predecessor, conducted anti-Armenian policies. Christian Europe was silent in the face of the horrific massacre of the Armenians by an Islamic state. For the politicians of Christian states, Christianity existed only under the arches of their beautiful gothic cathedrals. Outside of that everything was money, profit, and materialism. It appeared that there was no hope for the Armenians from Christian Europe.[39]

On February 28, 1917, Russia's first revolution exploded in Saint Petersburg. The throne of the Romanovs was toppling, and the tsar abandoned it. The viceroy of the Caucasus, Nicholas Nicholayevich, saved his skin only by fleeing.

Dro rushed to Tbilisi once again to dive wholeheartedly into the whirl of national work. The National Bureau, which was worried about the collapse of the frontline and the security of Armenian-populated areas, sent Aram to Yerevan as a fully authorized delegate. Dro was appointed commissar of the armed forces of the Araratian region with the Russian armies of the Caucasus front [40]

## 1917—A YEAR OF HOPE AND EMOTION FOR ARMENIANS

After the collapse of the tsarist dictatorship, the Armenian Question was rekindled. Survivors of the Great Slaughter (the Armenian Genocide) returned to their ruined towns and villages. National assembly, organization of national strength and resources, formulation of national rights—a new ascendancy took place in every aspect of national life.

Dro had one foot in Yerevan, the other in Tbilisi. The director of the National Council's military section was Stepan Mamikonian, the president of Moscow's Armenian Committee, having as his assistant Ruben Ter Minassian. Neither the director nor his assistant had the necessary familiarity with the workings of the military. For this reason, sometimes complications and friction arose, particularly between Andranik and his followers and the directors of the National Council. As an individual who enjoyed the trust of everyone, Dro was a counterbalancing force.

He often had to restrain everyone from turning sharp disputes into fights. Even someone as irrepressible and bold as Andranik respected him.[41]

At one session of the National Council, chaired by Avetis Aharonian, the subject under scrutiny was the securing of the frontline. Andranik was preparing to go to Erzrum, as commander of the National Guard forces. Along with members of the Western-Armenian Security Council, such as Vahan Papazian *(Koms)*, et al, he had arrived to consult with the National Council.

Dikran Bekzatian, Stepan Mamikonian, Andranik, Khachatur Karjikian, and Ruben gave speeches. Almost all of them stressed similar things—to declare mobilization, to take strict measures against desertion, etc.—actions already tried without success.

Dro also gave a speech, and the main point he made was that the frontline should be shortened and the Payazit-Basen line reinforced and defended.

Deep silence in the room. Andranik, who was sitting next to Vratsian, was agitated and "ready to explode like a black cloud. . . ."

Ruben spoke:

"I agree with Dro, but . . . ." He could not continue. The black cloud exploded with a horrific thunder . . . .

Andranik, lunging furiously like a tiger, jumped up and, shaking his fists, rushed on Ruben. The poor man, taken aback, was silent for a moment, then stepping to the other side of the table, began to shout in Andranik's face, waving his fists. The meeting was disrupted.

It was not Ruben's fault. The subject of Andranik's rage was Dro, but he could not yell at Dro, just as he could not yell at *Keri* or Rostom . . . . Andranik liked Dro and venerated him, despite their age difference.[42] (Andranik was nineteen years older than Dro.)


## ANDRANIK BEATS UP ANASTAS MIKOYAN[2]

As an aside, Vratsian relates that Anastas Mikoyan, after serving in the volunteer regiments' command for a

---

[2] The future Soviet Communist Party leader (1895–1978).

short time, had gone to the front near Andranik. "There he was beaten up by Andranik and he departed not only from the volunteer regiment, but also from the ARF."[43] Vratsian does not say why Andranik beat up Mikoyan. I will tell you that, with a short introduction.

In the days following the battle of Tilman (April 18, 1915), Andranik and his troops arrived at a village, and soldiers pitched a tent for their commander nearby.

Andranik and Sebuh entered the tent to drink coffee. Suddenly a blood-soaked soldier by the name of Gaspar Ipekian entered the tent and complained that another soldier had struck him on the forehead with his sword because he had initially struck the other with his whip.

Andranik laughed and Gaspar Ipekian, taken aback, did not understand why the commander was laughing.

Sebuh pulled Gaspar aside and whispered in his ear, "Only commanders like Andranik and Smbad are authorized to beat a soldier. Do not raise a hand on a soldier again!" Nevertheless, the soldier was punished.[44]

A couple of days later, emissaries accompanied reporter Anastas Mikoyan, who had brought with him Armenian newspapers from Tbilisi; in one of them Mikoyan had described a battle Andranik had waged in a way which did not please the commander. Andranik scolded Mikoyan severely and took away from him the horse that was provided by the army.[45] It was then that Andranik, according to Vratsian, had slapped Mikoyan. Vratsian continued, "I was one of the few, whom he never beat or cursed nor criticized. Who was the lucky one who did not taste Andranik's fist or tongue-lashing? Andranik had beaten up Gaspar Ipekian, Ashkharhbek Galandarian [archeologist, had been Andranik's chronicler and translator], Anastas Mikoyan, Shirvanzade, he had even tried to put his hands on Rostom, Dr. Zavrian (Hakob Zavriev) and Ruben Ter Minasian."[46]

When Dro traveled from Beirut to America for the last time, accompanied by S. Vratsian, he repeatedly recalled the incident wherein Andranik had put his hands on Ruben Ter Minasian. "He (Dro) was convinced that if his proposal had been accepted at the time, a lot of calamities would have been prevented. And from a purely military-strategic point of view perhaps he was right, but in the psychological conditions of those days, was it possible to implement such a plan? Was it possible to, without a fight, surrender to the enemy Van, Mush, and Karin, and then depart? Andranik's rage was natural and understandable,"[47] concludes Simon Vratsian.

# NOTES

1. Gr. Gutulian, *General Andranik and His Life and Wars.* 2nd ed, Beirut, 1929, p 27.
2. *Hairenik* (Homeland) Newspaper. August 30, 1977, p 2, Editorial.
3. Antranig Chalabian, *General Andranik and the Armenian Revolutionary Movement.* 3rd ed, Michigan, 1988, p 287.
4. Simon Vratsian, *Along Life's Pathways. Events, Personalities, Experiences.* Vol 4, p 168.
5. L. Martirosian, *A Life's Album.* Beirut, 1959, p 115.
6. *General Andranik's Historic Diaries of the Caucasus Front.* p 7.
7. Lieutenant M. Avetian, *Armenian National Liberation Movement's Jubilee (1870–1920) Album and General Andranik.* Paris, 1954, pp 159–160.
8. Simon Vratsian, *Along Life's Pathways.* Vol 4, pp 168, 169.
9. Ibid, p 169.
10. Ibid, pp 170–171.
11. *General Andranik's Historic Diaries of the Caucasus Front.* p 35.
12. Ibid, p 36.
13. Ibid, p 36.
14. Vardges Aharonian, *Andranik.* Boston, 1957, pp 31–32.
15. Lieutenant M. Avetian, p 171.
16. *General Andranik's Historic Diaries of the Caucasus Front.* p 114.
17. Ibid, p 28.
18. Ibid, pp 28–29.
19. *Hairenik* (Homeland) Monthly. 1967, May, p 2.
20. *Alik* (Wave) Special Edition. 1956, May 4, p 18 (see Hamlet Gevorgian, *Dro,* p 49).
21. Simon Vratsian, *Along Life's Pathways.* Vol 4, p 172.
22. Ibid, p 172.
23. Ibid, pp 172–173.

24. Ibid, pp 173–174.
25. Manuk Krzlian, *Dro, The Immortal Soldier of the Armenian Liberation Struggle. Asbarez,* May 21, 2002, p 6.
26. Lieutenant M. Avetian, pp 357–362.
27. Ibid, pp 361–362.
28. Ruben, *Memoirs of an Armenian Revolutionary.* Vol 7, Beirut, 1979, pp 82–96.
29. Karo Sasuni, *History of Taron.* Beirut, 1957, pp 1003, 1004.
30. Ibid, p 1004.
31. Ibid, pp 1004–1005.
32. Ibid, p 1005.
33. Ibid, p 1006.
34. Ibid, p 1010.
35. Ibid, p 1010.
36. *Hairenik* (Homeland) Monthly. 1934, January, p 82.
37. Ibid, p 82.
38. Vratsian, *Along Life's Pathways.* Vol 4, pp 174–176.
39. Ibid, p 176.
40. Ibid, pp 176–177.
41. Ibid, pp 178–179.
42. Ibid, 179–181.
43. Vratsian, *Along Life's Pathways.* Vol 3, p 34.
44. Sebuh, *Pages From My Memories.* 1st ed, Boston, 1925, pp 222–223.
45. Ibid, p 223.
46. Vratsian, *Along Life's Pathways.* Vol 3, Beirut, 1963, p 106.
47. Vratsian, *Along Life's Pathways.* Vol 4, p 181.

# FEDAYEE SONG

Armenian-Singer
(Avetik Isahakian)


Water is streaming down
From the misty mountains of Mush
Swallows came singing
The arrival of Spring.

There is no Spring for the Armenian,
No need for flowers, swallows,
My tomb is level with the earth,
Let thistles grow on me . . .
Depart, swallow . . . leave me alone
My heart broken, under the earth.

But when you see against the enemy
The Armenian nation like a mountain
Standing proud with gun in hand,
Armenians, mountains, like each other . . .

# CHAPTER III

## FAVORABLE CONDITIONS FOR THE PARTIAL LIBERATION OF TURKISH-ARMENIA IN EARLY 1918

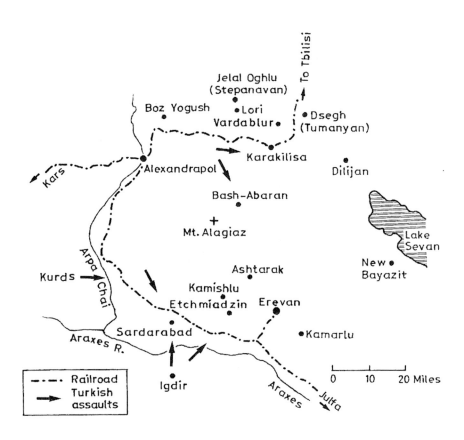

TURKISH PENETRATION MID-MAY, 1918

The Battle of Sardarabad

74

# INCORRECT IMPUTATIONS ABOUT ANDRANIK

(Note. An Armenian historian, Hamlet Gevorgian, wrote a 174-page book titled "Dro." Another writer, Arthur Andranikian, assembled additional writings along with Gevorgian's book and then published the collection in 1991, again titled "Dro." This collection was reprinted in 2000, edited further and with a more attractive format.)

Hamlet Gevorgian makes some imputations regarding General Andranik which do not correspond to the truth. Indeed, Gevorgian writes:

"The National Council (of Tbilisi) decides to maintain the current frontline and appoints commander Andranik of the 3rd division of the Armenian military forces—who by the way was the most fervent advocate of defending the frontline extending from Yerzunka to Van and Bitlis—as commander of the Karin (Erzrum) front national guard, with the conviction that the famous guerilla leader with his authority and martial skills would be able to inspire the soldiers and the people to defend the fortress-city of Erzrum, which had decisive military-strategic importance.[1]

"In February 1918, the Turks, violating the Yerznka ceasefire, commenced an offensive. What Dro had foreseen took place. Despite heroic resistance the Armenian forces, limited in number, were unable to maintain steadfast resistance against the Turkish onslaught, retreating from Baberd, Yerznka, Van, Baghesh and finally from the most important fulcrum of Western Armenia, the fortress-city of Erzrum. The roads leading to Western Armenia were thus open."[2]

For the sake of historical accuracy, I feel obliged to briefly refer to the February 1918 events in Erzrum, to show that first, Andranik was never an advocate of defending the frontline extending from "Yerznka to Van and Bitlis."

Second, the Armenian forces in Erzrum were not

"limited in number," but rather, they had more manpower and munitions than Vehib Pasha.

Third, in February 1918—to be exact, February 26—"heroic resistance" did not take place, because fighting did not take place.

Fourth, the Armenians had a hundredfold more munitions, supplies, and clothing than the Turks; thus, why were they "unable...." to put up "steadfast resistance"?

Fifth, the Armenians were protected with fortified ramparts, with trenches dug around the fortress-city and barbed wire. How could they not show "resistance," when the enemy, from the open field, would attack the fortress protected by hundreds of cannons?

Sixth, the "roads leading to Erzrum, the capital of Western Armenia, opened up" finally in front of Vehib Pasha because commander Bejanbekov (Bejanbekian) of the remains of the tsarist army, who was to defend the center of the front with his 4,600 professional soldiers, became a deserter and treacherously retreated without firing a shot. . . .

Now let us "open" history's roads . . . to the reader!

(I have 49 pages regarding the February 1918 tragic events in Erzrum in my *Andranik* book—the Armenian edition. Here I will present a summary of those events.)


## THE SITUATION IN TURKEY AND THE CAUCASUS IN EARLY 1918

As a consequence of the October 1917 Bolshevik Revolution, the tsarist army on the Caucasus front had deteriorated. Many soldiers had pulled back from Western Armenian regions and returned to their homeland, where they hoped redistribution of land to peasants would take place. The 200,000 Eastern Armenian conscripts serving in the tsarist armies had also returned to the Caucasus—or Russia—careless and indifferent as to the fate of Western Armenia. The cohesion and integrity of the 30,000-strong army under the command of General Andranik, consisting of Turkish (Western)-Armenian soldiers was also undermined by the political upheaval in Russia. The USA, England, and Russia (the Kerenski faction) had assumed responsibility for the organization and financing of this army.

The 320,000-strong tsarist army of the Caucasus front had left its entire stores of munitions, food, uniforms, and so on, to the Western-Armenian National Guard army, under the command of Andranik. This army was subject to the Armenian National Council of Tbilisi. Thus, the Russians had left to the Armenians 300 cannons, 3,000 machine guns, one billion bullets, 100,000 rifles, large supplies of food, clothing, etc.[3]

There was horrific famine in Turkey in 1917–1918. 600,000 out of the 800,000-strong Turkish imperial army had deserted, invading villages in hopes of securing a piece of bread.[4] Richard Hovannisian estimates the number of Turkish army deserters at half a million as a consequence of the famine, which approximates the figure given above.

Vehip Pasha was able to assemble only 400–500 soldiers in front of Erzrum, a division "torn to shreds," with half-starving and half-naked soldiers, whereas the Armenians, as we saw, had much more manpower, and many more munitions and stores behind the ramparts and barbed wire of Erzrum.

The Armenians had not seen so much munitions in their history, whereas the Turks had not been as weak in their history, from a military as well as economic perspective, as they were in early 1918.

In those days, December 3, 1917 to March 18, 1918, the Brest-Litovsk summit conference was convened between the Axis states (Germany, Turkey, Austro-Hungary, and Bulgaria) and Soviet Russia. According to the resolutions of this summit conference, Turkey supposedly was not going to cross the 1914 Russo-Turkish border . . . .

Two and a half years before the Brest-Litovsk conference, when the tsarist army and the Armenian volunteer regiments with victorious expeditions were advancing deep into Western Armenia, Andranik had astutely foreseen that before the war was over, the Turks would invade the Caucasus. As regards the resolution of the conference, the legendary Armenian general had said that the Turks would not even pause a moment on the 1914 border in their quest to reach Baku, and that is what happened.

In the fall of 1916, in the large hall of the Tbilisi prelacy, 1,500 individuals assembled to confer on the day's critical issues.[5]

Andranik gave a passionate speech the main point of which is as follows:

"Last June, at a dinner hosted by Mr. Samson Harutiunian (one of Tbilisi's aristocrats) I said that the Turks will invade the Caucasus. With what are you going to be able to defend yourselves, your children, your honor?"[6]

The Russian-Armenian prosperous elite of Tbilisi did not heed the word of the Great Man and even decided to retreat from the fortress-city of Erzrum. Influenced by Andranik's prophesy and the eleventh-hour intervention of Avetis Aharonian, they resolved to make "an attempt" at defending Turkish Armenia, "so as not to be liable in the judgment of history . . . ."

(For details of these very important but also sad events read my *General Andranik* book, pages 386–435.)


## GENERAL ANDRANIK SETS OUT TO DEFEND THE FORTRESS-CITY OF ERZRUM

To send off General Andranik as he began his journey to Erzrum, Council members Avetis Aharonian and Samson Harutiunian, and from the Turkish-Armenian Security Council Vahan Papazian, Avetis Terzibashian, and Baruir Levonian went to the Tbilisi railroad station.[7]

The station had a specific section for military transport, with a vast courtyard, which was crowded by young Turkish-Armenian soldiers and recently commissioned officers in their new and neat uniforms.

"Before long the bugle sounded. The officers rushed to head their detachments, the soldiers peered at the entrance of the courtyard, through the resounding of their files as they stood to attention. And then from a distance appeared Andranik's car. As soon as the national hero stepped down, there roared the order to attention, and the rifles, like one, rose to greet their general, under whose command the regiment would go to defend the homeland, free and independent Armenia's capital, Erzrum.

"Andranik, frisky as a young man, with martial steps, head held high, eyes stern, with military salute, passed from one end of the regiment to the other."[8]

Farewell speeches followed each other. Avetis Aharonian, in front of a thousand soldiers, solemnly kissed Andranik's forehead and said:

"Soldiers, see to it that this forehead never reaches the ground. This forehead has reached for the stars for 30 years."[9]

Vahan Papazian and others recited similar speeches.

When it was Andranik's turn, he made some bitter and some sweet remarks to the other speakers; and when he needed to mention Stepan Mamikonian's name, who had remained to the end opposed to the idea of Andranik's departure to Erzrum, suddenly a ray of anger shone in the hero's eyes. With a loud, quivering voice he said:

"Poghos Nubar did not wire us, that if Mamikonian, sitting in Sololak [an aristocratic neighborhood of Tbilisi], issues orders, the Allies will recognize Armenia's independence. The price of that independence is blood. And how could I not go to shed my blood, when this lad . . . ."

Andranik entered the ranks of the soldiers and singled out a handsome adolescent boy, barely thirteen years old, whose hands were lost in the sleeves of his military jacket, and his feet in the legs of his pants.

With the adolescent's arm in his hand Andranik continued,

"How could I not go to shed my blood, when this boy,

whom I myself released from his uniform three times, has for the fourth time managed to get into uniform, get a rifle and set out to shed his blood."

An emotional quiver passed over everyone. Paruir Levonian started to sob like a boy, tears flowing down his face.

"Go, my son," continued Andranik, releasing the adolescent's arm. "Go! I will not release you this time. Hold your rifle well. Let the valor of your spirit compensate for the shortcoming of your age." Then the lad, charming those present with his sharp military salute and turnaround, went with martial steps to reclaim his place. [10]

Andranik continued his speech:

"When this race can send such adolescents to the front, be assured that our liberty is near. The Russian departed, he left our homeland to us. The Turk threatens to come and wrest our homeland from our hands. Let us not allow the Turk to soak his hands in our blood. Let us create our homeland and be the master of our family, our water, our land, our rocks. Long live our army which fights for our liberty! Long live our martyrdom! May God grant that we are not abandoned in our faith."[11]

The bugle sounded and the soldiers, with their commander Andranik, went to take their places in the train cars.

On his way to Erzrum, Andranik sent a telegram to Murat of Sebastia, who was positioned to defend Yerznka, instructing him to leave the city and come to Mamakhatun, thus holding the Jevidge gorge.

When General Andranik reached Alexandropol, Sebuh came to him and requested that he order the military administration of Karin to deliver to him 200 rifles, to defend Babert. Andranik replied, "Sebuh, I will forthwith order the Karin authorities to give you 200 rifles, but neither 200 nor 500 riflemen will be able to hold Babert. I telegrammed Murat to come from Yerznka to Mamakhatun, but he is still lingering there. If you too go and harbor the refugee Armenians of Babert, you will subject both the soldiers and the refugees to massacre. Yerznka and Babert are unnaturally forward positions and our present forces are not sufficient to fight the Turkish army and mob."[12]

(Thus Andranik did not even want to defend Yerznka and Babert, which are not very far from Erzrum, so he could hardly have been a "most fervent advocate" of defending the vast expanse extending from "Yerznka to Van and Pitlis . . ." as per Hamlet Gevorgian.)

## BEZHANBEKOV RETREATS WITHOUT FIRING A SHOT

A golden opportunity had presented to accomplish the Armenian nation's centuries-old dream. Unfortunately, the dream was not realized as a consequence of the desertion of a certain commander Bezhanbekov.

Brigadier Bezhanbekov was the commander of the Tbilisi Armenian National Council's Regiments A and D, comprised of 4,600 professional soldiers.

With his two regiments, Bezhanbekov was the commander of the center of the frontline. On his right flank was Sebuh and on his left flank Brigadier Torgom. As for Murat of Sebastia, he had instructions to outflank the enemy from the left. On the eve of the attack on Vehip Pasha's division, Bezhanbekov deceived Andranik, telling him that the regiments' morale was high.

On the morning of February 26, 1918, with the attack barely launched, word arrived to Andranik that Bezhanbekov and his regiments were treacherously retreating without alerting the right and left flanks and without even firing a shot.

Andranik went to Bezhanbekov and said:

"If you only endure two more days, I will send you to the Caucasus, because you will be replaced with homeland guard troops, who will quickly arrive in Karin."[13]

The Russian-Armenian commander promised to wait.

At night, there arrived 600 troops, hailing from Mush and loyal to Andranik. At midnight, Andranik went to bed and instructed his guards to awaken him in two hours.

Before the commander got into bed, there was a knock on the door.

Vahan Totovents went to open it. A soldier had brought a note to the general. Andranik read, "Turkish soldiers are walking toward our right flank through the valley. What is your order?"

The general turned pale. He had read the content of the note in an audible voice. Torgom gave him a quizzical look.

"Let them pass," said Andranik to the soldier

The soldier saluted and stepped out.

General Andranik, with distinct insight, had immediately guessed the identity of those passing through the valley. He turned to his intimates and said, "They are not Turks, they are our (Bezhanbekov's) perfidious soldiers, who are fleeing through that valley. Those rascals!"[14]

(Hamlet Gevorgian wrote in *DRO*, "Despite heroic resistance . . . Andranik was unable to defend Erzrum.")

Simon Vratsian, about Erzrum's fall:

"On February 27 Erzrum fell most ignominiously, where under Andranik's command there were assembled 8,000 well-armed soldiers, more than a hundred functional cannons and countless munitions and supplies."[15]

(I wish that the esteemed Simon Vratsian had identified by name-surname the rascal who had precipitated Erzrum's fall "most ignominiously," like Baku's former mayor Novikov had done with regards to Nakashidze, openly, in the press:

"You are more wicked than Cain."

"You are more wicked than Judas."

"Let your name be forever in infamy."

Why had deserter-traitor Bezhanbekov gone to Erzrum with 4,600 professional soldiers, if he was going to return to his province without firing a shot . . . ?)

Thus, the frontline broke down. Everyone fled the fortress-town out of breath, leaving behind mountains of munitions and supplies to the starving enemy.

Andranik would later bemoan the lost opportunity, saying:

"The ammunition was so plentiful in Erzrum that if for four years we had shot ceaselessly at the moon, it would not have run out."

The Armenian liberation movement's first revolutionary song's lyrics:

A voice resounded from Erzrum Armenians' mountains
Armenian hearts palpitated from the din of rifles

I wish they had resounded. I wish the Armenians' thousands of rifles and cannons had thundered from the ramparts of Erzrum. Instead of the thunder of rifles, Bezhanbekov's and his soldiers' (hailing from Gharabagh) panting in flight resounded "from the Erzrum Armenians' mountains. . . ."

Andranik, through his personal example, tried to persuade the soldiers to return to the front, but "We will not fight here, we will not!" they yelled at Andranik's face.

"If you do not fight here and instead go to your province, you will not fight there either and will not be able to defend your homeland," replied the commander.[16]

Those who did not want to fight "here," that is, on the soil of Turkish Armenia, were Bezhanbekov's 1st and 4th regimental soldiers, hailing from Gharabagh, who became deserters, and on their way back to their province, near Goris, were massacred by Turkish and Tatar bandits waiting in ambush on the sides of the Zapugh-Herkelu gorge.[17]

"This is not our country! We want to go to our country! Down with war! Let the Turkish Armenians themselves defend their country," shouted the Russian-Armenian soldiers everywhere.[18]

When Andranik, drawing his sword, led the troops forward, the Russian-Armenian soldiers did not follow him.

And when the General, sword in hand, set upon one of the recoiling Russian Armenians, the latter did not hesitate to reach for his rifle . . . .[19]

On another occasion, a Russian-Armenian deserter took a shot at the "Lord and Protector of the Homeland," Andranik. Luckily the bullet missed its target. Murat of Sebastia lost his patience; grabbing the soldier firmly by his arm he said:

"Hey man! What are you doing? We who defended you for years against the Tatar [Azeri] assaults in the Azeri-Tatar battles (1905–1906 and 1918), now you do not want to be with us?"[20]

In the 1905–1906 Armeno-Tatar war, without the assistance of the Turkish-Armenian fedayeen, who were fighting under the authority of the ARF, the genocide of the Russian Armenians would have taken place ten years before the genocide of the Turkish Armenians, because the tsarist authorities had sided with the Azeris. And in September 1918, the Great Warrior Murat of Sebastia, who for 25 years had fought loyally next to Andranik, gave his life, shedding his blood on the "rocky mountains of Baku," where he had gone for the defense of his Russian-Armenian brothers and sisters.

The Russian Armenians were ungrateful for the countless sacrifices of the selfless and experienced Turkish-Armenian fedayeen, and they deserted Andranik in front of the ramparts of Erzrum.

Traitor Bezhanbekov, while retreating, sent two deceitful telegrams to Tbilisi's Armenian National Council, with the ulterior motive of covering up his treachery. One had the signature of Gen. Nazarbekian, with the following content:

"General Andranik, without my order, taking with him the Siberian regiment and 700,000 bullets went to Kars."[21]

The second was sent from Kars and had the signatures of Colonel Morel (of French origin, and one of Andranik's most loyal officers from the tsarist army) and that of army Commissar Misha Arzumanian, with the following content:

"Andranik arrived in Kars with the Siberian regiment. The Turkish-Armenian force mutinied, abandoned the positions. We are not responsible for the defense of Kars."[22]

These two telegrams were sent by neither General Nazarbekian nor Colonel Morel, whereas the liar who sent them was Bezhanbekov.[23]

In those days, an officer named Bagramian, leading a dozen horsemen as a communications agent between Russian army units, had assumed the task of monitoring the enemy's movements.

On March 11 when Bagramian, setting out from Kars heading to the frontline, encountered General Andranik on the way, the latter related to him the circumstances of Erzrum's fall without a fight. Later on, Bagramian would write the following in his *Memoirs:* "At that moment I clearly grasped the extent of the serious catastrophe our people had been subjected to."[24]

Dro's plan to shorten the frontline was rejected not only by the Western-Armenian Security Council, but also by the Armenian military chiefs, because, according to them, to abandon Erzrum without a struggle would have dire consequences for morale.[25]


**COURT MARTIAL**

After the retreat from Erzrum without firing a bullet, the National and the Western-Armenian Councils jointly convened. Intuiting that the Russian Armenian forces might not offer resistance on the 1914 Russian-Turkish border either, they resolved to send a delegation to Kars and Sarighamish to inspire martial spirit among the retreating forces and to halt the Turkish advance. The delegation included Nikol Aghbalian, Avetis Aharonian, Simon Vratsian, and a few others; Vahan Papazian represented the Turkish Armenians.[26]

When this attempt also failed, Dro, General Areshov, and Vratsian came to the front and this time organized a special court-martial and executed a couple of deserters by firing squad, but were unable to change the Eastern-Armenian soldiers' reluctance to fight on Turkish-Armenian soil.[27]

General Andranik did not hold a grudge against Eastern Armenians. In Alexandropol he formed his "Separate Armenian Strike Force," this time composed of Turkish-Armenian soldiers. In the fall of 1918, after saving the 60,000 people of Zangezur from certain annihilation, the hero, with his Separate Armenian Strike Force, set out to also save Gharabagh (in Eastern Armenia). After destroying the dens of Turk and Tatar bandits on both sides of the Zabul-Hekerlu defile, he came across the remains of the Armenian deserters hailing from Gharabagh. The hero reached the outskirts of Shushi, but the chief of the British military delegation at Baku, General William Montgomery Thomson, obstructed Andranik's advance and the hero returned to Zangezur.

Richard Hovanisian wrote:

"Had General Thomson not intervened to stay Andranik's advance in December 1918, Armenia would have established control over Gharabagh as well."[28]

By the way, if the British had not impeded General Andranik's advance, after liberating Gharabagh, the hero would have marched straight on Baku, to avenge the slaughter of 30,000 Eastern Armenians, on September 15, 1918, in Baku's Ermenikent neighborhoods.

As for the fanciful fable that Andranik was "the most fervent advocate of defending the frontline stretching from Yerznka to Van and Bitlis," as we saw, no one advocated the idea of defending that vast landmass. Andranik wanted to defend the land between Erzrum and the 1914 border; whereas Dro was intent on defending the line stretching from Payazit to Basen,[29] probably because his hometown, Igdir, was inside that line.

## ARAM'S AND DRO'S ROLES IN
## HOMELAND BUILDING

The year 1918 had become mortal for the Armenian population of the Araratian plain. While Andranik had assumed the role of guardian angel for some 35,000 Turkish-Armenian refugees who did not stray from Anranik's shadow, Dro and Aram exerted every effort for the sake of the rebirth of the Armenian people of the Araratian plain, because, Eastern-Armenia, in the words of Vratsian, was "a thorn in the chest of Turkey. It was necessary to expel this thorn, and in every direction, in the provinces of Yerevan and Gandzak, in the whole expanse of Baku and in the back of the Armenian division (Andranik's 'Separate Armenian Strike Force'), Turkish disturbances were breaking out, with attacks on Armenians, pogroms and deportations."[30]

The *Asbarez* daily newspaper, published in America, wrote the following about the military and political situation on the Araratian plain, in 1918:

"The 300,000 surviving individuals, a remnant of the nearly two million Armenian population, who had put their hopes on the (March 1917) Russian (first) revolutionary provisional government, are today under a looming threat.

"The neglected condition of the Caucasus military frontline, the likelihood of the Turks' counterstrike, the endemic Kurdish looting and killing, the local Tatars' rapid arming and the Georgians' two-faced policy pose new dangers for the Armenians.

"We are alone in our impotence and misery; we are surrounded by those who dislike us and are our rivals, who do not miss an opportunity to strike us."[31]

Aram and Dro, collaboratively, formed military squads to stabilize the frontline, and exerted much effort to keep the Armenian soldiers' martial spirit high. Until August 1918, Dro was nominally the military commissar of the Araratian plain, whereas Aram was the civilian administrator.[32]

## THE BATUM CONFERENCE

In early May, the Trabizond conciliation negotiations continued in Batum. The Armenian delegation (Hovannes Kadjaznuni, Alexander Khadisian, and Vratsian as advisor) arrived in Batum on May 6.

One of the first things the Armenian delegates did was to go and visit Khalil Bey, chief of the Turkish delegation.

(This was the same Khalil Bey who had found refuge with Krikor Zohrab, the famous Armenian author, and delegate of the Ottoman Parliament, when the Young Turks were being persecuted during the March 31, 1909, subversion of Nazim Pasha. But when in 1915 Zohrab's wife desperately had appealed to Khalil Bey, pleading with him to defend her husband, Khalil Bey had decisively refused to offer any assistance. On the same occasion, on March 31, 1909, the Minister of the Interior, Talaat had found refuge in an Armenian club and was saved.)[33]

The first official meeting of the Transcaucasian and Turkish delegations took place on May 11, 1918. Khalil Bey, after exchanging a few words with Chekhenkeli, put the plan of the conciliation treaty on the table, a copy of which he gave to the Armenian delegation, in a sealed envelope.

The Armenian delegates went home under "an exceedingly somber and gloomy impression." They opened the envelope and glanced at the map. From Armenia were annexed the regions of Kars, Artahan, Kaghzuan, and Olti, from the Yerevan province the most fertile region of Surmalu, three-fourths of the counties of Alexandropol and Edjmiadsin, half of Yerevan county, and a fifth of Sharur-Daralagiaz county.[34]

With the humiliating terms set by the Turks in Batum, "Armenia was condemned to suffocate in unbearably narrow borders."[35]

The Armenian delegates complained to the German

representative at the conference, General Otto von Lossov, to no avail.

On May 14, the Turks presented yet another demand to the Armenian delegation—to allow the Turkish forces transit rights through Alexandropol to Djulfa. Khadisian communicated with Aharonian and Karjikian in Tbilisi, but before they got a response, they told the Turks that their forces could transit through Armenian lands.[36]

On the morning of May 15, the Turks attacked Alexandropol, occupied the city, and continued their march toward Lori.

In Batum the Tatar delegates insisted that the capital of the Armenian Republic should be the village of Edjmiadsin (the former Vagharshabad), and demanded that Yerevan, being a Tatar city, should be annexed to Azerbaijan.[37]

On May 22, Jemal Pasha arrived in Batum. Chekhenkeli, Rasul Zade, and Khadisian greeted him with words of welcome.

When it was his turn to reply to the Armenian delegate, Jemal said with a somber face, "The Turks' quarrel with the Armenians is old and the Armenians do not take any step to reconcile with us. This course will lead to new misfortunes for the Armenians."[38]

The attempts to reconcile with the Turks in Batum were completely fruitless, whereas, in the meantime, in the Armenian provinces a fateful and agonizing struggle was taking place between the Armenian forces and the invading Turkish Armies.

## THE HEROIC BATTLE OF SARTARAPAT

The Turks had assigned altogether nine well-armed divisions to the Caucasus, 55,000–60,000 infantrymen, for military operations. Five of these nine divisions were assigned to fight the Armenians, around 30,000 soldiers.[39]

The Armenians were able to pull together 20,000 rifles against this force.[40]

As to the desperate and hopeless spirit prevalent in the people early in those days, S. Vratsian relates:

"The Turks' general onslaught initially brought about unspeakable chaos and terror in Yerevan. For many resistance seemed futile and meaningless. The information reaching us from the army did not inspire confidence in victory either. Gen. Silikian's communications painted a gloomy picture of the divisions' capacity to resist."[41]

To inspire hope, courage, and vigor in the hearts of the people, General Silikian made the following appeal:

"Armenians! Rush to liberate the homeland. The time has come when each Armenian, putting aside his individual interest for the sake of our great task, the salvation of the Homeland, and for the defense of his wife's and daughters' honor, will exert every last effort to strike at the enemy . . . .

"Armenians! It is not time to linger; every man up to the age of 50 has a duty to carry arms. I demand all of you, for the defense of the Homeland, to present yourselves with your rifle and bullets.

"Armenian women! Remember the delicate ladies of the 5th century, who inspired their husbands for the great task, at the time of the immortal Vartan's struggle. Follow their example; if you do not want to have your honor trampled, encourage your men! Curse the timid! Collect munitions, bread, clothes.

"We did not want to fight; for the sake of peace we were ready to sacrifice a lot, but our duplicitous enemy persists in his set way; he wishes not only to oppress us, but to annihilate and wipe out our long-suffering nation. But if it is our lot to be annihilated, is it not preferable to defend ourselves holding our rifles and attain in the battlefields our right of existence? As for our capacity for self-defense, that was manifest in our recent battles, on our front, where our enemy who outnumbered us had taken to retreat in the face of our forces' onslaught. Armenians! Stand up! On to work, to holy war!"[42]

To inspire the people with martial spirit, General Nazarbekian also made this appeal:

"Armenians! Our people are living through critical and dangerous times. After many centuries of Islamic bondage our people, understanding that it is no longer possible to continue that way, resolved to either achieve freedom and a bright future through armed struggle, or die with honor. Violating the ceasefire in a most barbaric way, the Turks began their offensive without warning and occupied Alexandropol. It seemed that all was lost. The only thing left for our deceitful enemy to do was to continue his victorious onslaught deep into Armenia, forcing the people to leave our homeland, losing everything. But God's mercy is great.

"The brave division of Yerevan did not waver. On the contrary, resisting their strikes, it counterattacked and after the second battle rolled back the enemy and is now in pursuit. The Yerevan detachment's victory inspired the troops of the Alexandropol division, who regrouped and quickly turned on their enemy, spirited with one wish and one will: victory or death. Armenians! If you want to rescue your families and your honor, if you do not want a more terrible serfdom which our brothers have tasted under Turkish yoke, if you do not want our whole nation destroyed, everyone capable of bearing arms stand up for the defense of your nation. Tardiness at present is destructive. If we do not rise up today and with rifle in hand defend our freedom and honor, then we do not deserve to exist as a distinct nation and there will be great sorrow— our future generations will remember us with curses. We have to put our hopes only in our strength, and if we do not assist the army forthwith, we will be destroyed. Remember, we are now going to attain our best future or we will never see it, nor will our future generations."[43]

— — — — —

These were encouraging appeals, but I think the most effective appeal was made by Aram Pasha (Manukian), which I will relate shortly.

General Movses Silikian, overall commander, set up headquarters at the St. Edjmiadsin seminary building, a couple of hundred yards from the Mother Cathedral.

91

On May 18, Silikian declared that the situation was desperate, because he had lost authority over the armed forces. The next day, accompanied by provost marshal Arshavir Shahkhatumian of Yerevan, Silikian visited Catholicos Gevorg V (Surenian, 1911-1930) and suggested that, for security considerations, His Venerable Holiness relocate to the region of Sevan.

His Holiness replied that if the Armenian forces were unable to defend this sacred place, then he himself would defend it and die on its millennial threshold.[44]

On May 15, Gen. Silikian concentrated his main force, 6,000–7,000 soldiers, between Edjmiadsin and Sartarapat.[45]

On May 21, two Turkish regiments of the 11th division of their Caucasus army attacked Silikian's positions. The Armenians were resisting along the line connecting the villages of Kurakanlu, Kerpalu, and Zeyva.[46]

To retreat was out of the question. It was necessary to vanquish the enemy, or to die.

Everyone was bewildered and panic-stricken. Where else could they retreat to? Retreat from Yerevan also?

Bezhanbekov's deserters from Erzrum had wanted to abandon Yerevan also and retreat toward New Bayazit.

The populace had jammed in front of the Yerevan theatre building (the future parliament); ninety percent of them were women.[47] Some, discouraged, were sobbing. And behold, mighty Aram rose to the stage, "lacking rhetorical skills,"[48] but with iron will and thumping his hand on the table, he roared—"Not one step back!" "Shaking his lion's mane" and "with his strong physique pacing the small stage with decisive steps," he addressed the Armenian mothers:

"If Armenian mothers do not sacrifice their offspring, all of our lives and honor are doomed. The time has arrived when the Armenian woman should feel the eminence of her calling and fulfill her holy duty."[49]

An old lady rose to the stage and addressing Aram, said:

"I have three offspring. All three are offered for the homeland. I am sorry that I don't have more. . . ."[50]

The steel-willed Aram with his enchanting communication skills was able to effect a turnaround in the Armenian soul which was then in retreat.

Aram transmitted his decision to General Silikian that the city should be defended at all costs.

The commander hesitated at first, but then, with his assistant Colonel Vekilov drew up the military plan and transmitted it to General Daniel Pek Pirumian and his assistant Major Alexander Chnéour, for implementation.

(Alexander K. Chnéour, hailing from Alzace in France, had served in the tsar's armies. On April 18 he was promoted in rank to Lieutenant Colonel, but he was still called "major.")[51]

The frontline extended from the Arax River to Mt. Aragads, but beyond that, the Bash-Aparan front was to be defended by Dro with his regiment.[52]

The church bells rang, sounding the alarm for the decisive battle. People and army, women and clerics, started heading to the Sartarapat plain.

From May 24 through May 29, General Silikian threw his reserves as well into the front for an assault which completely destroyed Shefki Pasha's forces, on the plain of Sartarapat. The Armenian cavalry chased the enemy to the heights of Alexandropol.

At the same time, on May 25, the Turkish forces engaged in battle the first Armenian regiment near Gharakilisa. The Armenians resisted for four days but then yielded to the enemy's superior artillery fire. The surviving soldiers retreated to Yerevan. The barbarian Turks, with their insatiable thirst for the blood of innocent people, massacred 7,000 of the Armenians in the region.[53]

The Armenians found themselves in a blind alley in Batum also. The Tatars and Georgians did not want to fight. The Tatars appealed for reconciliation with the Turks at all costs, whereas the Georgians had secured themselves with German support. The Armenians were left alone against the Turks, near Sartarapat, Bash-Aparan, and Gharakilisa.

## THE BATTLE OF BASH-APARAN

In May of 1918, when the Armenian nation's struggle for existence was taking place on the Sartarapat plain, Dro, with his warriors, heroically fought the Turks in the battle of Bash-Aparan and emerged crowned with victory, a victory with fateful significance for the Armenian nation and the building of statehood.

Some details regarding the Bash-Aparan battle:

Dro at first was not enthusiastic about the idea of defending the Bash-Aparan front. His opinion was that considering the premise that the Armenian forces, in quantity and quality, could measure up to the Turkish forces advancing toward Sartarapat, the Armenian command should keep the Armenian regiments together. A concentrated strike could destroy the Turks' forces congregating at Sartarapat, and this could be followed by moving the united Armenian forces to the Bash-Aparan front, encircling the Turkish forces there, and vanquishing them.

A dispute between Dro and Silikian arose about this military-strategic perspective. Silikian said, "I appoint you commander of Bash-Aparan." Dro replied, "I will go wherever you want, just do not divide the army. Let us, with full force, attack the Turkish forces advancing toward Sartarapat and massacre them. What is our information? We are informed that they have altogether two battalions. Even if they reach Ashtarak, we can massacre them."[54]

After considering this scenario of how events might unfold, Silikian did not accept Dro's perspective and sent him to the Bash-Aparan front.

Dro went to Bash-Aparan with a relatively small number of troops. From the division he commanded, Silikian kept with him the strongest combat detachment, the special operations battalion. Under Dro's command remained the companies led by Martiros, Kuro Tarkhanian, the cavalry forces led by Zemliak, Colonel Korolkov, Zalinian, and a part of Sakelian's company. Some other forces would arrive at the Bash-Aparan front later.

Before the arrival of Dro in Bash-Aparan, a notable portion of the region's population able to bear arms had resorted to self-defense. Following Aram's instructions, some groups of partisan fighters led by Arsen Ter Poghosian, Setrak Djalalian, and others moved from Edjmiadsin to Bash-Aparan and raised the banner of self-defense without waiting for the arrival of organized regiments.[55]

H. G. Turshian in his *Heroic Battle of Sartarapat:*

"At the Bash-Aparan front, where there were no Armenian regimental cadres, the resistance, as we have said, was started by partisans gathered at the village of Kuludja, led by locals, communist David Maliksetian and Mathew Hovanesian. On May 23, Arsen Agha (Ter Poghosian) and Sedo (Sedrak Djalalian) with their groups reached them to lend a hand."[56]

When Dro arrived at Bash-Aparan, he was informed that the Turkish 3rd division's command, having already occupied the heights near Aragads, was planning to exploit those favorable positions to outflank and surround the Armenian detachments in a pincer movement. For that reason, the Armenian forces were deprived of the possibility of organizing an attack in the direction of the Aragads heights.

To forestall this dangerous situation, Dro conceived a military plan of striking the enemy at its center, unexpectedly and fast, thus depriving it of gaining the upper hand on the right and left flanks.

"At Alagiaz," relates Dro, "I had a battalion; I left two companies there. The other two I deployed at the center. I also sent two companies from the reserve battalion to the center. Thus I had six companies at the center."[57]

Dro attacked the enemy with the assembled forces and, throwing them back, seized Aparan.

The successful outcome of the assault initiated by the Armenian forces was, however, short lived. The enemy, rapidly deploying fresh forces to the battlefield, mounted a massive counter-strike against the Armenian forces.

Dro admitted, "At first we mounted a successful assault but they also successfully threw us back . . . so far back, that they seized Bash-Aparan from us."[58]

After pulling back from Bash-Aparan, Dro retreated to the south of Ali-Kochak and took up positions at the villages of Khanzafar and Garakilisa. On May 24, Dro received military assistance, the 200 horsemen of Djhankir Agha (sent by General Silikian). Altogether (including the local forces) there were approximately 5,000 men at the Bash-Aparan front.[59]

On May 25, the Turks, exploiting their success, reached the vicinity of Ali-Kochak and Zamrlu (Kasakh) villages, where, ready and lying in wait to ambush them, were the companies led by Kuro Tarkhanian and Martiros of Bashgarn. All attempts by the enemy forces to advance failed. Dro's companies, with the cooperation of the natives of Aparan, blocked the Turkish forces' assaults.

Although the Armenian forces' initial assaults were inconclusive, Dro gained time. A day later, on May 26, Colonel Dolukhanian's 3rd regiment and the remainder of Sakelian's battalion reached Bash-Aparan. These fresh forces were sent by General Silikian.[60] By now almost all the forces of Dro's division were available to serve under his command. Having reorganized, they arrived at the front. On May 27, with a strong counterattack, Dro threw back the Turks from the vicinity of Ali Kochak and approached Aparan.

Dro transferred two out of four companies positioned on each flank to the center. He transferred the cavalry of Sakelian, Korolkov, and Djhangir Agha from the frontline to the rear. There was a severe rain and hail storm the evening before the battle. Dro's scouts, exploiting the cover provided by nature, revealed the details of the enemy's positions with his scouts.[61]

At dawn on May 28, Dro issued the command to attack straight at the center. The Turks, unable to withstand the Armenians' withering fire and forceful assaults, abandoned their positions and began retreating toward Aparan.

The Turkish command, exploiting the advantage of its higher positions, tried to strike the Armenians' flanks, and then their back. Under Sahakian's command, the resistance displayed by the two companies and the armed populace of Aparan was steadfast and resolute. After numerous attacks, when the enemy could not overcome the resistance of the Armenian soldiers, the Turkish command threw the bulk of its forces to the center and tried to develop an advance in that direction. Thus, the Turkish forces moved from their impregnable positions on the heights along the flanks to the center, where Dro, hidden from them, had concentrated most of his forces.

The critical moment was approaching. A daring assault was necessary. Under cover of heavy artillery fire, Dro threw into battle his forces in the center.[62]

Recalling that historic moment, Dro would later relate:

"It was then that Korolkov [the commander of the cavalry] fulfilled his historic role. I said, 'I'm sending the cavalry to a mortal combat.'

"I sent the Yezidis too, under the command of Djhankir Agha. I threw all the forces to the attack.[3]

"You know, Vardges [Aharonian], of the 700 horsemen in the cavalry, 160 were casualties, unheard of in the history of cavalry.

"But, they penetrated, tore apart the Turkish formations.

"Djemlyak was also killed, many lads were killed.

"We threw Sakeli's company [into the attack] too.

"But I did not expect such a quick rout of the Turks."[63]

---

[3] Belonging to the Yezidi sect.

By the evening of May 29, the enemy was defeated, sustaining more than two hundred dead and leaving behind two artillery pieces, along with more than 100 rifles and supplies.[64]

The defeated enemy retreated from Aparan toward the North.[65]

A failure in any one of the three main battles (of Sartarapat, Bash-Aparan and Gharakilisa) in the heroic struggle of the Armenian nation in May of 1918 could have led to negative and tragic consequences in the other two. In this respect, Dro was well aware of the importance of the frontline entrusted to him. The May 2 counterstrike had greatly enhanced the morale of the soldiers and the region's populace.

Misak Torlakian, a hero who took part in the battle of Bash-Aparan, relates:

"Irregular bands, some armed, some holding axes and swords, some old, some young, were approaching one after the other and . . .

" 'Hello, dear Dro, here we are, at your command.'

"And Dro would make necessary arrangements to harness everyone's service for the sake of the homeland's salvation. Those were historic, fateful days. The old [battle of] Avarair was resurrected. The ancient Armenian nation had resurrected itself with its martial spirit."[66]

Thus, Silikian and Dro, fighting the enemy with approximately matching forces, each achieved an important victory. When Silikian felt that Nazarbekian could be heading to defeat, he sent the two companies from Van to the rescue. In the meantime, on June 4, a treaty was signed in Batum between the Armenians and the Turks. Surprisingly, the Turkish 12th division, without taking part in the battle of Sartarapat, had retreated and joined the 11th division of the Turkish Caucasus army.[67]

(I wonder if the commander of the Turkish 12th division had Armenian blood in his veins. Perhaps from his mother? Otherwise how to explain this riddle....)

News of the victory of the Armenian forces in the battle of Bash-Aparan reached Yerevan. Inspired by the good tidings, a large crowd gathered around Yerevan's National Council building, eagerly awaiting news from the Sartarapat front.

Avetis Aharonian describes that time, when emotions were stirred up with joy and national pride:

"The *raya* (serf/slave) Armenian has vanquished the Turk on the battlefield for the first time since the fall of the Cilician (Armenian) Kingdom. Rumors say we have won, but, is it true?

"Dro has squeezed the enemy and is chasing him mercilessly. As to the Sartarapat front, the breasts of the crowd in front of the National Council building's balcony were heaving with excitement and impatience. They were murmuring rumors of victory to each other. Hopeful, joyful anticipation was everywhere. Then Aram appeared on the balcony surrounded by colleagues. Everyone's gaze turned to him. Telegram in hand, pale with excitement, but with a smile on his face, this somber man is gladdened with the mysterious paper he is holding, like a child with a bird he has caught. Dead silence. As if the crowd had even stopped breathing. That whole amorphous, boiling mass of people had become one eye and one ear. Moses had not brought a bigger annunciation from the mountain to the Israelites.

"Armenian nation! Hear our intrepid commander General Silikian's telegram. 'The battle that lasted more than five days concluded with the complete defeat of the enemy'."[68]


## APPRAISAL OF THE GLORIOUS VICTORY OF SARTARAPAT

(From academician-historian Hrand A. Avetisian's book, *The Victory of the Armenian National Unity in May 1918*.)

"The threat of finally losing the homeland had rallied and aroused the entire Armenian nation. Hundreds of people were presenting themselves to the military divisions, to volunteer to go to the frontline. The villagers were providing means of transport and provisions, entering the ranks of local militias. Regardless of political persuasion, they were engaged in a life and death struggle for the sake of the Armenians' homeland and national dignity. To the battle had rallied the intelligentia and the devout, the laborer and the peasant, young and old, women and young girls, and representatives of all political parties. In the ranks of the defenders was the cleric and Armenologist Garegin Hovsepian. 'In the region of Yerevan, the entire reign was in the hands of Aram Manukian, who was working in solidarity with General Silikian and Dro, inspiring the people and the armed forces. Their notable competence in organizing and maximizing the military and economic resources of the Yerevan region enabled the Armenians to defend, rifles in hand, a fragment of their homeland, the one city, Yerevan, and the monastery of Holy Edjmiadsin, and if they were accountable to us Armenians, then as well as now, credit goes exclusively to three individuals, Aram, Genral Silikian and Dro, wrote on February 7, 1919, the commander of the Armenian artillery brigade and veteran of the battle of Sartarapat, Colonel Kh. Araratian.

" 'The Armenian forces relied on the support of the Armenian villages, which were giving their all, in terms of both volunteers and provisions,' witnessed Chnéour.

"Our first victory at Sartarapat—according to H. Turshian—like a miraculous flourish of a magic wand, lifted the refugees' and the locals' sad disposition, and steeping everyone with faith in victory, transformed the dejected people into a united and determined whole."[69]

— — — — —

A final appraisal from Marshal Hovannes Baghramian of the Soviet Union, "In those extremely complex political and military conditions, General Silikian made the only correct decision—comprehensively planned, without exaggeration, brilliant."

And later, "I cannot pass in silence over the distinguished role of Movses Silikian in destroying the

Turks at Sartarapat. In that daunting time he headed the Yerevan division of the Armenian forces. I am deeply convinced that of all the generals at that time, Silikian was the most talented."[70]

After declaring victory, the Armenian National Council of Tbilisi immediately embarked on forming a government. Hovannes Kadjaznouni was unanimously elected prime minister. His cabinet, which was in Tbilisi, arrived in Yerevan in August. In the meantime, Armenia was being governed by the National Council of Yerevan and the army.

The newly born Republic of Armenia's first legislative assembly convened on August 1. Aram became a minister. As for Dro, he became chief of the capital's armed forces and later, commander-in-chief.

Armenia had a defense minister, General Hovannes (Ivan) Hakvertian, and a chief of staff, Thomas Nazarbekian; each was a remnant of the disintegrated army of tsarist Russia.

According to Vratsian, "The government was willing to bestow military rank and epaulets to Dro, but he tersely declined. To the end he remained without titles."[71]


## GENERAL ANDRANIK, GUARDIAN ANGEL OF THE TURKISH-ARMENIAN REFUGEES

Where was Andranik in those glorious days of victory at Sartarapat and Bash-Aparan? The hero had set up a base at Dilidjan as guardian angel of the Turkish-Armenian refugees.

Around 35,000 Turkish-Armenian refugees, hungry and homeless, felt secure only in the shadow of Andranik. Wherever he went, they followed their venerated hero.

Andranik was well aware that there were around ten Russian-Armenian generals in Yerevan, left from the tsarist army, who were able to take care of the military needs of the Eastern Armenians.

While in Dilidjan, Andranik obtained a copy of the Batum treaty. On the day he read this document, the general was very upset. Because of the ineptitude of Armenian political leaders and the treachery of the likes of Bejanbekov, his life's vision was shattered. The golden opportunity to liberate at least a fragment of Turkish Armenia had eluded his hands in front of Erzrum's ramparts, and all hopes built on thirty years of struggles were vanished. And now the sliver of Russian-Armenia liberated under terribly heavy and oppressive conditions had not a single guarantee of survival without a miracle. Upon reading the unbearably oppressive terms of the black treaty of Batum, the hero's mind was tortured, his spirit in turmoil, and his heart in despair. He did not eat that day, but rather brooded in his tent in the Dilidjan valley, rolling cigarettes, smoking, and drinking.

At dusk, to ease his inner turmoil, the general came out of his tent and headed toward the nearby forest. Preoccupied and feeling sad, he could not relate to the beauty of Dilidjan's green valley and colorful flowers.

He noticed a young woman, carrying an urn of water on her shoulder, barely dragging herself along the trail. She put the urn on the ground, sat down panting. She looked skeletal, pale as death.

"Are you sick, sister?" asked Andranik.

The young woman could barely talk. She shook her head "no."

"What then?"

The woman pointed to her stomach, explaining that she was hungry.

Andranik's eyes moistened. He ordered his bodyguard to carry the woman's urn to her hut and then to take a sack of flour from the division's supplies to the same hut.[72]

## DECLARATION OF ARMENIA'S INDEPENDENCE

In Batum, the Turks gave an ultimatum to the

Armenian envoys, demanding that they declare Armenia's independence. They gave the Armenians three days to accept those humiliating conditions, which they presented in a sealed envelope.

The Armenian envoys hurried to Tbilisi. They arrived on the morning of May 27. On May 28, at 10:00 a.m., the delegates of the Armenian political parties revealed that they were in favor of a declaration of independence. A manifesto was composed, and Armenia's independence was declared at noon. Had they not declared independence, Armenia would have had the status of unclaimed territory *(res nullins)* and as such, would have been divided up among its neighbors.[73]

On May 29, the Armenian envoys returned to Batum and delivered the declaration of independence at 7:00 in the evening, one hour before the deadline of the ultimatum.

By the way, the intent of the Turks, in pressing by ultimatum for the Armenians' independence, was to separate and isolate them from the Russian empire. For as long as Eastern Armenia was part of the Russian empire, the Turks could not massacre the Eastern Armenians, as they had done to the Western Armenians. But if Armenia, in separating from Russia, became independent, then at the first opportunity they could invade inside the borders of Armenia and annihilate and wipe out Armenia and Armenians—just like Kemalist Kiazim Karapekir tried to do on September 21, 1920; but after the Turks' arrival at the gates of Yerevan, this plan failed with the entry of the Red Army into Armenia.

Later, referring to the circumstances of the creation of the Republic of Armenia, S. Vratsian would write:

"Whereas the Georgians and the Turks (Azeri Tatars) had declared their independence, the Armenian National Council was hesitating, considering independence under such horrible conditions a bitter irony. For the salvation of the Armenian nation, everyone's gaze remained turned to the North.

"That is why the session of the National Council which examined 'independence' resembled a wake."[74]

# NOTES

1. Hamlet Gevorgian, *Dro,* Yerevan, 1991, p 72.
2. Ibid, p 72.
3. *General Andranik Speaks and Additional Articles,* Los Angeles, 1974, pp 54–55.
4. Gersam Aharonian, *On the Way to Our Grand Vision,* 2nd ed, Beirut, 1964, p 82.
5. *The Historic Diary of General Andranik on the Caucasus Front,* pp 50–51.
6. Ibid, p 51.
7. Avetis Terzipashian, *Nubar,* Paris, 1939, p 199.
8. Ibid, p 200.
9. *The Historic Diary of General Andranik on the Caucasus Front,* p 76.
10. Avetis Terzipashian, *Nubar,* pp 200–202.
11. *The Historic Diary of General Andranik on the Caucasus Front,* p 77.
12. Ibid, pp 75–76.
13. Levon Tutunjian, *The Tragedy of Karin's Fall.* See *Memorial Book of the Great Atrocit,* Beirut, 1965, pp 823–824.
14. Ibid, p 826.
15. Simon Vratsian, *Independent and United Armenia,* Boston, 1920, p 19.
16. *The Historic Diary of General Andranik on the Caucasus Front,* p 91.
17. Ibid, p 91.
18. Avetis Terzipashian, *Andranik,* 1942, p 335.
19. Ibid, p 35.
20. Lieutenant M. Avetian, *National Jubilee (1870–1920) Memomrial Book of the Armenian Liberation Movement and General Andranik,* 1954, p 183.
21. Avetis Yapujian, *The Political, Military, Economic, and Social Conditions of the Republic of Armenia,* Cairo, 1972, p 260.
22. Ibid, p 260.

23. Ibid, p 261. *Note—Serge Afanasyan, in his *La Victoire de Sardarabad* book, p 109, confuses this Bagramian with Marshal Bagramian. This Bagramian has no relation to Marshal Ivan Kristoforovich Bagramian. See Jacques Kayaloff, *The Battle of Saradarabad,* p 54.
24. Serge Afanasyan, *La Victoire de Sardarabad. Arménie, 21–29 Mai, 1918,* Éditions L'Harmattam Paris, 1985, p 28. Bagramian, *Mémoirs,* p 57.
25. Ibid, pp 27–28.
26. Vahan Papazian, *My Recollections,* vol 2, Beirut, 1952, p 467.
27. Ibid, p 470.
28. Richard G. Hovannisian, *The Republic of Armenia,* vol I, 1918–1919, The University of California Press, Berkeley, Los Angeles, London, p 162.
29. Simon Vratsian, *Along Life's Pathways,* vol 4, p 180.
30. Ibid, p 181.
31. Hamlet Gevorgian, *Dro,* Yerevan 1991, p 73.
32. Vratsian, *Along Life's Pathways,* vol 4, p 182.
33. Alexander Khadisian, *The Beginning and Development of the Republic of Armenia,* 2nd ed, Beirut, 1968, p 67.
34. A. M. Poghosian, *Socio-Economic Relationships in the Province of Kars, 1878–1920,* Yerevan, 1961, p 307.
35. Alexander Khadisian, p 69.
36. Ibid, p 72.
37. Ibid, p 74.
38. Ibid, p 76.
39. W.E.D. Allen and Paul Muratoff, *Caucasian Battlefields.* Cambridge University Press, 1953. Reprinted with permission, the Battery Press, Inc., Nashville, TN 1999, p 470.
40. Ibid, p 470.
41. Hrand A. Avetisian, *The Victory Achieved by Armenian National Unity in May 1918,* Yerevan, p 94.
42. Ibid, p 100.
43. Ibid, p 100–101.
44. Serge Afanasyan, p 45.

45. W.E.D. Allen and Paul Muratoff, p 475.
46. Ibid, p 475.
47. *Asbarez Daily,* Los Angeles, May 28, 1980. p 6.
48. Ibid, p 6.
49. Ibid, p 6.
50. Ibid, p 6.
51. Jacques Kayaloff, *The Battle of Sardarabad,* Mouton, The Hague, Paris, 1973, p 17, n 17, also p 36, note 10.
52. Serge Afanasyan, p 45.
53. Alexander Khadisian, p 80.
54. Hamlet Gevorgian, p 90.
55. Ibid, p 91.
56. H. G. Turshian, The *Heroic Battle of Sardarabad,* Yerevan, 1969, pp 163-164 (H. Gevorgian, p 92).
57. *Hairenic Daily,* 1956, May 28 (H. Gevorgian, p 96).
58. Ibid, May 27 (H. Gevorgian p 94).
59. Serge Afanasyan, p 61.
60. W.E.D. Allen and Paul Muratoff, pp 475–476.
61. Hamlet Gevorgian, pp 96–97.
62. Ibid, p 97.
63. Ibid, p 98.
64. Journal Q. G. pp 21–23; Serge Afanasyan, p 62.
65. W.E.D. Allen and Paul Muratoff, pp 475–476.
66. Misak Torlakian, *Memoirs,* Beirut, 1963, pp 408–409.
67. W.E.D. Allen and Paul Muratoff, p 476.
68. *Alik* (Wave), Extra Edition, *In Memory of Dro,* 1956, p 43. (Hamlet Gevorkian, p 99.)
69. Hrand Avetisian, *The Victory Achieved by Armenian National Unity in May 1918.* Yerevan, 2001, pp 98–99.
70. Ibid, p 94.
71. Simon Vratsian, *Along Life's Pathways,* vol 4, p 185.
72. Antranig Chalabian, *General Andranik and the Armenian Revolutionary Movement,* p 507.
73. Hovhannes Kadjaznuni, *The A.R.F. Has Nothing Left To Do,* Cairo, 1954, p 31.

74. M. Serobian, *On the Occasion of the Independence of Armenia,* Cairo, 1050, p 11 (see S. Vratsian, *Independent and United Armenia,* pp 45–46).

# FEDAYEE SONG

Armenian Troubadour
(Avetik Isahakian)

In unequal, intrepid struggle
You fell, my eminent friends.
Oh, your tomb is in my heart,
My eminent, my sacred friends. . .

— — — — —

In the valleys, battlegrounds of Salno
The fedayee has fallen with deeply wounded heart,
His wound open like a red rose,
His hand gripping his broken rifle.

In the bloodied fields the cricket is chirping
The fedayee has fallen into death's deep sleep
The fedayee is seeing a dream in his soul,—
Our homeland free . . . secure . . .

# CHAPTER IV

## THE FIRST REPUBLIC OF ARMENIA
## FACES POLITICAL AND ECONOMIC
## DIFFICULTIES

## WHY GENERAL ANDRANIK REFUSED TO RECOGNIZE THE REPUBLIC OF ARMENIA CREATED BY THE TREATY OF BATUM

From the day the Eastern Armenians' National Council of Tbilisi signed a conciliation agreement with the Turks in Batum, General Andranik's Separate Armenian Strike Force ceased having any link with the Republic of Armenia.

"General Andranik did not have faith in the Turks, nor in the future of the Republic of Armenia created by the 'dictates' of the Turks at the Batum Congress. He was certain that the Turks were being deceptive in Batum, by bestowing independence upon the Armenians . . . . The existence of an independent Armenian Republic may serve the Turks' temporary calculations, but not their permanent interests."[1]

As always, Andranik had guessed correctly the Turks' mind.

What had happened that the Turks, after committing the Great Atrocity (the Armenian Genocide), suddenly were bestowing "independence" on some thousands of Armenians who had survived? The reason was the following:

In early 1918, the Turks had become convinced that their side (Germany, Austria-Hungary, Turkey, and Bulgaria) was going to lose the war. As shrewd politicians they had decided to create a tiny Armenia outside their borders, of a temporary nature, so that if the Genocide of the Armenians got on the agenda of the peace conference, and if the *Ittihad* (Young Turk) Party's inner circle were put on trial as war criminals (as in Nuremberg), the Turkish representative would say, "Genocide? We solved the Armenian question by creating the independent Republic of Armenia!"[2]

Whereas, if the Armenian Genocide were not put on the agenda of the peace conference, they would simply destroy the temporarily created Armenian Republic, which indeed they tried to do under the command of Kiazim

Karabekir Pasha on September 21, 1920, when the Turkish army rushed across the borders of Armenia. The details follow:

In the summer of 1919, a peace treaty was signed with Germany, and until then the victorious allies—Britain, France, USA, tsarist Russia, Belgium, Italy, Japan, Serbia, Montenegro, Greece, Romania, and Portugal—had not even mentioned the Armenian Genocide. The Turks, noticing that nobody was questioning them about the Armenian massacres, instructed Kiazim Karabekir Pasha to prepare to destroy the Republic of Armenia created shortly before with ulterior motives.

By the way, about the concept of creating a tiny Armenia of a temporary nature and with ulterior motives, read *The Origin and Development of the Republic of Armenia,* 2nd ed, by Alexander Khadisian, published by Hamazkain in Beirut, 1968, starting on page 89. He was prime minister from September 1919 to May 5, 1920.

The Turkish rationale for the scheme of creating a tiny Armenia was, first, that *"There are around two million surviving Armenians now and it is not possible to annihilate them all, thus it is preferable to mollify them because, even if only 100,000 Armenians remain on the face of the earth, they will not leave us alone, ever,"* (per Talaat, the Young Turk interior minister), and second, that *"By creating a little Armenia we would have solved the Armenian question and as such can be present at the international peace conference . . . ."* (Also per Talaat. Emphasis mine.)[3]

Not every member of the Young Turk Committee of Constantinople was in agreement with Talaat's scheme to establish a small Armenia based on the considerations noted above. Some, led by Enver,[4] wanted to annihilate the Armenians of the Caucasus (Russian or Eastern Armenian) too, but Talaat's viewpoint prevailed and "the Turks created little Armenia."[4]

---

[4] Enver Pasha, the defense minister, part of the Young Turk troika (Talaat, Enver, and
Jemal Pasha) ruling Turkey during WWI.

For Andranik to endorse the Treaty of Batum would have meant accepting the Republic of Yerevan, around 9,000 square kilometers, as resolution of the Armenian question and legitimizing the loss of Turkish Armenia. He could not submit to the humiliating Turkish conditions of the Treaty of Batum and concede the loss of Turkish Armenia, for whose liberation he had struggled for around 30 years and failed . . . solely because of the treason of Colonel Bezhanbekov on February 26, 1918.

In regard to this, Montreal's *Horizon* Weekly wrote, "The soaring hawk in the sky does not turn into a reptile . . . ."[5]

Andranik's negative stance toward the Republic of Armenia was not of a personal nature; it was generally the stance of the entire Turkish- Armenian community, both the people and the leadership, from Poghos Nubar Pasha to Turkish-Armenian ARF leaders Michael Varandian, Garegin Pastrmajian, and Hamo Ohandjanian, who, while remaining loyal to the Republic of Armenia, had the same worries about the Turkish Armenian cause and its future, as did General Andranik.[6]

For General Andranik and all Turkish-Armenian people and leaders, the real Armenia was the Armenian Highlands—Erzrum, Van, Mush, Sassun, Pitlis. The Yerevan Republic of the Russian Armenians was merely a small province on the eastern frontier of the real Armenia; Armenians were scarce in the new Republic and the liberation of that province would not bring any resolution to the liberation of Turkish Armenia.

Armenians were indeed scarce in Yerevan because the affluent and the elite of the Eastern Armenians generally resided in Baku or Tbilisi, more developed and prosperous cities than Yerevan, which was a country town buried in dust during summers and filled with mud during winters, and which for the most part was  inhabited by Tatars.

Until 1920, the population of Yerevan was around 30,000; more than half were Azeri Tatars. In Tbilisi and its environs resided more than 300,000 Armenians, the same as in Baku.

What follows is the common people's stance toward the Yerevan Republic: "The Armenian Delegation in Paris, headed by Poghos Nubar Pasha, enjoyed more authority among Western Armenians than the government of the Republic of Armenia. The term 'Republic of Armenia' was not acceptable for many—for it was merely the 'Araratian (or Yerevanian) Republic'."[7]

## ANDRANIK MARCHES ON YEREVAN

There are a few versions of this story noted in my *General Andranik* (the original Armenian edition), pages 551–554. I will relate the last of those, which I deem the most accurate.

In 1954, when Dro was in New York, Vardges Aharonian, the son of the notably talented writer of the early twentieth century Avetis Aharonian, asked Dro to relate the circumstances under which Andranik's "invasion" of Yerevan had taken place.

Dro related that in February or March 1919, news came to the effect that Andranik had arrived at Davaloo having come from Zangezur via Daralagiaz. Dro arranged to have Sulukidze's wagon prepared for his trip to Davaloo. When he got there he found out that Andranik had left for Ghamarlu. Dro ordered the horses to be prepared and went on to Ghamarlu. He did not find Andranik there either, and continued his pursuit until he caught up with him in the vineyards region of Yerevan.

(During the Armenian-Georgian war, the Armenians had captured from Commander Sulukidze that posh wagon, which they utilized for the transport of state officials and foreign dignitaries.)

The meeting was friendly, they embraced, and Dro invited Andranik to Yerevan as the government's guest.

Andranik refused.

"If you do not want to be the government's guest," said Dro, "be my guest. Yerevan's people welcome you as an honored guest."

"I would be your guest wherever you wish," replied Andranik, "but I will not come to Yerevan."

Andranik headed toward Edjmiadsin with his soldiers. Dro went with him, and after arranging for the provision of Andranik's soldiers' needs from the army's stores, returned to Yerevan.

After midnight the same day, Yerevan's Archbishop Khoren Muratbekian and Father Garegin Hovsepian informed Dro that Andranik was marching on Yerevan.

Dro sent Colonel Kuro Tarkhanian to restore order.

To suppress some uncontrolled renegades, Tarkhanian ordered his soldiers to fire over their heads. Nonetheless, one of Andranik's soldiers got shot in the leg. Andranik heard the news in exaggerated proportions and marched on Yerevan. Dro, with his companies, took up position facing Andranik and sent him the following letter:

"Andranik,

"We are the generation inspired and educated by your revolutionary spirit, by your revolutionary struggles in the mountains of Sassun. Today, based on untrue reports made up by some drunkards, you are marching on Yerevan.

"I implore my adored fedayee chieftain not to bring a black stain on your revolutionary record and to refrain from taking steps against Yerevan.

"At the same time, as commander of the Yerevan District, I feel it is my duty to warn you that if you do not desist from your intention, you will force me to resort to force of arms, and I assure you, you will not be able to enter Yerevan. I have issued the necessary orders in that regard. It is futile to try—you will not reach your goal."[8]

Andranik, calming down, returned to Edjmiadsin and whipped those captains who had relayed false information to him.[9]

114

## THE ARMENO-GEORGIAN WAR

The Georgians provoked this war by occupying Armenian lands, blocking the railroad transporting supplies from abroad to Armenia, and subjecting the people to famine. The Armenians had no choice but to resort to arms.

I will sum up a few scenes from that insane war:

In October 1918, because of border disputes, relations were strained between the Armenians and the Georgians.

When the Turks vacated the Armenian region of Lori-Pampak, Armenian forces under Dro's command occupied it. The government of Georgia considered this step illegitimate and commenced military operations on October 23. This behavior toward Armenia, which at that time was subjected to famine and diseases, was considered cruel and hostile. The Armenians made some attempts to resolve the border disputes peacefully, but to no avail.

Throughout November, and until early December, the government of Armenia kept getting endless complaints and protests from the people of Lori that the Georgian troops were living off of the Armenian peasants without compensation. Under the pretext of conducting investigations, they would enter homes and take away whatever they wanted. They would molest the women and confiscate the peasants' stores of wheat, cattle, hay, oil, cheese, potatoes, poultry, eggs, etc. The same barbarian atrocities were being inflicted on the people of Akhalkalaki. Regarding Lori, the historian Leo would write:

"Our history of the past two thousand years leads us to the conclusion that we could not imagine Armenia through the centuries without Lori. This would be considered all the more unimaginable today, because to cut off Lori form the body of Armenia means to dismember its entire past and its cultural treasures—to concede to looting the magnificent accomplishments of hundreds of generations through the centuries."[10]

On December 9, and again on December 12, the government of Armenia appealed to the government of

Georgia, begging for the sake of both nations, to end the oppression, to withdraw their forces from Lori, and to settle border disputes through peaceful negotiations.

The response of the government of Georgia being negative, the Armeno-Georgian war began on December 13.

The same day, the government of Armenia ordered the commander of the Dilidjan-Lori region, Dro, to clear out the Georgian forces from Lori.

The reaction in Tbilisi to the Armenians' audacious action:

"Until December 18, the Georgian forces retreated and congregated in the region of Sadakhlu. Little by little new forces arrived from Tbilisi. . . . All of Georgia was mobilized, conscription was implemented. In Tbilisi, threatening speeches were made in parliament sessions. The press spewed fire and lightning on the Armenians, who were delegitimized; hundreds of Armenian men were arrested and exiled to Kutais. As a whole, nationalist passions were aroused to an extreme degree.[11]

"On December 23, the Armenian forces reassembled to launch another offensive. The same day, after long and fierce battles, the 12 companies of the 4th regiment, under the command of Lieutenant-Colonel Aslanian, occupied Sadakhlu. The Armenians captured 6 officers, 126 soldiers, 2 machine guns, more than 100 wagons full of supplies, bullets and other munitions, 3 trains and other stores. The Armenian losses were Lieutenant-Colonel Alexandrov injured, 7 soldiers killed and 11 wounded."[12]

On December 25, the British General Rykroft and the French Colonel Shartini tried to reconcile the warring sides, but A. Djamalian remained opposed to the annexation of the district of Akhalkalak to Georgia.[13]

Despite A. Djamalian's protests, General Rykroft, Colonel Shartini, and President Zhordania of the Republic of Georgia decided that the delegates of Georgia and Armenia should go to Europe, where the question of borders would be resolved by the great states, and that the

116

military operations should end at midnight on December 31.[14]

In the meantime, both sides tried to gain advantages to end the war in favorable positions.

General conditions were becoming increasingly unfavorable to the Armenians. The Armenian soldiers had not had any rest for two weeks. The poorly clothed and meagerly supplied forces were exhausted, there were no reserves, and the government was busy with other issues. They were not receiving supplies from the rear. The troops were being fed by bread confiscated from the Georgians and were fighting with Georgian munitions.[15]

Finally, on December 31, at midnight, the warring sides ceased fire and the war ended.[16]

The suffering of the Armenian people did not end with the ceasefire. Armenia's legation in Tbilisi was shut down. Likewise, the Armenian National Council was shut down. Charitable organizations caring for the needs of refugees and orphans were shut down. Armenian newspapers were shut down. ARF members of the Tbilisi City Coucil were arrested. Armenian "militiamen" were fired from their jobs. A terrible persecution unfolded against Armenians in Tbilisi streets. The Armenian National Council presented to the government of Georgia a long memorandum regarding the terrible and arbitrary atrocities and violence being perpetrated against the Armenians. What follows is an excerpt from that memorandum:

". . . The half million Armenians living under Georgian rule have been denied all their rights; their honor, their estates, liberty and belongings have become subject to the unrestrained whims of the 'militia' and agents of the special forces. . . . The Armenian National Council's archives were sealed and all its material resources, as well as monies and medicines assigned for refugees, were confiscated. At the same time, entirely innocent individuals are being arrested, with the aim of extortion; in the event of refusal or complaining to authorities, they are threatened with execution. One can form an idea about the extent of degeneracy by the fact that the militiamen and special agents had set ransom prices ranging from 50 to 50,000 rubles, and there were not uncommon instances when representatives of both agencies submitted demands for money regarding the same individual, and if the naïve hapless person notes that he has already paid to the one then that fact reinforces the demands of the other claimant."[17]

On January 5, 1919, arrests of Armenians took place on a massive scale. "Militia agents," wrote the Georgian (Armenian) National Council, "like beasts in the literal sense of the word, went on a hunt against Armenians; within a few hours, they arrested 6,000. A few hundred were lucky enough to be able to pay, on the spot, in broad daylight, the demanded ransom or, securing permission to go home accompanied by the militiamen, they paid an even larger sum to get rid of these tyrants."[18]

Conditions in the provinces were worse than in Tbilisi. Besides unlawful extortions, looting, and jailing, rapes and murders took place there.

Thus, after occupying the village of Bolnis-Khachen, they looted everything and carried away staples in an organized fashion. They took away bread, wheat, grains, potatoes, beans, walnuts, fabrics, sewing machines, cutlery, pots and pans, agricultural implements, silver and gold, furniture, etc. Whatever they could not take away they destroyed. They laid to waste the houses' doors, windows, fixtures, beehives. They took away the livestock—the cows, horses, sheep, poultry. The soldiers and officers would drink wine and rape the young women remaining in the village.[19]

Similar atrocities took place in other villages. At the summer resort located in the center of Beli-Kluch, soldiers entered an orphanage and demanded women. When the latter fled, they raped a couple of pre-pubescent girls and left. A couple of days later the same thing occurred again in the same orphanage. The administration appealed to the local authorities but nothing came of it.[20]

During the Armenian-Georgian war, the enemy displayed barbaric behavior toward the Armenian populace, with the connivance of the state, whereas when a few dozen Georgian officers were captured and brought to Yerevan, the Armenians put out a feast in their honor, drinking and toasting Dro as well as the fraternal Georgian-Armenian friendship.[21]

## ANDRANIK GOES ABROAD

By the time it reached Edjmiadsin, General Andranik's 5,000-strong Separate Armenian Strike Force had dwindled down to 1,350 soldiers. As a result of difficulties he had with the Yerevan government and the diplomatic machinations of the British in the TransCaucasus, Andranik disbanded his division, handed the weapons to the Catholicos, and, accompanied by British Colonel Gibbons and twenty soldiers, set out toward foreign shores.

When they reached the Georgian border, Gibbons asked Andranik whether the Georgian government would allow him to enter Tbilisi with twenty soldiers. The general replied that he would immediately send a cable to the foreign minister of Georgia, Mr. Kekechkori, informing him that he is coming to Tbilisi. Andranik said in his cable, "I am coming to your capital accompanied by twenty soldiers, to be a guest for a few days and from there go to Batum and abroad."[22]

Kekechkori sent vehicles in the middle of the night to receive Andranik and his companions with honors.

When the General had been in Zangezur province, he had heard that units from the army of the Republic of Armenia, under the command of Dro, had clashed with Georgian border guards.

Five days after General Andranik arrived in Tbilisi, Minister Kekechkori sent him word that he would like to have a meeting.

The General picked the poet Hovannes Tumanian as his translator and, accompanied by a few bodyguards, went to Kekechkori's palace. (This was the palace of the former viceroy of the Caucasus, Grand Duke Nikolai Nikolayevich.)

After the formal reception, in a friendly and polite atmosphere, the conversation turned to the Armenian-Georgian clashes of recent days.

Andranik said, "I want to give my condolences for the soldiers fallen on both sides."

Kekechkori replied, "We are also sorry about the unpleasant event. We never imagined that Armenians would attack us. During the battle they told me that General Andranik is commanding the Armenian army.

"I told them, 'That is impossible. General Andranik would never take such a step; even if I were to see it with my own eyes I could not believe it.' I was right in my judgement. Conduct a small inquiry and ask the Armenians who is at fault. If we were the aggressor, and we are the guilty party, I am ready to redeem that wrong, General Andranik."

Mr. Kekechkori's voice quivered and he almost cried. The weight of his grief was choking his words.

Andranik answered, "I will depart tomorrow. I do not have the right to conduct an inquiry. How are the Armenians' thousands of orphans and refugees to blame for the incident? You closed the Batum-Yerevan railway subjecting them to famine. I appeal to your mercy to order the opening of the Batum-Yerevan railway and save the innocent people."

Kekechkori cradled his head in his hands as he contemplated. He was close to tears.

The following day when General Andranik, with his retinue, headed for Batum, he was greeted by Georgain honor-guards at all the stations.

When Andranik arrived in Batum, 70 wagons were being loaded with flour, destined for Yerevan.[23]

120

## MAUSERISTS

An excerpt from Simon Vratsian:

"Malicious and narrow-minded people even today malign the names of Dro and the so-called 'Mauserists,' as if Dro had patronized those elements who at one time had become a public menace. During wars and revolutions, Mauserism is a common phenomenon everywhere. Unemployed and accustomed to killing, people without moral restraints often resort to force of arms to ensure their survival. For a certain time such things occurred in Armenia also, as they did in America when the Civil War ended, and in the Soviet Union. And it is not unnatural that some of the 'Mauserists' might exploit Dro's and other famous activists' authority for their own ulterior motives. Dro, of course, was not the offender in this matter, and neither were Aram or Ruben when bandits were extorting money from the public in their names. On the contrary, Dro was a restraining and disciplining factor for such offenders. For the sake of historical truth, one has to add that 'Mauserism' in Armenia was no more than the same phenomenon in the aftermath of war in America or Europe. In comparison to Bolshevik 'Mauserism,' the Armenian variety was child's play.

"As I said, Dro enjoyed great charisma also among the youth. His ideological and social ties to Tbilisi's 'proletarian' group are well known. It was remarkable that Armenia's Western-Armenian youth also, particularly the lads who honed their mettle in the furnace of *Ashkhadank* (Labor—a publication) had intimate ties with him. The explanation lies not only in Dro's genuine humane nature, but also, from an ideological perspective, the likes of Barunak Kaputikian and Hemayak Manoogian, all of them had unreserved admiration and trust in him.

"The officer-corps actually venerated Dro. And again the reason was not only Dro's lively social temperament, but also, above all, his ideological patriotism, his selflessness, and his spirit of sacrifice. To die with—and

121

yes, for—Dro was considered an honor.

"I do not recognize, since Aram's demise, any other individual in Armenia in those days who was more popular, enjoyed more sympathy, and was more loved by all classes of the people, than Dro—Comrade Dro.

"He did not have any title. His title was comprised of three letters: DRO, at most, Comrade DRO, with the most intimate and genuine meaning of the word 'comrade'."[24]

Colonel Egor Ter Avetikian wrote the following about Mauserism:

"Another anecdote about Dro, on the occasion of his immortal death, and with that I will conclude my memoir about the great Armenian fighter, the unequalled warrior, about Dro who has passed on to eternity, because it seems daunting to me that we could replace him anytime soon with another new Dro.

"They 'blame' Dro, as being the founder of 'Mauserism.'

"The notion that Dro was the founder of Mauserism is true, completely true. I myself, being Dro's comrade and worshiper, declare and affirm that it was Dro, who, at a time when the Armenians of the Caucasus were in a deep slumber, founded 'Mauserism.' I will tell you how that took place, why Dro became a 'Mauserist.'

"All of you who do not like guns, who deny the value of guns, are aware that our misfortune, our losses are not to be attributed to the alleged timidity of the Armenian peasantry—our most valuable masses, nor to other reasons, but to the mostly internal factors, which are not loving guns, denying the value of guns.

"Our misfortune has been calamitous. Our losses have been invaluable, irreplaceable.

"The struggle for existence is based solely on force of arms, not on principles of morality, correctness, justice, humanity.

"The Creator—God Himself—has endowed all His creatures, the rational as well as animals, with the capacity

122

for self-defense.

"Show us that any creature of the Creator is denied means of self-defense and only then condemn us, for our expressed opinion, which essentially reflects Dro's viewpoint at the same time.

"Therefore, all nations and God's creatures are armed for self-defense, in the struggle for existence.

"If from among us, from the bosom of our nation, suddenly, unexpectedly, arises an individual who asserts a different law, a different vision, then without pausing, without deliberating, without any qualms, we rush to give the newborn new labels, and if we do not find a label pleasing to the heart, then at least with the expression 'Mauserist' we console ourselves.

"Therefore, since France is armed with the Lebel rifle, then 'Lebelist,' 'Lebelism' follow; in Germany, 'Mauserism,' since it is armed with the Mauser rifle. Austro-Hungary 'Manlikherist,' and in Russia 'Mosinov,' that is 'Mosinist,' 'Mosinism.'

"And when Armenia and Dro agreed that they also would find a weapon for the struggle for existence and in the first place obtained the Mauser handgun, the unjust, gun-hating Armenians who deny the value of arms could do nothing but console themselves by labeling us with a new title—'Mauserist.'

"The criminal element is not lacking in all nations, be they civilized, developing or wild, who would apply to an evil end their weapons which were manufactured or procured for self-defense.

"Civilized England, during the First World War, from among its forces deployed in France alone condemned 144 officers and soldiers to death for misusing their weapons" etc.[25]

————

In parentheses I should note that Colonel Egor Ter Avetikian's viewpoint on arms and martial training for a nation's defense and survival is correct and necessary. General Andranik also, when visiting a village and seeing that the youth had neither guns nor knowledge of how to use them, would get quite upset.

From centuries past to our present days, the naïve and guileless Armenian people have always prioritized the building of churches and praising the Lord, rather than having arms and martial training. On historic Armenia's hills there are countless ruins of monasteries, but fortresses are lacking.

Even the ruin of David Pek's "fortress," if you have seen it, reminds one of a garden wall . . . .

The Great Raffi, one of the greatest guides of the Armenian liberation movement, was well aware of this situation when he wrote:

*"Oh Fathers, oh Ancestors, if instead of all these monasteries with which our homeland is full, you had built fortresses, if instead of sacred crosses and vessels which consumed your riches, you had bought guns, if instead of burning aromatic incense in our temples, you had burnt gunpowder, now our homeland would have been fortunate. Kurds would no longer wreck our country, slaughter our sons, ravish our women. From those monasteries grew our homeland's destruction. They wrested our spirit and valor, they cast*
*us into serfdom, beginning with the day when [King] Trdat left his sword and crown, took up the cross and entered the Mania cave to become a hermit . . . . Oh Ancient Gods of Armenia, oh Anahit, oh Vahagn, oh Haik, I raise my chalice to your sacred memory, you save us . . . ."[26]*

Nevertheless, we have to accept that in the Diaspora, where there is no national homeland under our feet, the biggest factor in Armenian preservation—its footing and security—lies in the Armenian Church, whether apostolic, catholic, or evangelical, and, of course, Armenian schools and press.

— — — —

Countless monasteries but not a single fortress.

To get back to our topic, whatever the motives in issuing to certain individuals the right to carry Mauser handguns, some exploited that right to their own advantage. When there is famine in the country, principles of morality, law, justice, or humanity evaporate for the most part. If the aim of the government was martial training, then this should have been done in camps and retreats away from population centers.

125

## SLIGHT IMPROVEMENT IN THE ECONOMY

By the fall of 1919, the Republic of Armenia had become an adequately strengthened and stable country. The British, through their military presence, had expelled the Turks from the TransCaucasus, re-establishing the 1914 pre-war border between Turkey and Russia, which also extended Armenia's borders from 9,000 sq. kilometers to 50,000 sq. kilometers.

In other words, from the Spring of 1919 until September 21, 1920, around a year and a half, the expanded borders of the Republic of Armenia encompassed Nakhichevan, the province of fortress Surmalu with its majestic mountain, Ararat; the ruins of Ani; Dro's birthplace, Igdir; and Kars-Artahan. The British, in those years the world's number one superpower, had not officially annexed Gharabagh and Akhalkalak to Armenia, but the Armenians of those provinces considered themselves part of Armenia.

As of the Spring of 1919, with the destruction of the Turks in the TransCaucasus, Armenia became a de-facto independent and sovereign state. The people, of whom 150,000 had succumbed to the horrible famine of the Winter of 1918–1919, as well as cholera and typhoid epidemics (as for the whole year around 200,000 victims), had by the fall of 1919, with famine and epidemics lightening up and the delivery of flour and grain sent by the United States of America, reached a degree of relief from crisis.

Dro was no longer commander of the armed forces in Yerevan. Armenia was divided into new administrative districts, and Yerevan as the capital was a separate unit. Dro became division commander and member of parliament.[27]

At the ARF 9th General Assembly, convened in Bucharest, Romania, heated discussions took place about the Party's new by-laws and about the composition of the future regime in the Republic of Armenia.

The ARF Bureau had delegated Vratsian to report on both questions. As soon as he was done reporting, Ruben responded, contradicting him by asserting that Armenia was not developed enough to become a free democracy.[28]

Vratsian agreed that under current conditions in Armenia it would not be useful to fundamentally decentralize the authority of the Party, and that the Bureau and the Central Committees should be endowed with expanded powers; however, "the state should be a state with a democratic parliament, and a government accountable to parliament whose freedom of action should not be restricted by partisan monopoly."[29]

Vratsian's viewpoints were endorsed by the Bureau and were also supported by the readers of the *Ashkhadank* (Labor) newspaper in Tbilisi, who considered Vratsian a "left-wing ARF" member.

As for Dro, "[h]e was a Russophile in the full meaning of the term. Maybe the reason was that he had not had much to do with Europe. He did not have faith in European diplomacy, nor did he see sincerity among neighbors (Azerbaijan, Georgia); he was convinced that Armenia's national interest required that it remain allied with Russia, whether red or white.[30]

"In those days many were convinced of that. For that reason, the separation from Russia was so painful."[31]

The next issue for the Republic of Armenia was Gharabagh. The government of Azerbaijan had appointed Dr. Khosrov Bek Sultanov governor of the Province of Gharabagh and had mobilized the entire army to repress the rebellion of the Gharabagh Armenians against the Sultanov regime. The Armenian government sent Dro with his division to assist the rebels.

## DRO IN ZANGEZUR

In December 1919, Dro reached Goris from Gharalagez. His expeditionary forces consisted of 400 infantry, and 300 swordsmen. They also had two cannons and 30 machine guns. Forthwith Dro sent to Gharabagh Manuk of Sassun, Kostia Atayan, and Captain Jacob Ter Martirosian, with 400,000 rubles and instructions to support the local self-defense committee until the arrival of Arsen Mikaelian, under whose command they were to serve. The young and inexperienced Arsen was a native of Gharabagh. He had lived in America for a time.[32]

The Armenian government's political appointee in Gharabagh, Serkey Melik-Yolchian, and Dro were in agreement that force of arms would be necessary to unite Gharabagh to Armenia, but during the Winter months a campaign would be unwise. Melik-Yolchian was a native of Gharabagh and governor of Siunik Province. Because of lack of provisions, the local soldiers were sent to their homes and some of the officers were sent on prolonged leave. Dro himself returned to Yerevan, where he stayed until the end of February. An uprising in Gharabagh in winter was unlikely.[33]

On February 15, Dro reported to the government in Yerevan that the self-defense measures in the provinces of Zangezur and Gharabagh were insufficient to effect their sovereignty. At the same time, he emphasized that establishing control over Gharabagh was necessary for the security of the quarter million Armenians of the region of Gandzak, as well as from the point of view of preventing a land linkage between Turkey and Azerbaijan.[34]

In the meantime, relations remained tense between the two nations, and clashes were not uncommon. According to Armenian sources, on February 22, around 400 Armenians were killed in Khankendi and Aghdam. Some of them were lynched.[35]

On March 10 and 12, Arsen Mikaelian sent couriers to Goris with the message that the Azeris were preparing for a general offensive and that his soldiers were getting restless, eager to confront the threat. Melik-Yolchian and General Hovannes Ghazarian (Ivan Ghazarov) replied that they should be patient and await Dro's return from Yerevan.[36]

In this period of waiting, Lieutenant Colonel Garegin

Nzhdeh (Harutiunian), leading his partisans, had unleashed an offenseive to occupy the birthplace of Christopher Mikaelian, Agulis, which was destroyed by the Azeris in December of 1919. He succeeded in occupying upper Agulis, but on March 25 before he could reach Ortupat in the region of Meghri, a courier arrived with a message from Colonel Ruben Narinian that the Azeris were attacking the province of Zangezur. Nzhdeh halted his advance and before long asserted control of the situation, tossing out the enemy and securing Zangezur's eastern flank.[37]

Arsen Mikaelian, Lieutenant Colonel Zakhar Mesian of Gharabagh, and *Teli* (Crazy) Ghazar from Gandzak had already started the uprising. A number of other positions also raised the flag of revolt, but as a consequence of lack of means of communication and flaws in the general coordination of the uprising, it became a disastrous failure, especially in Shushi.

The people of Shushi had not rebelled. On the contrary, they had greeted the Azeris with salt and bread and submitted to their rule. Yet they were to pay the highest price.

On the night of March 22, 100 Armenian armed men under the command of Nerses Azbekian secretly slipped into the town with the aim of disarming the garrison, but everything went wrong. The city's Azeris, the garrison, and outside reinforcements turned Shushi into a flaming hell from March 23 to 26. Six thousand people from the Armenian community, taking advantage of the darkness and smoke, escaped. Around 2,000 structures—home, church, school, library, etc.—burned to the ground. Chief of police Avetis Ter-Ghougasian was turned into a human torch. Bishop Vahan Ter-Grigorian, who was opposed to the use of force and agreeable to living with the Azeris in peace, was tortured to death. First they cut his tongue, and then beheaded him, displaying his head in the streets. Communist leader Alexander Dsarougian and 500 other Armenians were hacked to death.[38]

Responding to the exhortations of Assistant Governor Kika Kalandarian and school superintendent Ruben

Shahnazarian, many people had taken refuge in the courtyard of the Beklarian Palace, but the Azeri soldiers and mob wrecked the walls and rushed inside, massacring everyone in sight.

The *Mshak* (Farmer) newspaper echoed the massacre of the Shushi Armenians, with the following words:

"This is that Shushi which hurried to submit to the rule of the Azeris, prevented the peasants of Gharabagh from uprising, greeted the Turks with salt and bread and submitted to Sultanov."

Sultanov did not spare his loyal Armenians. And who was responsible for this tragedy? They were the British generals who stood by Sultanov against 200,000 Armenians. The hands of Thompson, Shuttleworth, and Corey were stained with the blood of Armenians. The grim fate of Shushi should serve as an example to every Armenian. "Poor Shushi. It was ill-starred due to its love of peace. Unforntunately, it turned into a slaughterhouse."[39]

On April 3, the enemy unleashed a fierce attack on Askeran with the thunder of eight cannons. *Teli* Ghazar and his men fought valiantly, but without artillery they could not withstand the attacks for very long. *Teli* Ghazar ordered his men to retreat immediately, but he remained steadfast on his rampart with a few braves. They fought to the last bullet and fell with rifle in hand.[40]

On April 13, Dro finally arrived in Gharabagh with a large force and encamped at Tumi Village, 35 km south of Shushi. His absence in the preceding weeks had played a decisive role in the tragic development of events in the political and military arena. Arsen Mikaelian and *Teli* Ghazar had expected to have the military force that Dro had brought with him on the first day of the uprising.

Dro's first task was the detailed planning of military operations. He mobilized 3,000 infantry and 500 cavalry from the provinces of Shushi and Dizak. Nzhdeh also arrived with his 300 fighters from the province of Ghapan. The province of Zangezur supplied Dro with 900,000 bullets, 2,000 artillery shells, and numerous rifles and hand grenades. The Commander formed an auxiliary committee to supply the army with munitions, barley, wheat, medicines, as well as hay and other provisions for the horses.[41]

Before commencing a general offensive, Dro convened a general assembly of Gharabagh Armenians on April 23, to ascertain whether they would endorse the offensive and participate in it.

The assembly condemned the destruction of 32 villages and the slaughter of 4,000 innocent peasants.

After all these preparations, Dro did not issue the order to attack. Events had taken a new course in the TransCaucasus. The Red Army had concentrated forces on the borders of Azerbaijan. Dro, armed, prepared, and ready, hesitated. The commander's 45 days in Gharabagh were wasted and for naught.[42]

# NOTES

1. Antranig Chalabian, *General Andranik and the Armenian Revolutionary Movement,* p 500.
2. Alexander Khadisian, *The Origin and Development of the Republic of Armenia,* 2nd ed, Beirut, 1968, p 89.
3. Ibid, p 89.
4. Ibid, p 89.
5. Haigal, *We Will Not Bow, Horizon* Weekly, Montreal, June 21, 1982, p 1.
6. Richard Hovannissian, *The Republic of Armenia,* Vol 1, p 260.
7. Simon Vratsian, *The Republic of Armenia,* 2nd ed, Beirut, 1958, p 254.
8. *Hairenik* Daily, November 29, 1978, p 2.
9. Ibid, pp 2–3.
10. Leo (Arakel Babkhanian), *Border Disputes,* Tbilisi, 1919, p 24 (see also Vratsian, *Republic of Armenia,* 2nd ed, p 217).
11. Ibid, p 222.
12. Ibid, p 223.
13. Ibid, p 224.
14. Ibid, p 225.
15. Ibid, p 226.
16. Ibid, p 230.
17. Ibid, p 232.
18. Ibid, pp 232–233.
19. Ibid, p 233.
20. Ibid, pp 233–234.
21. Simon Vratsian, *Through Life's Pathways,* Vol 4, p 186.
22. *General Andranik's Historic Diary of the Caucasus Front,* p 149.
23. Ibid, pp 150–152.
24. Simon Vratsian, *Through Life's Pathways,* Vol 4, pp 187–188.
25. HamletGevorgian, *Dro,* Collectiion. Yerevan, 1991, pp 267–269.

26. Raffi (Hakob Melik-Hakobian), *Collected Works,* Vol 3, *Djalaleddin,* Yerevan, 1962, pp 56–57.
27. Simon Vratsian, *Through Life's Pathways,* Vol 4, pp 189–190.
28. Ibid, p 190.
29. Ibid, p 190.
30. Ibid, p 191.
31. Ibid, p 191.
32. Richard Hovannisian, *The Republic of Armenia,* Vol 3, p 135.
33. Ibid, p 141.
34. Ibid, p 141.
35. Ibid, p 142.
36. Ibid, p 148.
37. Ibid, pp 149–150.
38. Ibid, p 152.
39. Ibid, pp 152–153.
40. Ibid, p 157.
41. Ibid, p 159.
42. Ibid, pp 159–160.

# CHAPTER V

## SOVIET RUSSIA EXPANDS
## INTO THE TRANSCAUCASUS

Alexander Khatisian

## AZERBAIJAN'S SOVIETIZATION

On the night of April 26–27, 1920, an armored train of the Soviet army entered Azerbaijan. The Communist Party of Azerbaijan, which had schemed to organize a coup d'état on April 27, learned that the armored train was rapidly approaching Palajari which leads to Baku. The *Musawat* (Equality) Party's secretary general, Mehmet Rasulzade, declared that the aim of the Red Army was to annex the Caucasus to the Soviet Union and to re-establish the Russian Empire's old frontiers. On the same night, April 27, the government handed over sovereignty to the Communist Party of the country. The next day, April 28, Azerbaijan's *Revcom* (Revolutionary Committee) welcomed the Soviet armored train and formally declared the Soviet Republic of Azerbaijan. The country's Communist Party chief, Nariman Narimanov, was appointed president of the *Revcom* as well as of the Popular Commissars. M. T. Huseinov was appointed commissar of foreign affairs, and Hamit Sultanov of internal affairs. On April 29, having barely attained power, the president of Azerbaijan's *Revcom,* Nariman Narimanov declared that the districts of Gharabagh and Zangezur would be annexed to Azerbaijan by force of arms. In other words, whether it be Azerbaijan's Communist Party or the *Musawat* Party, they had the same hostile stance towards Armenia.[1]


## THE REACTION IN ARMENIA

The initial reaction in Armenia to news of the Communist coup d'état in Baku was cautious optimism, given that Armenians in general had Russophilic tendencies. The Western states, aside from providing American flour to Armenia, had been of no use whatsoever politically. The ARF was ready to establish fraternal relations with Soviet Russia on condition that Russia's Popular Commissars' Council respect the Armenian nation's steadfast will to live free in united and independent

Armenia.

At a parliament meeting, the Socialist Revolutionary Party's delegate, Arsham Khondkarian, observed, "Although it is desirable that a nation be the master of its fate, in order to reach that ideal, power is necessary. It is senseless to wage a struggle against the whole world in defense of ideals which are not achievable. We should wrest the utmost, but if we do not succeed, we should be ready to make concessions, including independence, because the physical survival of the Armenian nation overrides any other consideration."[2]

When Levon Tumanian asked what had we gained from the imperialists, Minister of Communications Arshak Djamalian replied that Europe kept alive the starving Armenians. Former ARF member Vahan Minakhorian added, "It is true that the Allied states threw breadcrumbs to us, but that was only because they had played a big role in the tragedy of the Armenian holocaust. The ARF should confess that its policy of clinging to Europe's skirts has been disastrous. The physical existence of the Armenian nation, above any other consideration, compels us to turn towards Revolutionary Russia."[3]

The talented orator Vahan Navasardian said in his speech that while the parliament debated, Armenian blood was being shed in the highlands of Gharabagh and Zangezur. The jewel of Khachen province, Paludjan, was annihilated, and similarly Varanta's diamond, Shosh. The peasants of the charming and lively village of Gulistan were put to the sword. Shushi, that glorious, legendary, and long impregnable fortress-town of the Caucasus, was obliterated, along with its people. The Armenian nation is peace-loving and, despite everything that had happened, extended a hand to Turkey, but that blood-soaked country refused to take our hand. He concluded his speech with the following words: "Esteemed gentlemen of the opposition, listen to me carefully. We are neither Russophiles nor Russophobes, neither Turkophiles nor Turkophobes. We love the Armenian people blindly and passionately, and will defend its existence by all means. We are ready to negotiate with everyone who is willing to accept the Armenian nation's existence and the homeland's independence."[4]

## LEVON SHANT'S MISSION TO MOSCOW

The Armenian government's attention was focused on the Allies and Europe, yet it could not overlook the Bolshevik advance to the TransCaucasus. During the war the Allies had lavished promises on the Armenian people, and also provided certain quantities of food, but had not kept their promises. By necessity the government had to have a dialogue with Russia's new masters, without entirely terminating hope from the West.[5]

Having in mind the ideal of United Armenia, the government approached Western-Armenian Levon Shant (Seghbosian) to head the special delegation. Levon Shant was born in Constantinople but educated in Tbilisi, and was at the time vice-chairman of the Armenian parliament. Accompanying Shant would be the left-leaning ARF members Hambardzum Terterian and Levon Zarafian. Attorney Terterian, born in New-Nakhidjevan, in the region of Rostov, had been a classmate of the renowned Communist leader Alexander Miasnikian. A native of Gharabagh, Levon Zarafian had been a left-wing activist in Baku and was acquainted with famous Communists.[6]

For Vratsian, Hambardzum Terterian, with whom he had been a classmate both at the New-Nakhidjevan parish school and at Petrokrat University, was the most appropriate person to represent Armenia in Moscow. "Intellectually advanced, judicious, duteous, a patriot, he also had friends in Bolshevik circles; he was particularly close to Alexander Miasnikian and to Sargis Srabionian (Lukashin) from his hometown." [7]

As for Levon Shant, according to Vratsian, he was "never suitable for this role. Dry by temperament, an introvert, contemptuous of worldly affairs, anti-Bolshevik to his core, he did not have any inclination to deal with politics. He was particularly interested in literary-philosophical questions. Hambardzum Terterian related that in Moscow, except for official relationships, his contacts were minimal. He isolated himself in his room, working on his play, *The Chained.*[8]

On April 30, 1920, the Armenian delegation left for Moscow. Author and playwright Levon Shant's works were familiar in Russian literary circles.[9]

The delegation which arrived in Moscow on May 20, had the authority to sign a treaty with Soviet Russia on the basis of the following main points:

1. Soviet Russia is obliged to recognize the independence of Armenia and Gharabagh.

2. Russia would, at least in principle, accept annexation of the provinces of Turkish Armenia to Armenia.

3. Russia should not interfere in the internal affairs of Armenia, directly or indirectly.[10]

The Armenian delegation had meetings with the minister of foreign affairs of Soviet Russia, K. V. Chicherin, and his deputy, L. M. Garakhanov (of Armenian heritage). Chicherin was of the opinion that Russia's friendship with Kemalist Turkey could lead to that country's sovietization. Terterian responded, "We understand the Turks best. They will exploit your assistance first to attack the Armenians, and then the Greeks. They will then abandon you and join the Allies."[11]

In late June the Russians presented a new proposal to Shant's delegation: The district of Nakhidjevan to Armenia, Gharabagh to Azerbaijan. As for Zangezur, its status would be decided between Soviet Russia's plenipotentiary in Armenia, Legrand, a Russian-Jew of French extraction, and the government of Armenia.[12]

Levon Shant did not sign any treaty. He sent a telegram to Yerevan and asked the government for instructions. He received a reply a month later. In the meantime Chicherin announced that the negotiations were over and would recommence in Yerevan, between Legrand and the government of Armenia.[13]

## DRO'S RETREAT FROM GHARABAGH

After Baku's pseudo-Communist coup d'état, the governor of Gharabagh, Dr. Khosrov Sultanov, changed colors from one day to the next, declaring himself a Sovietophile and appealing to Gharabagh's Armenian population with the message that the fratricidal bloodshed should cease and that Armenians and Azeris should coexist peacefully. (It would have been more accurate if Sultanov had said "Armenocidal bloodshed.") He also demanded that Dro disband his force and depart from Gharabagh.

On May 6 Dro sent a letter to Sultanov, with copies to Lenin in Moscow and Dr. Nariman Narimanov in Baku, pointing out that "Gharabagh's Armenian villagers had for years led an unequal struggle against Russian despotic governors and Azeri Khans and Peks. Gharabagh's Armenian villagers have friendly motivations towards Soviet Russia, but they cannot support a revolution announced by an infamous individual, whose bloodthirsty and regressive essence is well known to all. For as long as Khosrov Pek Sultanov remains as the chief of Gharabagh's *Revcom,* Armenians will remain in their position of resistance. The will of the Armenians of Mountainous Gharabagh to be a part of the Republic of Armenia remains unchanged."[14]

Narimanov appointed Tatash Puniazate as Gharabagh's extraordinary commissar who in turn, according to his instructions, dismissed Sultanov and liquidated his *Revcom.* In mid-May the chief of the Caucasus Bureau, Orzhonikidze, also arrived in Shushi. He sent a delegation, including a liaison officer, Sahak Ter-Gabrielian, to Karapulagh, Dro's encampment. The delegation first encountered Armenian military units in the village of Shosh, in the northern outskirts of Shushi. Ter-Gabrielian announced that the Red Army had arrived not to wage war, but to restore peace and tranquility in the TransCaucasus.

Dro received the delegates on May 19. They demanded that Dro send away his forces from Gharabagh and transport them to Zangezur. Dro wanted to

140

understand the goal of their mission. Ter-Gabrielian replied that the Red Army had to occupy Mountainous Gharabagh and that the government in Yerevan was agreeable to this plan. Dro replied that he had entered Gharabagh because Azerbaijan's army had massacred the Armenians of Shushi and destroyed numerous Armenian villages. He would withdraw from Gharabagh only by orders issued from Yerevan and that the Red Army should expel from Gharabagh all the Azeris and Moslems. He then offered to come by arbitration to mutual concessions: the Red Army would withdraw 20 miles, and he would withdraw 30 miles toward Zangezur.

Ter-Gabrielian's delegation returned to Shushi with the impression that Dro would not be in opposition if the Red Army were to occupy Mountainous Gharabagh and install an administration there.[15]

On May 24 Dro, Nzhdeh, and Arsen Mikaelian had a meeting with Shushi's Communist leader, Dr. Sargis Hambardzumian. The outcome was a concensus that it would be prudent for Dro to withdraw from Gharabagh and go to Zangezur before the Red Army closed the routes of retreat, and hand over Mountainous Gharabagh to the Red Army.

Dro and his soldiers set out toward Zangezur, over the snow-bound peaks of Kirz and Khdsaberd, "with weary steps and downcast looks."[16]

## THE MAY MUTINY

In late April of 1920 when the Red Army entered Baku, and Azerbaijan installed a Soviet administration, the country's Communist leaders—just like the bigwigs of (Islamist) *Musawat*—threatened to declare war on Armenia if Yerevan's government did not cede Gharabagh and Zangezur to Azerbaijan.

Yerevan, spurning Baku's threats, organized a splendid martial parade on the occasion of International Labor Day on May 1, to show Nariman Narimanov and his comrades that the government of Armenia was neither intimidated nor discouraged by Baku's threats. The whole city was decorated with red flags, carpets, and flowers. The capital's left-wing ARF paraded displaying pictures of Lenin and Stepan Shahumian alongside those of the ARF icons Christopher, Rostom, and Zavarian. After the parade, a magnificent public assembly took place in front of the parliament building, where the chairman of the parliament Avetik Isahakian, foreign minister Hamazasp Ohandjanian, Sebuh, and others gave speeches.[17]

Here and there disturbances took place, particularly in Alexandropol, where, because of the railroad network, the working class constituted a large number. The ARF formed a bureau government with Hamazasp Ohandjanian as Prime Minister to forestall additional disturbances. Catholicos Gevorg V issued a call to the nation, to guard the republic so that the blood spilled by countless martyrs would not go to waste. The Liberal Democratic Party announced that "Turk *Ittihadists* [the inner circle of the Young Turk government which orchestrated the Armenian Genocide] under the label of 'Bolshevik' are operating in Baku and only someone blind in both eyes could fail to see the danger that threatened the Armenian nation."[18]

Before the October revolution, there were hardly any Communists in Armenia. The country being agrarian, the peasants did not understand anything about socialism or other ideologies.

During the era of the first republic, Armenian Communists in Azerbaijan and Georgia were subjected to ruthless persecution. The national government in Armenia gave them refuge, on condition that during their residence in Armenia they would not engage in politics. Many of these Armenian Communists from abroad, such as Sargis Kasian, Askenaz Mravian, S. Khanoyan, D. Shahverdian, Avetik Sahakian, Aramais Yerznkian, Avis Nuridjanian, and others saved their lives thanks to the national state, and most of them kept their promise. However, when the Red Army approached the TransCaucasus, the Bolsheviks who were hosted in Armenia began to secretly plot against the state.[19]

Armenia's Communists were relatively powerful and active in Alexandropol. They received large sums from Tbilisi and Russia and published a newspaper. The state was aware of their activities but procrastinated in taking decisive measures.

The national state was more concerned about the cooperation of Russia with Kemalist Turkey than about Armenia's Communists. Because of this, the ARF Bureau, in early January 1920, sent a delegation to Tbilisi, comprised of A. Djamalian, R. Ter-Minasian, and S. Vratsian to establish contact with the Russian Communist Party's Caucasus Bureau and clarify the details of the Lenin-Kemal Ataturk relations.

The meeting took place with the Caucasus Bureau's General Secretary Hmayak Nazaretian, who did not leave a good impression with the Armenian delegates.

He was questioned as to whether there was an anti-Armenian treaty between the Bolsheviks and Kemalists. He did not deny that there was a treaty. As to its anti-Armenian nature, he stated that the Communist revolution supported all oppressed people; thus, it was not possible that it would not also support the Armenian people. The Armenian delegates said that the Armenian people's interest required a certain understanding between the Armenian state and the Bolsheviks. The reply was a dry and contemptuous smirk.[20]

The historian Christopher J. Walker analyzes the people's feelings and instinctive desires in those days, in Armenia, thus:

"Now, on May Day, three days after the Bolsheviks had taken Baku, their comrades in Armenia were full of confidence. There was also another current of feeling prevalent among many of the ordinary people—a current which was to broaden and swell in the coming months. This was a yearning to be rejoined with Russia, and an almost instinctive belief that only this way would the starvation and suffering end—only this way would the prevailing conditions of Armenia change; the silent winter deaths, and the chronic diseases of summer. It was as though they

143

guessed that the European diplomats, who in a year and a half had only delivered to them few crumbs, might now desert them completely, and instead they looked to their old protector, Russia."[21]

Indeed, the tsarist dictatorship, which vigorously persecuted Armenian revolutionaries, had not exerted any impediment or pressure on the industrious, peaceful Armenian people. An ordinary Armenian was free in Russia, had no fear or worry that a Turk or a Kurd could come and kill him, take possession of his belongings, his estate or . . . his honor. In Turkey, at any time, a Kurdish or Turkish officer or bureaucrat could kill an Armenian *raya* (literally meaning "cattle"), violate his wife, kidnap his pubescent daughter, or expropriate his estate, without fear of judicial prosecution, because a Christian's testimony was not acceptable in Turkish courts. If a Turk heard that in a certain village an Armenian wedding was taking place, he could well go over there with a few armed cohorts and kidnap the bride. If anyone opened his mouth to object, they could kill him on the spot. For this reason, when an Armenian woman or girl would come out of her house, she would wear rags and cover her face or rub it with soot in order to avoid attracting the attention of any passing Kurd. Because of these practices prevailing for centuries, wrote the great Raffi,[5] the Kurds' features became nobler, whereas that of the Armenians, uglier.


## UPRISING IN ALEXANDROPOL

Attempts were made in Yerevan to give the May 1 holiday a Bolshevik character. Anti-government speeches were made, etc., yet as a whole the people remained unmoved by the Bolsheviks' commotion and agitation. Yerevan was not with the Bolsheviks, but Bolshevik elements and tendencies were not so easily dispensable.[22]

In Alexandropol, however, the Communists raised

---

[5] The famous 19th century Armenian writer.

the Soviet flag and from an armored train proclaimed a Soviet regime. From this train Captain Sarkis Mousayelian sent telegrams in all directions, proclaiming war against ARF anti-revolutionaries and asking Baku to send assistance. The rebels attacked the ARF club and took down framed portraits of Christopher, Rostom, et al, from the walls, smashing them on the ground and stomping on them.[23]

When the news reached Yerevan, the minister of defense ordered Mousayelian to depart to the Ghamarlu front. The latter not only refused, but also sent an ultimatum by telegram to Yerevan, demanding that the government hand over all powers to him. Almost simultaneously, uprisings broke out in various regions of Armenia. Telegrams arriving from all directions about disturbances and uprisings temporarily confused the government. The administration was unable to put out all these fires. A swift and resolute government was needed.[24]

An extraordinary session of parliament was convened on May 5. Khadisian's administration resigned. The ARF bureau became the government. In effect, an ARF dictatorship was declared. The new government issued an appeal warning of the danger shadowing the homeland and inviting the people to rally around the government to defend Armenia's independence and liberty. The appeal was signed by H. Ohandjanian, A. Gulkhandanian, A. Djamalian, G. Ghazarian, and S. Araratian.[25]

Mobilization of ARF cadres was declared everywhere, and to recapture Alexandropol a division was formed under the command of General Sebouh.

In those critical and dangerous times, the Armenian Social-Democrat, Democrat-Liberal, and Populist parties stood by the side of the government and issued specific appeals, condemning the Bolshevik rebellion.[26]

To avoid civil war and bloodshed, and before taking decisive steps, the government tried to resolve the problem peacefully. Prime Minister Ohandjanian sent a telegram to the rebellion's leader, Mousayelian, to end the uprising, promising amnesty to the guilty. Mousayelian rejected the offer and asserted that the Military-Revolutionary Committee was the legitimate government and that the government in Yerevan should recognize his authority immediately.[27]

The government, seeing that all efforts for peace had proved to be in vain, deployed armed forces. These were also bolstered by volunteer units. On the morning of May 13, a clash took place between Mousayelian's armored train and government forces between the Ani and Aghin stations. Among the rebels six were wounded. The armored train did not withstand the government's pressure and attempted to flee.

On behalf of the rebels, their commissar of internal affairs, Dr. Artashes Melkonian, offered to cease military operations.

The government's minister of the interior, Sahak Torosian, replied, "We do not recognize you as a legitimate side, but as a band of adventurers," and added, "for you there is only one way of salvation—to surrender."[28]

The rebels' position was not favorable in Alexandropol either. ARF partisans dismantled the railway and blocked the road between Alexandropol and Gharakilise at the Jejur Tunnel. To pressure the rebels, Sebouh had under his disposal hundreds of Western-Armenian partisans, a part of the 6th infantry division, a machine gun, and eight field cannons. Those who declared a Soviet regime were in disarray within 48 hours. By May 15, the situation was hopeless for the May rebels to such a degree that when General Andranik's deputy, Smbat (Baroyan) of Mush, offered to mediate, saying that continuing the rebellion could lead to bloodshed, they gladly accepted the offer. The city of Alexandropol surrendered on May 15. Mousayelian and Malkonian were arrested, and Avis Nuridjanian was able to flee.[29]

When the May rebellion began, Dro was still in Gharabagh. When he reached Yerevan, the uprising was almost liquidated.[30]

"Dro had no faith in the representatives of the [Western] allies in Yerevan. Europe and America were too

146

far from Armenia and would not be able to come to the rescue. Instead of waiting for salvation from a distant saint, he considered it wiser to rely on the more proximate saint. The proximate saint was the Russian or Russia, whether white or red was all the same. Some time had to pass before he would be disillusioned and resigned from that saint too. . . ."[31]

## PREPARATIONS FOR THE ARMENO-TURKISH WAR

I have noted earlier that with the Treaty of Batum (May 11, 1918) the Turks created a tiny Armenia (9,000 sq km), of temporary nature, so that if at the Versailles Peace Conference a delegate questioned the head of the Turkish delegation about the Armenian Genocide, the latter could answer, "Genocide? We solved the Armenian Question by creating an independent Armenian Republic!" And if nobody questioned them, they would proceed to destroy Armenia.

The Turks executed this wily stratagem because they were apprehensive; first, they had raised arms against the Allies and were vanquished; second, they had committed genocide. Let us quote Armenia's second prime minister, Alexander Khadisian (July 1919–May 5, 1920):

"We have to consider that the Turks were very afraid of the Armenian Question in the anticipated peace conference. About this I have heard from Raouf Bey, Vehib Pasha, Khalil Bey, Enver Pasha, and many other Turkish officials. That was the reason why the Turks wanted to solve the Armenian Question before the International Peace Conference.[32]

"Later on I was informed that when we were conducting negotiations in Batum, fierce disputes took place among the Young Turk committee members of Istanbul as to what extent it served their purpose to maintain an Armenian state in the Caucasus. About this, in the fall of 1918 in Istanbul, Grand vezier Talaat Pasha told me the following:

" 'Enver Pasha was of the opinion that since the Armenians have been and are bound to be our enemies and will not leave alone our Anatolian provinces, it would be better to fundamentally annihilate them in the Caucasus also, as they have been in Turkey. But a small Armenia in the Caucasus could well become the impetus for Armenians to always aspire to expand their borders and become a perpetual danger for Turkey. Whereas I,' continued Talaat, 'replied that that plan is impossible if only because one way or another there are some two million Armenians remaining alive at the present and it is impossible to annihilate them all; thus it would be better to satisfy them, because even if there remain only 100,000 Armenians on the face of the earth, they will never let us rest in peace. And finally, by creating a small Armenia, we would have solved the Armenian Question and presented such to the International Peace Conference.'[33]

"Talaat Pasha's opinion prevailed and the Turks created the small Armenia. After that Enver Pasha one day bragged to me: 'I solved a very complex problem; I created Armenia, satisfied the Armenians' national demands, but I accomplished this in such a way that I did not concede a single inch of Turkish lands.' "[34]

In early 1920, according to the Turks' timetable and political accounts, the time was drawing near to put an end to the game called "independent Armenia." The reason was that the Paris Peace Conference had ended its sessions without anyone demanding accountability from them for the Armenian Genocide. The Versailles Treaty with the main state of the Axis, Germany, was signed on June 28, 1919, and was put in effect on January 10, 1920.[35] The victorious allies had not only acquitted the *Ittihadist* hyenas of shedding a sea of blood, but on the contrary, the vanquished Turkey's new prime minister and head of the Turkish delegation to the Peace Conference, Tamat Ferid Pasha, on February 12, 1919, in his report to the peace conference, had hurled the ultimate accusation at the brow of the Armenians, saying that the Armenians had killed one million Turks in the Eastern provinces between 1915 and 1918 . . . ."[36]

In February 1920, Nationalist (Kemalist) Turkey was already making preparations to attack the Republic of Armenia.[37]

By early May, the preparations for the offensive were completed, yet Kiazim Karabekir Pasha did not begin offensive operations until September 20. What was the reason?

Before commencing its offensive, Kemalist Turkey's only worry was Revolutionary Russia. What position would Russia take in such an event?

On April 26, the commander of Turkey's eastern front, Kiazim Karabekir Pasha, after informing the Grand National Assembly that preparations for the offensive would be completed in "two weeks," received the following reply from the chair of the assembly:

"Your proposals were taken into consideration. We would like you to continue preparation. Naturally, the order to cross the border would be issued from here."[38]

## WHY DID THE KEMALISTS POSTPONE THE OFFENSIVE AGAINST ARMENIA?

In early May, the Kemalists suddenly decided to postpone the offensive and conveyed the following to Karabekir:

"The question of annihilating the government of Armenia, which is a political instrument of the Allies, was taken into consideration by the Executive Council today.

"As such:

"1. Until the decisions of the Peace Conference regarding us are completely identified, our internal and external circumstances do not allow us to deprive ourselves of a probability of reaching an understanding with the Allies.

"2. For this reason, prior to becoming more or less

acquainted with the terms of an understanding with the Bolsheviks, and identifying their material support, the [offensive] operation was found to be objectionable.

"3. The Armenian events have been the most important of the factors arousing the Christian world against us; to exterminate the Armenian government, which was ratified by us before others, by our military force, for a reason proffered by us, would constitute a new Armenian massacre, halting the tide that is beginning to turn more or less in our favor. It would arouse American public opinion against us, and it would secure the approval of everyone for the implementation of British designs. For these considerations, we must beware our army formally and explicitly attacking the Armenian government, but it has been considered more convenient instead, to fortify the local forces in the three provinces (Kars, Artahan, and Ardou) along with the Moslem Bolsheviks who have advanced to Kenjo, to launch an offensive, as much as possible stealthily."[39]

Therefore, due to certain clear "considerations," in the spring of 1920, to launch a direct offensive against the Republic of Armenia was not considered suitable by Ankara's Grand Assembly. Accordingly, it was necessary to wait a bit longer until the time became more "suitable."

In the summer of 1920, the nationalist government of Mustafa Kemal commenced contacts with Lenin, using "anti-imperialist" rhetoric. The Turks, who are skillful at deception, did not have any difficulty in deceiving the leader of Revolutionary Russia, Vladimir Ilych Lenin, by pretending to be Bolsheviks. Indeed, to reward the Nationalist Turks' "anti-imperialist" declamations, on August 24, 1920, in Moscow, a Russian-Turkish Treaty was signed, whereby Soviet Russia gave "free rein to the nationalist Turk to deal with Armenia as it saw fit, without fear of any Russian intervention in favor of Armenians."[40]

Soviet Russia not only left the Turks free to attack the newly created Republic of Armenia, but also provided them with large amounts of money and munitions to utilize against the Armenians.

150

Manuk Krzelian relates that "Lenin prioritized granting Turkey 200.6 kilos of gold, 6,000 rifles and one million bullets."[41]

The road was leveled for the Turks' unfortunate scheme and the Soviet government had given the green light to the Turkish invasion.

Again, before commencing action, the Kemalist Turks also wanted to know for certain what Georgia's position would be in such an eventuality.

For this purpose the Kemalists sent a secret delegation to Tbilisi, led by Youssef Kemal.[42] He had meetings with Prime Minister Noi Zhortania and Foreign Minister Yevgeni P. Gegechkori of Georgia's Menshevik government. He received assurances that "in the event of an Armenian-Kemalist conflict, Georgia would declare its strict neutrality."[43]

In return for its "strict neutrality," Georgia would receive the provinces of Borchalou and Akhalkalaki, and the region of Artahan.[44]

So, while the Turks were preparing and awaiting an opportune time to commence military operations against the Republic of Armenia, what were Armenia's government ministers thinking?

In truth, they were not thinking much at all, because, as ministers of a new state, they had neither experience in international diplomacy, nor the means (such as an intelligence service) to be able to know what was transpiring on the other side of the border. To quote Karo Sassouni:

"Whereas Turkey had put its hope in its own strength to secure its sovereignty, despite unfavorable conditions, Armenia, dazzled by very favorable conditions and believing the Allies, underestimated the work to be done by its own strength and waited for diplomacy."[45]

In this regard, the following instance is eloquent:

In the fall of 1920, unaware of goings-on around them, Ashkharh Bek Kalandarian, Toros Toramanian, and

151

Archbishop Karekin Hovsepian conducted archeological expeditions in various regions of Armenia. Kalandarian went to the region of Tigori and Kadjaran, Toramanian went to Ani, whereas Archbishop Karekin, with architect Yeghiazarian and others, went to the region of Kotaik.[46] Archbishop Karekin (who was later anointed Catholicos of the Great House of Cilicia in 1945) relates:

"Our expedition was interrupted by a sudden accident on September 20; however, we were content with the results we obtained.

"Our hearts were rejoicing, filled with the vision of our nation's intellectual, spiritual, and cultural rebirth. The horizon for our intellectual, scientific, and artistic workers was wide and expansive.

"But we had anticipated Saturday, before Friday.

"For us it was totally unexpected to hear, upon our return to Yerevan, that Armenia was at war with the Tajiks."[47]

General Andranik in distant America, having a presentiment of the danger threatening the Republic of Armenia, issued a heart-rending appeal to the U.S. government, which was translated and published in the March 27, 1920, issue of *The Independent*. Later, in the summer of 1971, it was also published in New York's *Ararat* quarterly. The following are some excerpts from this appeal:

## GENERAL ANDRANIK'S APPEAL TO THE GOVERNMENT OF THE UNITED STATES

*WE ARE DESPERATE!*
*By General Andranik*

*In the name of all those Armenians, whose story you can read in more than a million nameless graves, and in the name of the million living Armenians, I express my thanks to the Americans for their interest in my country. But I must also endeavor to make you see that, while we sit here, hundreds of Christian women are in captivity under the very guns of the Allied fleet in the Harbor of Constantinople; and every Armenian in the valleys and mountains of our country is in danger of death.*

*The plan of the Turks is the complete extermination of all Armenians. The world knows the unspeakable methods used. We know that they have been buying ammunition in large quantities. We hear that they are mobilizing. They plan to finish their horrible work in the spring. Only America can prevent their doing so.*

— — — — —

*We cast our lot with the Allies at the beginning. We remained faithful to the end. To illustrate, my detachment of volunteers fought without interruption from the first days of the war. After the collapse of Russia and the Treaty of Brest-Litovsk, deceived and abandoned by the Georgians, betrayed by the Tatars, we defended the front alone for seven months, retarded the Turkish advance, and rendered signal service to the British Army in Mesopotamia, as Lord Robert Cecil officially testified. We were fighting to protect our refugees long after the armistice was signed. Now, eighteen months after the armistice, the Turks and others go on exterminating our people because we are Christians.*

— — — — —

*By raising her mighty hand, even semi-officially, America can save Armenia and the East. In the name of all the martyred hosts of my countrymen, in the name of three million Armenians, I pray it can and will.*

*According to the Allies, we were to expect help from America in the reconstruction of Armenia. We expected that America would accept a mandate for Armenia. We put our great hope in America. We expected troops and officers and administrators to help us reorganize our country. The aid and voice of America would help Armenia to stand on her feet. We would have a chance. We could reconstruct our country. We are accustomed to doing things. Our people are responsible and industrious. But how shall we begin when*

153

*our country is, as now, surrounded and invaded by
enemies?*

*Again, we were led to expect a mandate for Armenia,
but it is eighteen months since the armistice was signed and
the Turks are preparing, without interference, to destroy our
people.*

— — — — —

*If America cannot help us diplomatically, then I
beseech you, let us defend ourselves against the Turks and
Kurds and Tatars, the enemies of Christianity. We fought
during the war with antiquated Russian ammunition. We
fought well. If we had ammunition and supplies we could
raise 100,000 men, 50,000 in Turkish Armenia plus, 50,000
in Russian Armenia. The first month I could mobilize 20,000
Turkish Armenians. In three months 40,000 or even 60,000
would be ready and most of them would be expert soldiers.
Here in America there are 10,000 to 15,000 young
Armenians ready to go to the defense of our country. But
before we can do this, we need supplies and some officers to
help train our men. Everything all over the world is in the
hands of the Americans. The little we need to take a stand
for our country and our flag would not be much to ask.*

— — — — —

*This spring we are without hope unless America
intervenes. The Turks are preparing. We have news that they
are already mobilizing. The Near East will be in a turmoil
unless America raises her mighty voice before it is too late.
My personal judgment is that America can prevent disaster.*

(A few months before "Andranik's appeal," in
November 1919, the government of Armenia sent a
delegation to America, headed by General Hakob Bagratuni,
to seek military assistance from the United States
government. When the delegation arrived in Paris, Boghos
Nubar Pasha asked General Andranik to join the delegation.
The hero accepted.)

The historian Richard Hovannisian wrote the
following about those days:

154

"More than fifteen years Bagratuni's senior, Andranik was undoubtedly the most popular living Armenian hero."[48]

The military mission arrived in New York City on November 22, 1919. It was welcomed with the same enthusiasm and fanfare with which an Armenian civil mission, headed by Hovhannes Kachaznuni, had been received six weeks earlier.

"Happy crowds, a beaming reception committee, bouquets held out by trembling schoolgirls, fluttering flags, honor escorts in cars and on horseback, a procession down Fifth Avenue. At the Holland House, Armenian scouts and uniformed veterans lined the way to the grand ballroom, where Bagratuni exhorted the youngsters to stand tall as the sons of Haik, the epic progenitor of the nation and to emulate Andranik, Armenia's soaring eagle."[49]

Armenian Americans from coast to coast gave the delegates, particularly General Andranik, such a warm reception that many other Americans began wondering who this Andranik might be. When they were told that he was the George Washington of the Armenians, they took him to Philadelphia and had him seated in Washington's historic chair—a great honor accorded only to prominent foreign dignitaries.[50]

—  —  —  —  —  —

On one occasion, Senator John Sharp Williams escorted the Armenian dignitaries to the White House. The President's secretary, Joseph P. Tumulty, conveyed Wilson's "abiding sympathy for the Armenian Cause," but regretted that his health did not permit a personal interwiew.[51]

The Republic of Armenia's formal military mission to the U.S. was received enthusiastically everywhere, except . . . in the capital, Washington, D.C. General Andranik was so frustrated and angered by the State Department's cool attitude toward the problems of the independent Republic of Armenia, that he made a policy of refusing to attend public functions that did not include fundraising for the Armenian armed forces in the Caucasus.[52]

In conclusion:

General Andranik's heart-rending appeal to the U.S. Government, pleading for the United States "to raise her mighty voice" and exert her influence to prevent Kemalist Turkey's offensive against the Republic of Armenia, remained unanswered; Armenia's two missions, one financial, headed by Kadjaznuni, the other military, by General Bagratuni, returned empty-handed to their country.

Under the harsh and dispassionate conditions of the post-Genocide era, when the Armenian people were abandoned by virtually the entire world, it was not possible to preserve for long an "independence" that was dependent on the pitiful terms of the Treaty of Batum, while facing the whirlpool of the Russian Revolution on the one side, and the open jaws of the "grey wolf" on the other. It was necessary to make a choice between Revolutionary Russia, no matter what color it had, and Kemalist Turkey; because, as Simon Vratsian would later confess:

"It was understandable to any mature individual that under the conditions of that time, it was not possible to create an independent Republic of Armenia."[53]

The Russian-Armenian leaders of Armenia, at the eleventh hour when Karabekir Pasha was at the gates of Yerevan and had occupied 80 percent of the country, made that choice between the Russians and the Turks, but it was too late for the following reasons:

The reader already understands that in the spring of 1919, the British General William Henry Beach with his 1,500 soldiers along with 1,200 soldiers from the Armenian Army had expelled the Turks from the TransCaucasus and expanded Armenia's borders from 9,000 to 50,000 sq km. In other words, the mighty Albion had created three countries with almost equal size in the TransCaucasus— Azerbaijan, Georgia, and Armenia.

Why did the British give these alms to Armenia? Nakhidjevan, Sourmalou, Kars, and Artahan—Armenian provinces that were part of the tsarist empire since 1879— were joined to Armenia in the spring of 1919, rather than being left to the Turks.

Great Britain, having occupied Baku, was hopeful that the Bolshevik Revolution would not be able to withstand internal and external military pressures for long. With the idea that they, the British, would remain in the TransCaucasus, they created three countries of equal size to make it easier to dominate them.

The 50,000 sq km Armenia created by almighty England was five to six times larger than the earlier 9,000 sq km Republic of Armenia.

This relatively expansive state, recognized by the great states, preserved its existence around a year and a half, from the spring of 1919 to September 20, 1920.

## SHOULD ARMENIA HAVE FOLLOWED AZERBAIJAN'S EXAMPLE?

On the night of April 26–27, as we said, the Azeris accepted the Soviets with open arms and handed over power to them.

Had the Russian-Armenian leaders of Eastern Armenia followed Azerbaijan's example and handed over power to the Soviets, if not immediately, then without much delay, and declared the country a Soviet Socialist Republic, today Nakhidjevan, Sourmalou, Kars, and Artahan could have been a part of Armenia, because these provinces had already constituted a part of the Russian Empire since 1879; second, the provinces which constituted Soviet Azerbaijan, Soviet Armenia, and Soviet Georgia, when they submitted to Soviet rule, have remained the same to this day, with inviolable borders.

When Vratsian himself admits that "it was understandable to any mature individual that under the conditions of that time, it was not possible to create an independent Republic of Armenia," then what did he and his Russian-Armenian friends gain by prolonging Armenia's independence by a few more months?

I have pondered this question which had also occupied Vratsian's mind for a long time, disturbing his conscience. He probably wondered with regret (as he has indirectly confessed) "would it not have been better if along with Azerbaijan, we too had sovietized our country?"

Let us quote one of the titans of our contemporary historiography, the same Simon Vratsian:

"There are those who say that if the government of Armenia had been able to find common ground with Soviet Moscow at that time, future disasters could have been avoided and Armenia, albeit Soviet, could have had more expansive borders, encompassing even territories from Turkish Armenia.

"This idea, undoubtedly, has long occupied and continues to occupy Armenian politicians. *I confess it has not let me rest either, and continuously torments me. Did we not perhaps commit a fatal mistake? Should we not have sovietized Armenia right along with Azerbaijan, or soon after, in the months of July and August? Should we not have spat on Europe, the Sevres Treaty and [President] Wilson and tied our hope with Moscow?*"[54]

This long-suffering people would live horrific days under the dictatorial Soviet Regime; their body, mind, and spirit would be consumed for decades, until Stalin's death, but those provinces which were part of the Republic from the spring of 1919 to the Fall of 1920 could have remained a part of Soviet Armenia and today's Armenia.

Vratsian continues:

"Of course, it was exceedingly difficult in those days to have dared to take such a step. Who would have dared to even think that [the Treaty of] Sevres would be voided . . . [the Treaty of] Lausanne and Europe's and America's promises and commitments would not be worth an eggshell. But psychologically, were not the Turks also bitterly depressed? But there did arise a Mustafa Kemal, a Raouf Bey, and the course of history was changed.

"Was it not possible for us also to have had an ARMENIAN Mustafa Kemal? An undaunted revolt against

158

wicked Europe, a separate agreement with the Bolsheviks. . . ."55

(*That ARMENIAN Mustafa Kemal, ARMENIAN Garibaldi, ARMENIAN Simon Bolivar, Mr. Vratsian, was Andranik! Brave of the Brave! The man the renowned writer, Shahan Shahnur, has classified as "one of the three peak figures" of the Armenians' 3,000-year history; on whom the talented and famous writer of the turn of the twentieth century, Avetis Aharonian, has bestowed the following accolades: "beyond criticism," "unmatched," and "tempestuous Aramazd."6 Alas, that you lost the unmatched hero that you had produced, due to his having told you:*
    *"Do not believe the deceptive rhetoric of the Young Turks, because they are insincere.*
    *"Do not get involved in boundless Russia's revolutionary conflicts, because our resources are not sufficient to struggle against both the sultan and the tsar at the same time.*
    *"Do not believe in the Brest-Litovsk Treaty, because the Turks will not even pause a minute on the 1914 border."*
    *You, the luminaries of the Russian Armenians! You did not listen to the Great Man's word and did not hear the Wise Hero's exhortations, when in all three cases the unmatched Andranik, with his prophetic vision, had correctly judged the coming development of political events; as for the Armenian political parties and the nation as a whole . . . you fell into tragic error and catastrophic blunder.*
    *I wish Dashnakist Andranik's Turkish-Armenian Dashnakist comrades, warriors, and intellectuals had been alive; perhaps the fate of the Armenian people and homeland could have been different.*
    *Will this poor nation once again see a man of Andranik's caliber, brave and wise?)*

---

6 A pagan god.

## THE REASONS FOR THE DELAY OF
## TRANSFER OF POWER

Just as the question of transferring Armenia's reign to the Soviets a few months earlier had tormented Simon Vratsian's mind for days on end, it had also occupied my mind for years until I was able to untie the knot, I think.

When in the last days of April 1920 a few divisions of the Red Army approached Azerbaijan, the Azeris handed over the country without ifs, ands, or buts, who knows with what logic—probably opportunistically. Armenia and Georgia were not sovietized yet, for Russia's Red Army and Communist Party were very far from mastering the situation in their boundless country.

In fact, across the entire expanse of the tsarist empire, fierce battles, both civil and interventionist, were taking place.

White Russian Admiral A. V. Kolchak had established an anti-Bolshevik government in Siberia.

General Anton Ivanovich Denikin, one of Alexander Fyodorovich Kerenski's former commanders, had achieved resounding victories against units of the Red Army in the Ukraine, and General N. N. Yudenich had made a stand against the Bolsheviks across Estonia, whereas Kerenski's defense minister, Boris Savinov, embodied anti-Bolshevik sentiments in the whole country. The Allies had provided a lot of money, armaments, and military experts to these anti-Bolshevik commanders,[56] and the Allies, as well as the Axis powers, were convinced that Bolshevism could not endure for long.

As for the interventionist forces, 30,000 Czechs were fighting against the Bolsheviks in Siberia. By the end of 1918, 15,000 British and American soldiers had landed in northern Russia, and 70,000 Japanese were in eastern Siberia. Also battling Bolsheviks were forces from Germany, Norway, and Austria, while 7,000 Americans were defending the Trans-Siberian railway.[57]

After his defeat, Boris Savinkov, the right-wing "Social Revolutionary" (SR), resurrected his terrorist base, which in the more distant past (before Kerenski) he had used to assassinate tsarist officials. On August 30, 1918, one of his agents, a girl named Fanny (Anna) Kaplan, shot and wounded Lenin when he was returning from a labor meeting, in Moscow. The next day, another agent killed M. S. Yuritskin, St. Petersburg's CEKA Chief.

For the wounding of Lenin, that same night, the Bolsheviks arrested 500 renowned tsarist individuals in Moscow and shot them.[58]

Denikin's, Yudenich's, and Kolchak's anti-Bolshevik forces not only held their positions until 1919, but some of them got as close as 200 miles from Moscow.

The Czechs, tiring of their struggles in boundless Russia, betrayed Kolchak to the Red Army units. The latter arrested and shot him on February 7, 1920.[59]

Denikin had already been defeated a year earlier and escaped to England.

After that, new interventionist armies did not appear on the battlefield, but the anti-Bolshevik struggle continued until England sealed a peace and commerce treaty with the Soviets on March 16, 1921, in London. The Germans did the same on May 6, Norway on September 2, Austria on December 7, and Italy on December 26, 1921.[60]

Why were the White Russian commanders and the interventionist armies finally defeated?

During the tsarist centuries, the Russian people were divided into two classes: prince-feudal lords, and *mujiks* (destitute peasant farmers) who cultivated the princes' estates like slaves. There was no middle class.

When Bolshevism arrived, the poor peasants and laborers were deceived by the slogans about justice and equality trumpeted by the Communists. They were told that the laborer peasants would become the lords of the princes' estates, and that Bolshevism would create a paradise-like country for the laboring class. Instead of paradise the Kremlin's Red Dictator created hellish conditions across the country, not sparing even the loyal and faithful Communist chiefs, the high-ranking commanders of the army, and the intellectual class. That was the reason why the unfortunate

Russian people, the masses of the country who had not seen the light of day for centuries, sided with the Bolsheviks and caused the collapse of the anti-Bolshevik front.

Thus, in 1920, when the question of handing over power to the Bolsheviks (or not) was occupying the minds of Yerevan's Eastern- Armenian leaders, they were not in a hurry, because, in my estimation, it was not clear yet whether the Bolsheviks would win or lose in the civil and interventionist battles raging in all corners of the country.


## TURKEY INVADES ARMENIA

On September 20–21, 1920, the Turkish army began advancing to Sareghamish, and thus began the Armenian-Turkish War.

The government of Armenia appealed to the Turkish state to begin negotiations in order to establish peace between the two governments. The Turks proposed that the Armenian government reject the Treaty of Sevres and accept the Treaty of Batum.

The Armenian Government appealed to the representatives of the Allies in Tbilisi, but the latter did not show any inclination to come to the aid of Armenia.

Responding to the repeated appeals of the Armenian Government, Karabekir Pasha accepted the cease-fire proposal "and on his part offered heavy conditions, chief among them the military occupation of Alexandropol's fortress and railway station, the withdrawal of Armenian forces 15 *verst*[7] from the Arpachai river, the occupation of an area around the City of Alexandropol by a nine-*verst* radius," etc.

The Armenian Government accepted those terms, but on November 8, Karabekir Pasha changed the terms of the cease fire, making them much graver with the explanation that "the earlier terms were developed by

---

[7] Russian measure of length.

himself, whereas the new terms were instructed by the government in Ankara."[62]

Indeed, with the new and heavier terms put forth by Karabekir on November 8, the Armenians were obliged in 24 hours to turn over to the Turks 2,000 rifles in good condition, 20 heavy and 40 light machine guns, 3 artillery batteries, 4,000 cases of munitions, 6,000 bombs, 2 trains and 50 wagons, and numerous other terms regarding the withdrawal of Armenian forces to new lines.[63]

Armenia's leaders rejected these terms and appealed for help in all directions, but did not receive a response from anywhere.

Upon receiving the Armenian Government's rejection, Kiazim Karabekir Pasha replied, "Since the government of Armenia does not accept the terms of the government in Ankara, the latter is forced to commence military operations."[64]

On November 11, the government of Armenia expressed regret regarding the Turks' latest terms and nevertheless expressed hope that a way out could be found which would satisfy "the interests and honor of both nations. . . ."[65]

"To satisfy" the terms of the two nations' interests and honor, the government of Ankara, with a bulletin, added new and heavier terms to the demands it had presented so far.

A few days after commencing military operations, on November 16, Yerevan "decided to accept the Turks' terms and begin negotiations for peace."[66]

Alexander Khadisian, Sarkis Araratian, and others hastily went to Alexandropol to seal "peace" with the Turks at any price, and to accept terms, "very grave" terms, which albeit would "put an end to Armenia's independent existence."

In Alexandropol, the Turks further intensified their terms, demanding the Armenian state's "cannons, with their shells and mules."[67] The republic's delegates turned these also over to the Turks, remaining completely dependent on the Turks' mercy and charity.

In those days, the Armenian Patriarchate and political parties in Constantinople held commemorations to protest for the Armenians left defenseless against the Turks. Karabekir, meanwhile, had reached the gates of Yerevan and occupied 80 percent of the expanse of the Republic of Armenia, i.e., 40,000 sq km of the 50,000 sq km area.

In these critical days of the Armenian-Turkish War, Georgia declared itself neutral. . . .


## ARMENIA UNDER SOVIET RULE

On November 26, Armenian-Turkish negotiations began in Alexandropol. On November 29, an Armenian Communist uprising began in Karvansarai and Dilijan, declaring Armenia to be a "Soviet Socialist Republic."[68]

On the same day, a group of Armenian Bosheviks from Baku came to Idjevan village in Armenia and unofficially declared the sovietization of Armenia.

On December 2, by the so-called "Yerevan Accord" signed by the "left-wing ARF" members Dro and Hambardzum Terterian of the Republic of Armenia and Soviet Russia's representative Legrand, Armenia was officially declared a "Soviet Socialist Republic."

Simon Vratsian's government resigned, a provisional "coalition" government led by Dro was formed, pending the arrival in Yerevan of sovietized Armenia's Revolutionary Committee.

In Alexandropol, Khadisian demanded instruction from Yerevan as to whether to sign the treaty or not. The deposed government's head, Vratsian, replied, "We are forced to accept the Turks' terms. You are authorized to sign the treaty."[69]

Actually, it was up to Dro's government to issue such an instruction to Khadisian. But Dro was also obligated to repeat that which Vratsian had already instructed to Khadisian.[70]

164

"I already told you. Act according to your understanding. I am speaking in the name of comrade Silin." (Armenia's military commissar.)[71]

Thus, with the deposed Prime Minister Vratsian's and new Prime Minister Dro's instructions was sealed Alexandropol's black and grim treaty, legitimizing the lands occupied by the Turks, fifteen hours after Armenia's sovietization.[72]

About this K. Sasuni would write the following:

"The government of Armenia and the ARF had all the means to avoid the obligation of signing this treaty."[73]

According to the 2nd clause of the humiliating terms signed on December 2 in Alexandropol, "Armenia would lose Alexandropol, Kars, Artahan, Sareghamish, Kaghzuan, a portion of the Araratian Plain, the richest and most fertile Surmalu district of the Province of Yerevan, including Koghb" (as well as Igdir, Ani, and Mount Ararat).[74] What remained for Armenia were the regions of Yerevan, Zangezur, Sevan, and Daralagiaz, which would de facto become a Turkish protectorate.[75]

Vratsian writes, "The Treaty of Alexandropol was terrible and from a Bolshevik perspective illicit, but in the conditions of those days, it was necessary and unavoidable."[76]

Khadisian, upon his return from Alexandropol to Yerevan, delivered to Dro the historical documents of the "Black Treaty" of Alexandropol and obtained the following receipt:

"Received from Alexander Khadisian:
"(1) Treaty with Turkey (in French language);
"(2) The same in Turkish;
"(3) Three maps, attached to the Treaty;
"(4) An accounting regarding the funds spent by the delegation;
"(5) A report by Alexander Khadisian.

165

"Signed by
"Commander of All Military Forces of the
"Soviet Socialist Republic of Armenia
"DRO
"Yerevan, December 5, 1920"

Delivering to Dro and Silin all the documents, treaties, and maps, Khadisian considered his service completed.[77]

Khadisian's epilogue about the Treaty:

"The original text of the Treaty of Alexandropol is kept in Yerevan, with the Soviet Government.

"Let those who have the means and the power change the terms of the Treaty of Alexandropol. We, the signatories of that Treaty, would be the first to applaud. But already a number of years have passed and unfortunately the situation has not changed."[78]


## DRO THE SUPREME LEADER OF ARMENIA

About Dro becoming a member of Armenia's Bolshevik *Revcom* (revolutionary committee), Vratsian would write:

"I am closely acquainted with Dro's feelings in those days. We would examine together the ardent issues of those days during our frequent meetings. He believed, and getting agitated would push back my doubts, that the Red Army would arrive soon and lift the Damoclean sword from Armenia's head. He believed that 'Russian attention' would be a salvation for the Armenian people. He strove only to gain time, pending the arrival of Russian forces in Yerevan.

"By the Treaty signed with Legrand, Armenia was going to become an independent republic and a *Revcom* was going to be formed, comprising Bolsheviks and 'left-wing Dashnakists.' Dro and Terterian would be a part of the *Revcom,* as 'left-wing Dashnakists.' Members of the army and government, officers and political party members would not be persecuted for their previous activities. Pending the

166

arrival of the *Revcom* in Yerevan, the reign of power in the country would be in the hand of Dro as chief of staff, assisted by Silin. At midnight on December 2 power would be transferred to the Bolsheviks peacefully."[79]

But Dro and the others felt that not everything would transpire peacefully and that certain leaders would become victims of Bolshevik revenge. For this reason the ARF decided that some members of the government should move abroad. Dro offered every assistance to enable them to leave the country hastily. Among them were Dr. Hamo Ohandjanian, Ruben Ter-Minasian, Artashes Chilinguirian, Bashkhi Ishkhanian, Levon Galantarian, and others. Dro had ideological disputes with some of these, yet he helped them in their departure, even though he knew that his turn could come later.[80]

Armenia's army and administration submitted with discipline to the new regime, under the leadership of Dro and Silin. The latter was a delegate of the Russian Bolsheviks, with Legrand being the head of their delegation.

Dro did not remain long as the head of sovietized Armenia's interim government. On December 4 the new Soviet government's cabinet of ministers, headed by Kasian, arrived in Yerevan. On December 6 the forward divisions of the Red Army reached Yerevan. Dro received them with military honors. From Azerbaijan arrived members of the *Revcom*. The wonderfully attired Dro, heading similarly impeccably attired cavalry officers, accompanied by Hambardzum Terterian, Legrand, and others went forward to Kanaker and received them with honors, then led them to Yerevan.[81]

The *Revcom* commenced its activities within days. Terterian was appointed commissar of the state bank, whereas Dro remained as commander of Yerevan's garrison. The CEKA[8] was formed, headed by the notorious Atarbekov. Soon a ruthless crusade against the ARF commenced. Dro frequently visited Vratsian, on some occasions accompanied

---

[8] The progenitor of the KGB.

by Silin and General Bobrishchev. The latter was chief of the Red Army's intelligence division. Dro also took part in the Bolshevik commissars' feasts, but he appeared depressed. He still thought that the Bolshevik atrocities in Armenia were the work of local riff-raff.[82]

Before long it was revealed that some members of the former cabinet and parliament who had tried to cross over to Georgia (Hamo Ohandjanian, A. Chilinguirian, V. Babayan, Dr. H. Ter Davidian, V. Navasartian, and others), were arrested. It was feared that they might soon face a firing squad.

Alexander Khadisian, who was not a party member but in favor of the ARF, decided to visit S. Kasian, the head of the new government, in an effort to ameliorate the treatment of those under arrest.

On the morning when Khadisian went to meet Kasian, he was first received by a tall gentleman, Ayvazian, the chief of CEKA. He was then informed that Kasian had audited Khadisian's lectures in Tbilisi, in 1903–1905. Conversing with Kasian, he asked that the arrested not be executed. Kasian replied:

"We are not at all thinking about executing them. We want to subject them to a public show trial. It is important for us to expose the nature of the ARF and its impotence. We will begin the trial as soon as we complete the prosecutorial file. As for what the verdict would be—of course I do not know. Personally, I think two of them—he named the two—would in any event be condemned to death. The outrage against them is immense; but at the moment nobody is threatened with anything. Although our young people are eager to dispatch this matter forthwith, we will have to wait."[83]

The conversation then turned to the Treaty of Alexandropol. Khadisian revealed the process of this treaty and the "reasons" which prompted the delegation to sign it. Kasian replied:

"You acted legitimately. At that moment it was impossible to act any other way. But you understand that we are the Soviet government; we cannot assume responsibility for this Treaty. For that reason we fiercely criticize it in our press and blame you. But that is a tactical matter. Our aim is not to recognize that Treaty and form a new one."[84]

Khadisian did not remain much longer in Armenia. Certain Communists found it necessary to imprison him. The government investigated the matter and decided to deport him, A. Gulkhandanian, and General Ghorghanian. Khadisian took leave of Vratsian, Kadjaznuni, former foreign minister Sirakan Tigranian, and Dro. On December 16, Khadisian, Gulkhandanian, and Ghorghanian together crossed into Georgia and from there abroad.[85]

# NOTES

1. Richard Hovannisian, *The Republic of Armenia, Feb–Aug 192,* Vol 3, 1996, pp 180–185.
2. Ibid, pp 190–191.
3. Ibid, p 191.
4. Ibid, pp 191–192.
5. Christopher J. Walker, *Armenia, The Survival of a Nation,* Croom Helm, London, St. Martin's Press, New York, 1980, pp 287–288.
6. Richard Hovannisian, *The Republic of Armenia.* Between the Crescent and the Sickle, Vol 4, 1996, pp 46–47.
7. Simon Vratsian, *Along Life's Pathways,* Vol 5, Beirut, 1996, p 130.
8. Ibid, p 130.
9. Christopher J. Walker, *Armenia, The Survival of a Nation,* Croom Helm, London, St. Martin's Press, New York, 1980, p 288.
10. Ibid, p 288.
11. Ibid, p 288.
12. Ibid, p 289.
13. Ibid, p 290.
14. Richard Hovannisian, *The Republic of Armenia,* Vol 3, pp 193–194.
15. Ibid, pp 195–197.
16. Ibid, pp 198–199.
17. Simon Vratsian, *Republic of Armenia,* 2nd ed, Beirut, 1958, p 387.
18. Richard Hovannisian, *The Republic of Armenia,* Vol 3, pp 225–226.
19. Simon Vratsian, *Republic of Armenia,* 2nd ed, Beirut, 1958, p 378.
20. Ibid, pp 382–383.
21. Christopher J. Walker, *Armenia, The Survival of a Nation,* Croom Helm, London, St. Martin's Press, New York, 1980, pp 284–285.

22. Simon Vratsian, *Republic of Armenia,* 2nd ed, Beirut, 1958, p 388.
23. Ibid, p388.
24. Ibid, p 390.
25. Ibid, pp 390–392.
26. Ibid, pp 392–395.
27. Ibid, pp 395–396.
28. Ibid, p 396.
29. Richard Hovannisian, *The Republic of Armenia,* Vol 3, pp 232–235.
30. Simon Vratsian, *Along Life's Pathways,* Vol 4, p 194.
31. Ibid, p 194.
32. Alexander Khadisian, p 88.
33. Ibid, pp 88–89.
34. Ibid, p 89.
35. *Encyclopedia Britannica,* 1958, Vol 25, p 93.
36. Levon Vartan, *Chronicle of the Armenian Nineteen Fifteen, 1915–1923,* Beirut, 1975, p 168.
37. Avetis Yapujian, *And the Armenian Nation Resurrected From the Fire and the Sword.* Cairo, 1971, p 64.
38. Ibid, p 66.
39. Ibid, p 67.
40. Levon Vartan, *Chronicle of the Armenian Nineteen Fifteen, 1915–1923,* Beirut, 1975, p 202.
41. Manuk Krzlian, *Dro, the Invincible and Immortal Soldier of the Armenian Liberation Struggle, Asbarez* Daily, Saturday, May 18, 2002, p 12.
42. Avetis Yapujian, *And the Armenian Nation Resurrected From the Fire and the Sword.* Cairo, 1971, p 73.
43. Ibid, p 73.
44. Ibid, p 73.
45. Ibid, p 82 (see, K. Sassuni, *The Armenian-Turkish War,* p 24).
46. Archbishop Garegin S. Hovsepian, *The Most Calamitous Day of My Life (The Fall of Kars).* Cairo, 1945, p 3.
47. Ibid, p 9.

48. Richard Hovannisian, *The Republic of Armenia*, Vol 2, p 385.
49. Ibid, p 386.
50. Avetis Terzibashian, *Andranik,* Paris, 1942, pp 396–397.
51. Richard Hovannisian, *The Republic of Armenia*, Vol 2, p 384.
52. Ibid, p 390.
53. Simon Vratsian, *Armenia Between the Bolshevik Hammer and the Turkish Anvil,* Beirut, 1953, p 13.
54. Simon Vratsian, *Along Life's Pathways,* Vol 5, p 167.
55. Ibid, p 167.
56. *Encyclopedia Britannica.* 1958, Vol 19, p 713.
57. Ibid, p 712.
58. Ibid, p 712.
59. Ibid, p 713.
60. Ibid, p 713.
61. Khadisian, p 283.
62. Ibid, p 283.
63. A. M. Boghosian, *Social-Economic Relationships in the Region of Kars.* Yerevan, 1961, p 369.
64. Khadisian, p 283.
65. Ibid, p 283.
66. Ibid, p 288.
67. Ibid, p 288.
68. Levon Vartan, *Chronicle of the Armenian Nineteen Fifteen, 1915–1923,* Beirut, 1975, p 205.
69. Shahan, *Another Addendum on the "How" and "Why" of the Treaty of Alexandropol.* Boston, 1945, p 31.
70. Ibid, p 32.
71. Ibid, p 33.
72. Ibid, p 31.
73. Ibid, p 31 (See K. Sassuni, *The Armenian-Turkish War, Hairenik* Monthly, July 1926, p 116).
74. A. M. Poghosian, *Socio-Economic Relationships.* p 374.
75. Ibid, p 374.
76. Simon Vratsian, *Along Life's Pathways,* Vol 4, p 199.
77. Khadisian, *Republic,* p 313.

78. Ibid, p 314.
79. Simon Vratsian, *Along Life's Pathways,* Vol 4, pp 197–198.
80. Ibid, p 198.
81. Richard Hovannisian, *The Republic of Armenia,* Vol 4, p 389.
82. Simon Vratsian, *Along Life's Pathways,* Vol 4, p 199.
83. Khadisian, p 321.
84. Ibid, pp 321–322.
85. Ibid, pp 323–324.

# FEDAYEE SONG

## PRAISE TO SEROB PASHA

The golden peak of towering Nemrut
Shines luminous in Lake Van;
Your dear name, brave Serob Pasha,
Shines with wisdom in our hearts;
Let the worthy praise of your deeds,
In this wretched singer's unadorned lyrics
Flow like a clear, babbling spring.

— — — —

Nemrut Mountain has a thousand springs,
All of which flow to the Plain of Mush;
Only the spring from Serob's heart
Flows to the heart of the poor people—
To the heart of the homeland,
Thirsting for free days, verdant days.

# CHAPTER VI

## POPULAR UPRISING AGAINST
## THE BOLSHEVIK REGIME

Oliver Baldwin

## DRO IS BANISHED TO MOSCOW

Before departing from Yerevan, Hambardzum Terterian and Vratsian visited Dro to confer. Anticipating the inevitability of a popular uprising against the vile and unbearable Bolshevik regime of Armenia, they advised him not to go to Russia, but instead to withdraw to the Zangezur Province.

Dro refused to withdraw to Zangezur. First, he considered it dishonorable to resort to flight; second, he was sincerely convinced that Moscow was not of the same mind regarding the policy of Armenia's *Revcom*. He believed that if he reasoned with Moscow's leadership circles, he could effect a change in both the internal and external policies of the *Revcom*.

Before the guests had departed, some officers also arrived and pleaded with him not to leave the homeland, but instead to raise the flag of uprising. He replied that an uprising would be a reckless venture, that Armenia at present could not be independent, and that the only salvation of the Armenian people lay in remaining tied to Russia.[1]

News that Dro was summoned to Moscow spread like lightning throughout Yerevan. Vratsian, who was under surveillance by two Cekists, went to visit his friend of many years. Dro's wife, Arpenik, teary-eyed, greeted the guest. In a corner of the living room sat his father, who was drying his eyes with his handkerchief. Dro was lying down in the bedroom and chain-smoking.

"Is it true then?" asked Vratsian.

"True. They are calling me to Moscow," replied Dro.

"Calling you or taking you . . . ."

"Isn't it the same?"

Of course it was not the same, reasoned Vratsian.

"It was impossible for him [Dro] not to feel that they were banishing him from Armenia, but he was still convinced that in Moscow he would succeed in changing the central government's policy toward Armenia. He had his

177

subordinates prepare a series of reports about Armenia, which he was going to take with him to present to the Soviet Central Authority. He defended the thesis that Armenia and the Armenian people, under all circumstances, were and would remain friends with Russia, and that for Russia, Armenia was important as a bridge and a foothold in the direction of the Mediterranean Sea."[2]

After examining at length the pros and cons of the situation, Dro and Vratsian arrived at the following conclusion: Dro would go to Moscow. Vratsian would also go and together they would strive to be useful for Armenia. However, the plans changed and Dro went alone.

It was getting close to dusk. Representing the military, General A. Bobrishchev arrived to bid farewell. Other eminent Bolsheviks would also arrive to bid farewell. Vratsian left.

Dro's father, handkerchief in hand, remained seated in the corner of the living room, subdued and sad. In the dining room Arpenik was setting a table for the *Revcom* members and commissars. A storm was raging outside.

Later, it was said that they feasted until morning.

The following morning, Vratsian visited Dro again. The front door was open. Acquaintances as well as strangers had arrived to bid farewell. The luggage was lined up against a wall. Arpenik was sobbing in a side room. Dro's father, holding his handkerchief, was pacing the floor in the living room. Dro was in the bedroom, dressed and ready to go. After a brief meeting, Dro and Vratsian came out to the crowded living room. There were warm hugs and kisses. A crowd had formed outside.

The sleigh began to move. "Farewell." "God be with you." "Looking forward to your return."

Dro telephoned Vratsian from Baku to inform him that he had arrived safely and comfortably, and would soon depart for Moscow. He made some remarks about Zangezur, where Nzhdeh had refused to submit to the Bolsheviks. The gist of the conversation was that difficulties should not be created for the Soviet authorities.

After that there was no word from Dro. Some stated that he was exiled to Siberia. Others said that Stalin received him with great honors and offered him a high rank in the Red Army.[3]

## OLIVER BALDWIN DESCRIBES THE LAMENTABLE CONDITION OF THE ARMENIAN PEOPLE UNDER THE SOVIET REGIME

Lieutenant Colonel Oliver Baldwin, the son of the British Prime Minister Stanley Baldwin, had a chance encounter with Armenia's second Prime Minister, Alexander Ivanovich Khadisian, at the Savoy Palace in Alexandria, Egypt, in August 1920. Khadisian was touring Armenian settlements and communities abroad to raise funds for the homeland.

Khadisian persuaded Colonel Baldwin to come to Armenia to instruct the infantry.

Baldwin accepted the invitation and went to Armenia. Minister of Defense Ruben Ter Minasian appointed Baldwin to the rank of Lieutenant Colonel in the Armenian army.[4]

With Armenia's sovietisation, relates Baldwin, the country lost its independence because the Allied states failed to support Armenia.

One morning, Colonel Baldwin encountered an Armenian peasant sitting on a stone trying to keep himself warm in the sun, for his clothes were threadbare and the holes in them showed the bare flesh. The peasant began to sing "God save the King" in English. It turned out that he had been employed by the British in Batum and had come to Armenia to fight for his homeland. He had been imprisoned for refusing to hand over a pair of socks the American Near East Relief had given him, to a Bolshevik soldier during Red Week.

Red Week was an interesting institution. It occurred once every three months, during which time any Red soldier could do exactly what he liked to the civilian population:

take what he wished, sleep where he willed, go where he pleased.[5]

There were two prisons in Yerevan. The smaller one held around 250 inmates and the larger one around 1,000. Both were packed with inmates who were subjected to unspeakable tortures. Among the inmates were Russian soldiers who were arrested for the offense of intoxication.[6]

The people were exceedingly unhappy with the new regime. Everyone was terrorized. There were plenty of rumors about an impending uprising. Many escaped through secret routes to Persia. A popular uprising was inevitable. A story circulated among the people that the great national hero, Andranik, was in Persia and would shortly advance north, that he had hurried over from America, and that President Wilson was coming as well in order to see that the Armenian boundaries were in keeping with his former decision. Others said that the Tsar had been found in Siberia and was leading an army westward. Still others averred that Trotsky was dead and that Lenin had been killed.[7]

But nothing like that happened. Andranik was still in America, wondering why his country had had faith in the Western Allies . . . . The only people who thought themselves lucky to have Bolshevik rulers were the Tatar inhabitants of Yerevan; but even they would eventually have a shock, when their leader, Ali Khan, was arrested as a bourgeois for being overweight.[8]

Also arrested were Oliver Baldwin and an Italian merchant named Parmejani. The larger prison was so crowded that a nearby residence was also expropriated to house inmates. Periodically, some prisoners were taken out in groups never to be heard from again.

At this time, Armenia was not yet entirely under Bolshevik rule. There were two mountainous provinces which the Red Army had not invaded. One was Zangezur, where Ruben was secretly plotting resistance against the Bolsheviks; the second was Gharabagh, where Nzhdeh was active. The latter had served as a captain in the Bulgarian Army.[9]

After Baldwin was released from prison, he once encountered a starving, emaciated, almost naked child in the street, whimpering pitifully. He gave the child a piece of sausage he had. The child held the sausage without eating. Dr. Clarence Ussher later explained that if starvation is prolonged, the digestive organs cease to function and only come around gradually.[10]

The American missionary, Dr. Ussher, who had resided in Van since 1898,[11] was now settled in Yerevan as administrator of Near East Relief, managing ten orphanages in Armenia, each one of which held 200-300 orphans.[12]

During the last week of Baldwin's incarceration, a new CEKA chief by the name of Adarbekov (Adarbekian) was sent from Moscow to Yerevan. This man of Armenian and Russian descent was a notorious sadist, addicted to cocaine, and known for his hands-on approach to torturing his victims. Short in appearance, with small blue eyes, trimmed red beard, and dressed in black leather, he always had a pistol under his left arm, with his right hand often on it.

Upon arriving in Yerevan, Adarbekov's first act was to forbid stoves throughout both prisons. The second act took place when Baldwin was walking to Dr. Ussher's house. At a corner of one of the side streets was a detachment of Red cavalry, a small crowd of people, and an old carriage with two horses. Silin and Dro were seated within.[13]

Silin was sent by the Soviets as Commissar of the military command in Armenia as well as chargé d'affaires of Legrand.

As Baldwin came upon the carriage, its coachman drove off. When he enquired about the meaning of this, Baldwin was told that Dro had been called to Moscow. Wiser men recognized the reason. Dro was too great a power amongst Armenians. Dro was a national leader; therefore the sooner he was out of the way the easier the subjugation of the people. From the hour of his departure and through the next day rumors circulated of how the peasants had stopped the carriage, killed the escort, and allowed Dro to escape into Gharabagh.

But none of these rumors was true. Dro probably thought it better for his people to suffer persecution, rather than to rebel and be massacred. In any event, with Dro's exile, Chief Adarbekov of Armenia's CEKA took away a pillar of strength from the ARF organization in Armenia.


## "GLORIOUS HAMAZASP"

After Dro, the most central ARF figure in Armenia was "Glorious Hamazasp," who, while in prison, was felled by an axe in the hands of Adarbekov's Red henchmen.

Born in Van in 1873 and a goldsmith by trade, Hamazasp was Archbishop Garegin Srvandziants's nephew, his senior brother Khachatur's son.

During the 1905–1906 Armeno-Tatar war, Hamazasp had delivered a stunning blow to the Azeris in the Askeran Gorge. Of the 200 enemy cavalry, only six survived. Gharabagh's Armenians were elated and sang a song dedicated to "Glorious Hamazasp."

> The sun of freedom rose,
> Chasing clouds from the sky!
> Hamazasp with his band
> Arrived from the district of Khachen.
>
> The Armenians' lord, the ARF,
> Has thunderous braves;
> The whole world proclaimed
> Glorious Hamazasp.

Hamazasp was arrested in the Caucasus and exiled to Siberia, where he kept busy as a goldsmith. Hamo Ohandjanian's and his wife Rubina's wedding rings were prepared by Hamazasp in distant Siberia.[14]

In 1914, he was the Commander of the Armenian Volunteers' 3rd Regiment on the Caucasus front. He took part in the battles around Basen and Van. After the sovietization of Armenia on December 2, 1920, Hamazasp published a telegram of greeting to the Red Army in the January 11, 1921, issue of the *Communist* newspaper, to the effect that Armenia was delivered from the claws of the Turks. The devilish Adarbekov and his sycophants, who were inflicting what the Turks had left undone on the suffering people of the homeland, dispatched with axes, in a dastardly fashion, Glorious Commander Hamazasp and other inmates in the prisons.[15]

Alexander Khadisian wrote the following about the unfortunate Hamazasp, in the December 1923 issue of the monthly, *Hairenik* (Homeland):

"The first Armenian activists I encountered after my arrival in Tbilisi in the Summer of 1914 were Andranik and Hamazasp. The latter had escaped from exile in Siberia and after a long journey had come to Tbilisi. I had first met him in 1906 when he was leading the Armenian self-defense against the Tatars during the 1905–1906 Armeno-Tatar War. The second time I saw him, he was a defendant in a Russian court. Now it was the third time I was meeting him. One day, I noticed a man near my house, nodding to me with deference. I did not recognize him; he was still residing illegally in Tbilisi. He whispered his name to me. I invited him in. In an emotional voice he started explaining to me that a war with Turkey was inevitable and that he was putting himself at the disposal of the military command, requesting to be assigned any dangerous but important task in the army. He was the first swallow of the volunteer movement. Hamazasp's selfless proposal was accepted and he was given the task he wanted, which he fulfilled. He later became Commander of an Armenian Special Forces group in General Baratov's Division, from whom I have heard, as well as read, glowing reports of Hamazasp's military activities."[16]

## DR. CLARENCE DOUGLAS USSHER'S
## HOSPITABLE HOME

After watching Dro's departure, Baldwin continued up the street to Dr. Ussher's house. The doctor welcomed him with courtesy and the two had lunch. Dr. Ussher related that on a few occasions Red soldiers had knocked on his door seeking admission but they were dealt with firmly—on one occasion the burly American doctor himself picking up a Red soldier by the scruff of his neck and throwing him onto the street.

Another time a Russian woman had come to Dr. Ussher's house, begging him to look after her few remaining trinkets. Her husband, a general, had been murdered in Russia; her crippled son had been arrested in Baku for being the son of his father, and she had fled to Armenia. All her other belongings had been confiscated by the Bolsheviks.

One Sunday afternoon, three Protestant ministers, two Armenian Church priests, and two or three lay brethren of the orphanages came to the house. After conversing for some time with Dr. Ussher in Armenian, the small assembly sank to their knees in fervent prayer, beseeching God to save Armenia from the Bolshevik terror.[17]

## ARMENIAN OFFICERS EXILED

One day, Baldwin went for a walk through Yerevan and found the Parliament Building surrounded by the Red cavalry. After enquiring about it, he was informed that Adarbekov had issued an order that all former officers of the Armenian Army were to report to the Parliament Building for duty as officers in the Red Army. When they were all assembled inside, the doors were flung open and around a thousand officers were marched out of the building in fours between lines of cavalry, with the whole party turning on to the Dilijan road, the cold, snowbound

184

road that leads to Baku. Without food, without extra clothing, without snow boots, without being able to say good-bye to their families, the column left town.

Their mothers or wives tried to approach them with their overcoats or a piece of black bread and raisins, but they were sent back by the whiplash of the Cossack. It was said that Adarbekov had ordered this measure to prevent a counter-revolution.

The following day, five hundred more officers were sent off in the same way, on foot, including General Thomas Nazarbekian, 73 years old. The road to Baku was littered with bodies of poor officers, dead of hunger and cold. Women too fell on the road, wives and mothers who had followed their loved ones.

The ARF circulated this story in every village in the country, to prepare the public opinion in support of an uprising.[18]


## THE STALINIST ATROCITIES IN THE EYES OF ARMENIA'S ACADEMICIANS

The inhuman and widespread atrocities inflicted by the Soviet regime on the pitiful people who were already subject to famine and deprivation began in the days of Lenin and continued until the death of the dictator Stalin in 1953.

Unfortunately, Armenians in the Diaspora did not know what was going on behind the "iron curtain." For example, had they known the hellish conditions prevailing in Armenia then, I do not think that as many Armenians would have heeded the call for repatriation in the 1940s.

In the fall of 1994, my wife, Siran (short for Siranouche), and I went to Armenia. I was going to defend my dissertation for the title of Doctor of History. Our visit to the homeland coincided with the 75th Anniversary of the founding of Yerevan's State University, and we were invited to attend a reception in the Great Hall of the University.

Some of the speakers described the terrors of the

Stalinist dictatorship, whose bloody reach had penetrated the walls of academia. For example, in the years 1937–1939 six rectors succeeded each other, some of whom were subjected to the firing squad. One was shot because he had traveled from Azerbaijan to Yerevan in a vehicle which was deemed to be a "capitalist product." An Armenian academician translated Karl Marx's *Das Kapital* from the original German into Russian. He had finished the translation of the third volume in 1930. The translator wrote on the last page, "I have neither money nor bread to eat; long live Marx!" As wages for his work, sacrifices, and deprivation, he was shot by firing squad in 1938. Many other academicians at the University also became victims of the Stalinist terror.

## THE PEOPLE'S CONDITION WAS HOPELESS

The people's condition was tragic and the authorities of the day did nothing to improve their lot.

The local cinema had been commandeered and filled with men, women, and children who were at death's door. One day, Baldwin and Jack V. Arakelian, the Deputy of Arsho Shahkhatouni, the former Army Provost Marshal in Yerevan, were walking by the cinema and took a look inside. The hall was cold and dark. The floor was covered with the living, the dying, and the dead. No attempt was made to feed these wretched people nor to attend to them medically. The stench from this mass of humanity was indescribable, the groans heart wrenching. Every morning an ox wagon would draw up in front of the cinema and the dead would be placed therein. The wagons would take the bodies to the pits and return for more. Once in the hall, no one came out alive.

On one occasion, on the outskirts of town, Baldwin came upon a dead woman. By her side sat her husband, who was apparently to follow her shortly. He held a baby— their baby—whimpering, naked, starved, and cold. The father began to lick the child, trying to keep it warm.

Curiosity led Baldwin back there an hour later. All three were dead.[19]

## KARPIS DJERBASHIAN ABOUT
## THE SOVIET REGIME
(Excerpts)

"How heavy and hard became that ransom for salvation—the Stalinist terror—which meant that when you put your head on your pillow at night, you would be gripped by fear of whether there would be a knock on your door at an ungodly hour; whether you would make it to the dawn to be able to praise the Lord for survival through another night. The sanctity of family was wrecked. Marriage was limited to simply registering as a couple at the municipality. Divorce was accomplished with the same ease. Baptism was considered archaic and bourgeois. The father of any child who was baptized was considered a suspect Soviet citizen. It was hard to find any priest to perform baptisms anyway. The Holy See of Edjmiadsin was in dire straits. Around a thousand clerics were exiled, to vanish in Siberia. After the slaughter of the luminaries of Western Armenian literature in the Genocide of 1915, our national literature was dealt another great blow in the years of Soviet "nirvana." Many intellectuals perished: Charents, Bakunts, Yessayan, Totovents, and others. Even the Catholicos of All Armenians became the executioner's victim. That ransom for salvation also included the 300,000 Armenians who died in the Soviet Army.

———————

"But we are also obliged to consider, remember, and appreciate those honorable Armenian communists, who in the beginning had faith in Lenin's humanitarian ideals, who were virtuous citizens. They were conscientious, ardent Armenians. Steeped in the spirit of sacrifice, they dedicated themselves to the country's development. Thanks to them, the people's educational standards rose. They built schools and residential housing. Science, art, and literature

187

developed. The town of Yerevan was transformed to a radiant capital city, enriched with universities, institutes, museums, libraries, the metro, etc."[20]

## THE FEBRUARY UPRISING

The Bolsheviks who had come to power in the name of the people, particularly the working class, had been so evil and impudent in their dealings with the pitiful and impoverished population that an uprising had become inevitable. By violating the sanctity of homes and carting away the people's belongings, winter provisions, and furniture, the Red soldiers incited the people against the regime. The troika of Sargis Kasian, Kevork Atarbekian, and Avis Nuridjanian had created a suffocating atmosphere in the country which lasted six to seven months, until the arrival of Alexander Miasnikian in Yerevan, in the early summer of 1921.

The ARF wanted to submit and cooperate with the new regime, but for the bloodthirsty Adarbekov and his cohorts, even the left-wing ARF members, Dro and Hambartsum, were unacceptable.

After a brief respite during the Lenin era with the arrival of Miasnikian when the atmosphere became more bearable, political conditions would again become turbulent and the paranoid terror would spread so wide, that two of the troika of rulers of early Soviet Armenia, Sargis Kasian and Avis Nuridjanian, would themselves become victims of Stalin's universal purges, starting in 1937. I do not know what became of the bloodthirsty Adarbekov.

The first clashes of the uprising began on February 12, 1921.[21] That same evening, Oliver Baldwin, Madam Korotkova, and her husband, Shura Khansarian, were guests at Dr. Ussher's house for dinner. The latter had transferred to Yerevan after World War I, since there were no more Armenians left in Van-Vaspurakan in Turkish Armenia.

After dinner the conversation turned to the question

why the poor Armenians were being crucified again. Perhaps God was unaware of it? The missionary Dr. Ussher replied that all these were a matter of the earth and that God was aware of it all.

Two days later, on February 14, when Baldwin again visited Ussher, he heard that secret plans were underway to overthrow the Communist regime, that in many neighborhoods the ARF was holding clandestine meetings, that the number of new members being sworn into the ranks of the ARF had increased since the Bolsheviks came to power, and that first of all they would force open the prison gates and then occupy the barracks of the Red soldiers, etc. No one knew who was the leader of all this in Yerevan, but it was surmised that the leader of this general movement was Ruben Pasha.[22]

Neither Dr. Ussher nor Baldwin was hopeful about the success of this uprising.

On the morning of February 16, the Bolshevik press reported that "a light clash with bandits had taken place in the hills behind Yerevan."[23]

That same afternoon, Baldwin had sat down to dinner with Ussher. Baldwin lifted his glass of water to drink, and then stopped. He heard a distant noise. "Perhaps . . ." he thought. They ran to the balcony. It was true. From a distance, they could hear the faint crackle of rifle fire. Suddenly, they heard a brief burst from a machine gun. They looked at each other and smiled . . . .

The next day, when Baldwin went out to the street, he noticed fliers pasted on the walls. It was a long list of names. A neighbor translated for him. It was an edict signed by Defense Minister Avis Nuridjanian and Kevork Atarbekian, which stated that if the ARF did not cease the uprising, all the inmates in the prison would be gunned down.

There were famous names on that list: Hamazasp, Kadjaznouni, colonels, ministers, revolutionaries, journalists, doctors, etc.

The ARF re-established itself in power in Yerevan on February 18.[24] At 6:30 that same morning, Baldwin woke up to the crackle of gunfire. He got dressed and, picking up his pistol, went ouside. Young and old came out of many homes, guns in hand, and joined the growing crowd. "To the prison! To the prison!" they yelled as they headed there. They opened the gates. The prisoners stumbled into the light, emaciated, weak, crying. Feverishly they pointed to the center block. Twenty to thirty bodies were lying there, some naked, some half-clothed, soaked in blood, hacked to pieces. Some were identified: Colonel Korganov, Hamazasp. They opened another door. Half an inch of blood on the floor, pieces of flesh, cord, bits of clothes, more dead bodies. In another place they found a newly dug pit, full of dead bodies, seventy-five in all.[25]

Later they learned how it had happened:

On the night of February 16, the first fifty had been taken out and shot against the prison wall, then buried in the pit.

On the night of February 17, so many wardens had been withdrawn to swell the fighting ranks that it was left to a little Jewish Komissar to arrange the shooting of the others. He ordered the Armenian Red soldiery to help. They refused. He enlisted two Communists of Tatar extraction to help him execute the remaining twenty five.[26]


## VRATSIAN WAS OPPOSED TO THE UPRISING

During the February uprising, Vratsian had taken refuge at a certain Sako's home in the Kond neighborhood. The winter was bitterly cold that year, especially in February. Vratsian reminisces:

"Shut in at the home of Sako, on the Kond hillside, I was troubled with the following thoughts: I, who was an informed, persuaded advocate of Armeno-Russian friendship in both the fields of politics and culture; I, who believed in the coexistence and cooperation of Soviet Russia and Armenia; I, whose spiritual, ideological, and moral character was forged by immersion in Russian culture; I

now with eyes open could see the demolition of my hopes. .
. . I loved Pushkin and the wonderful Chekhov, but as
much and more I also loved our Armenian writers and
poets. *Volga-Volga* spoke a lot to my heart, but my whole
being was taken by *Maïr* (Mother) *Arax*. Why have armed
men come to our homeland to force us to think, sing, dress,
eat, and drink like them?"[27]

There was still gunfire here and there, but Kond was
free. Vratsian and a friend stepped out to the street. At the
corner of Aramian and Raffi Streets they were surrounded
by a tumultuous crowd, the heroes of the uprising in the
city, armed with rifles, men of all ranks and stature. "In
their midst, seated in a wagon, was Smbad of Mush with
his wounded hand on his chest. Around him were familiar
and well-known faces; they were both laughing and crying.
They were tears of unrestrained happiness, of joy and
victory.
" 'Hurray! Long live!' roared from every direction
ceaselessly."[28]
Vratsian and his friend headed to the city. From
Abovian Avenue to the Parliament, thousands were singing
the national anthem, *Mer Hairenik* (Our Homeland).
In that crowd, Vratsian noticed two individuals:
Artashes Chilingarian and Bashkhi Ishkhanian, who were
standing on the sidewalk in front of the Shahnazarian
Pharmacy. Chilingarian, *aka* Ruben Darpinian, would later
become the editor of the *Hairenik* (Homeland) newspaper in
Boston. As for Bashkhi Ishkhanian, together with David
Ananouni, he headed the Armenian Social Democratic
Labor Party in Yerevan. Although Marxist by orientation,
they were hostile to the Bolsheviks,[29] and Ishkhanian had
even called the Soviet Union the "Famine Union."[30]
With some difficulty, Vratsian and his friend were
able to reach and ascend to the top floor of the Parliament
Building. In order to topple the Soviet Regime in Armenia,
virtually all the parties had collaborated: the Populist,
Democratic Liberal, Social-Revolutionary, Social-Democrat,
and *Hunchakian,* whose members, elated and joyous, were

191

mingling in the Parliament.[31]

To topple the oppressive Soviet Regime in Armenia, a committee was formed, called the Salvation Committee. Without his knowledge, Simon Vratsian had been nominated to head it. After the success of the uprising, a government was formed comprised of:

Simon Vratsian, Prime Minister, Foreign Minister, and Director of Agriculture;

Garo Sassouni, Minister of the Interior;

Hambardzum Terterian, Finance Minister;

Hakob Ter-Hakobian, Minister of Provisions;

Dr. S. Yeghyazarian, Health Minister;

Yervant Sargisian, ARF Representative;

Kuro Tarkhanian, Defense Minister;

Garegin Sargisbekian, Chief of Staff.[32]

The government sent a telegram to Lenin, explaining that the coup d'état in Armenia was not directed against Soviet Russia, but was a consequence of the *Revcom's* ferocious policy.[33]

After the reestablishment of Armenia's independence, the government, at the recommendation of the Salvation Committee, sent a memorandum penned by Hovannes Kadjaznuni to its delegates in Constantinople, Europe, and America, from which I relate the following paragraph:

"To struggle against the Bolsheviks and generally to restore peaceful life in our country, we are in great need of neighboring Turkey's friendship, even alliance. Every step you take where you are, overseas, which undermines our effort to establish friendly ties with Turkey could have fatal consequences for us. Today we have two real powers by our sides: one is Soviet Russia and the other Turkey. The other powers are too distant from us. With the first, as our bitter experience showed, we cannot reconcile; we have to reconcile and normalize relations with the other. That is not impossible, because we and the Turks have common interests, which we can defend harmoniously with joined forces. The return of the Bolsheviks is considered as undesirable by Turkey as it is by us. The return of the

Bolsheviks means nothing but the annexation of Armenia by Russia. In that event Turkey would have on its border its enemy for centuries, the great and aggressive Russia. Aggressive, because it is clear to everyone that Soviet Russia is as imperialist as was tsarist Russia in its era. Having retained Azerbaijan, consolidating in Georgia, and overcoming Armenia, Soviet Russia would next attack Turkey also."[34]

## VRATSIAN'S WORRIES AFTER
## THE FEBRUARY UPRISING

"The heaviest and most worrisome aspect of the February uprising was the Turkish Question. The repressive atrocities conducted by the *Revcom* in Armenia had made people forget their instinctive fear of the Turk. Those who were advocating the civil conflict—Bolshevik or not—had forgotten that on the other side of the Arax River were the Turks, and the Magara Bridge was the border between Armenia and Turkey. As if they had forgotten that the Turks had occupied Alexandropol and had plundered and destroyed as well as violated Armenian women in the surrounding villages. They had forgotten that the protestations by Armenia's *Revcom* and the demand to evacuate Alexandropol had been dismissed with contempt by the Turks.

"Every time there was talk about the civil conflict, whether by us or the Bolsheviks, I pushed forward the troubling Turkish argument. Civil conflict terrified me, because it would unleash the Turks' anti-Armenian instinct. The Treaty of Alexandropol had showed that for the Turks Armenia was not a positive political factor, that for Turks intoxicated with Pan-Turanian vision, Armenia and Armenians were an obstacle, a harmful and dangerous thorn which should be eliminated.

— — — — —

"If the civil conflict had been a purely internal affair, particularly after the officers' exile and the Bolshevik

193

looting, it would not have been difficult to topple the *Revcom* regime; except for Communists in Armenia, not a single man remained in favor of the Bolsheviks. However, if the Turks were to attack Armenia, in my opinion the outcome would be worse than tragic for the Armenian people.

"The Armenian citizens, however, were so inflamed by the Bolsheviks that they were not thinking that far ahead, which is the reason why the February uprising succeeded quickly and easily. Public opinion was notably impressed also by the fact that the Turks' representative in Yerevan, Behaeddin Bey, was one of the first to praise the February 18 coup d'état with especially warm expressions. That signified, people concluded, that the Turks' attitude toward Armenia was now positive. This sentiment was quickly taking root among Armenians during the clashes.

"Very well, the enemy is toppled, but not finally vanquished. The struggle continues and will continue until final victory. But Armenia alone is incapable of securing victory. Friends, allies are needed. Arms and armaments are required. Whatever Armenians had would be exhausted in a short time.

"And who were those powers on whom Armenia could rely? Europe? Europe was very far and completely cut off from Armenia. From the perspective of engaging in warfare, one could not hope for any assistance from Europe.[35]

— — — —

"As we had occasion to confirm, the February 18 uprising was the result of pan-national sentiment and did not have a partisan or classist nature. Indeed, all Armenians had united to topple the Bolshevik dictatorship. On February 23, a band of sixty Armenian Democratic Liberal party volunteers departed Yerevan to the front and fought to the end against the Bolsheviks, taking casualties and inflicting casualties. In Armenia, in those days, there was not a single ADL member who opposed the February uprising. Now, they deny that fact, but as the Russians say, 'that which is inscribed by pen cannot be wiped by ax.' "[36]

## THE FEBRUARY UPRISING CURTAILED
## IN YEREVAN

Suppressing the February uprising in Yerevan was not difficult, as it turned out. When Georgia became sovietized on February 25, the Bolsheviks were able to tighten the noose around Yerevan with auxiliary forces.

In those critical days, Simon Vratsian, on March 1, through the Turkish attaché in Yerevan sought the aid of Ankara, emphasizing that the government of Armenia stood by the Treaty of Alexandropol. But the Turks, Christopher Walker writes, being shrewder, were keener on getting good terms from the Russians at the forthcoming Moscow conference than giving aid to the anti-Soviet rebellion in Armenia which would jeopardize their bargaining position. Thus, they left Vratsian's plea unanswered.[37]

Next, on March 9, Vratsian appealed to Moscow, to try to resolve the conflict with the Bolsheviks through negotiations, but again this plea was left unanswered as well.[38]

On March 18, 1921, Vratsian issued the following appeal to Ankara:

"To the Turkish Grand National Assembly Government's eastern front delegate Behaeddin,

"Please transmit this request quickly to your higher authorities and, as I explained to you personally, prompt them for a quick reply.

"The struggle of Armenia for its liberty and independence against the Bolsheviks, we are convinced, serves the interest not only of Armenia, but also all the nations of the Near East. For this reason Armenia hopes that in the course of its struggle it might receive assistance from its neighbors, and foremost among them the Turks, whose interests also demand that Armenia emerge victorious from this struggle and remain independent.

"Deriving from this position and perspective, the government of Armenia appeals to the Turkish Grand National Assembly government in the name of mutual interests of both nations, as soon as possible to:

"1. Repatriate all Armenian prisoners of war from the Yerevan frontline.

"2. With certain conditions provide to the Armenian army armaments, particularly Russian rifles or bullets for Mausers or Rossi and Lebel rifles.

"3. Inform us, as to whether the National Grand Assembly government finds it feasible to provide military assistance to Armenia, and if so, to what extent and in what time frame.

"In making this appeal, the government of Armenia relies on the friendly relations whose foundations were laid beginning with the Treaty of Alexandropol, and which were disturbed during the Bolshevik regime.

"Respectfully Yours,
"President of Armenia
"Simon Vratsian."[39]

"Naturally," adds Vratsian, "this appeal was not solely my initiative, but it was composed and submitted with the knowledge and approval of those around me. For example, H. Kadjaznouni, H. Ohandjanian, Commander-in-Chief Suren, A. Hovannisian, V. Minakhorian, Khondkarian, etc., were aware of it."[40]

(What the government of the First Republic of Armenia tried to accomplish by the hand of Simon Vratsian, that is, to establish good-neighborly relations between Armenia and Turkey, is nowadays being tried by the respectable Foreign Minister, Vartan Oskanian of the Third Republic of Armenia.

In this regard, reporting on the talks he held recently with the Turkish foreign minister in Istanbul, Minister Oskanian characterized the result as positive or hopeful.)

———————

The Kemalist Turks who had tricked Lenin and established "friendship" with the Bolsheviks after August 1920, sat down for a meeting with Soviet Russia's Commissar of Foreign Affairs, Chicherin, in Moscow on

February 26, 1921,[41] to delineate the new Russian-Turkish borders.

While the negotiations continued in Moscow, in the March 3 issue of the *Shizn Nationalistey* paper, A. Skachko wrote the following:

"For the sake of advancing the revolution in the East, Russia and Soviet Armenia can make certain concessions to Turkey . . . ."[42]

According to the slanted reasoning of Soviet leaders, by solving disputes with Turkey, "an era of ceaseless brilliant victories against imperialism, which is oppressing the world, would commence for the revolution in the East"; on the other hand, the existence of an anti-Soviet government in Armenia served as a reason for Soviet Russia and Kemalist Turkey to conclude "successful negotiations" in Moscow, and to sign the March 16, 1921, Moscow Treaty,[43] according to which:

Kars and Artahan, the province of Surmalu with its main town Igdir, Mount Ararat, and the ruins of Ani, as well as the Provinces of Olti and Arduin, would be given to Turkey, whereas Nakhidjevan would become "autonomous" under the patronage of Azerbaijan.[44]

On April 2, the Bolsheviks reached Kanaker on the outskirts of Yerevan; panic seized the people and thousands fled south toward Zangezur and Iran.[45]

## THE UPRISING CONTINUES IN THE MOUNTAINS OF ZANGEZUR

Yerevan fell to the Red soldiers, but Zangezur did not concede and continued raising the flag of liberty.

Zangezur had been independent since December 27. The ARF forces' commander there was Garegin Nzhdeh. In February, by spreading his authority over Daralagiaz also, he declared the region the Independent Republic of Mountainous Armenia. The ARF forces were so steadfast in their mountains that the Bolsheviks decided to negotiate with them, but the negotiations soon broke down.

The clashes resumed. The Red Army, after a few military thrusts in July 1921, finally suppressed the rebels and occupied Mountainous Armenia. A large number of fighters and refugees crossed the Araxes River to Persia.[46]

Christopher J. Walker cites three reasons why the Independent Republic of Armenia ended after two and a half years of her existence:

1. The Turkish offensive of Autumn 1920 against the First Republic of Armenia;
2. The unbreakable resolve of Kiazim Karabekir to crush Armenia;
3. The perfidy of Britain and France, who acted in a way contrary to all their declarations on Armenia.[47]

## "DID THE BOLSHEVIKS SAVE ARMENIA?"
(asks Christopher J. Walker)

Before answering the question, let us consider that:

"The Treaty of Moscow (March 1921) handed over large tracts of purely Armenian-inhabited land to the Turks. Also, when the Bolsheviks eventually arrived in Yerevan, the terror they created could not have failed to remind some inhabitants of the Turkish occupation. But the Bolsheviks did not murder Armenian women and children merely for the sake of exterminating them, as the Turks did. Even a shocking act such as the slaughter of the 75 officers is not in the same category as the utterly relentless, ruthless, and indiscriminate actions which accompanied the Turkish capture of a town. It is with this in mind that even Avis Nurijanian's murderous reign of terror must be seen as a saving grace, because it was backed by the might of the Eleventh Red Army, which was the only power capable of halting a Turkish advance. However cynical the Communist seizure of power in Armenia may have been, it resulted in a small area of the globe remaining to Armenia, and not being relegated to the history books."[48]

In early summer 1921, Lenin dispatched Akexander

198

Miasnikian to Yerevan with a letter addressed to local Bolshevik leaders whose sentiments were conciliatory, urging concessions to the petty bourgeoisie, the intelligentsia, and particularly the peasantry; initiation of an extensive irrigation project; encouragement of trade; and expulsion of arrogant and hot-headed intellectual youths (such as Avis Nurijanian) from Armenia, in order to effect a slower, more cautious transition to socialism.[49]

## IN MOSCOW

What Dro was doing in Moscow and how he was sustaining himself, no one knew. Vratsian received occasional news from Soviet representatives but they were not very trustworthy. He received more reliable news from the director of Yerevan's radio station.

Engineer Isahakian was a patriotic man who had come from Paris to take part in the reconstruction of the homeland, as many did in those days. He had joined the army as an engineer and was appointed director of Yerevan's radio station. After Armenia's sovietization, he was kept in his position because the Bolsheviks did not have a qualified replacement for him. But they did appoint a commissar by his side. However, that Bolshevik commissar was sympathetic to the ARF, and it was with his acquiescence that Isahakian was relaying news to Vratsian.[50]

Vratsian learned from Isahakian that Dro was living in Moscow in semi-exile and was in close contact with the city's Armenian Bolsheviks, particularly Sahak Ter Gabrielian. The latter was a member of the Soviets' Caucasus Front Military Revolutionary Council. Vratsian adds that in the days of the February uprising, they felt the absence of Dro. On the morning of February 18, when Vratsian met with Hovannes Kadjaznouni in the home of the latter's brother, the agronomist Vardges, Kadjaznouni's first words were, "Where is Dro?" He believed that Dro had taken refuge in the rural interior and was very surprised to

199

hear the truth.

Later on Dro would relate that on a daily basis he kept himself informed of news from Armenia through Ter Gabrielian and others.[51]

Dro was physically exiled, but spiritually he was in Armenia. Armen Tonoyan characterized Dro's exile in Moscow as "honorable exile."[52]

## MANUK KRZELIAN ABOUT DRO'S EXILE

(Note: Manuk Krzelian was the secretary of the Los Angeles branch of *Hamazkaïn* and the author of a series of articles about Dro—*The Invincible and Immortal Soldier of the Armenian Liberation Struggle, Dro,* published in the May11–May 25, 2002, issues of the *Azbarez,* a daily newspaper.

Krzelian's objective and correct approach to historical events and figures is commendable.

My only criticism regarding this series is the lack of references.

What follows is an excerpt from Krzelian's articles.)

"As soon as Dro arrived in Baku, developments took an altogether different course, of course under strictly secretive *Cekist* conditions. From here Dro departed to Moscow as an 'honorable exile,' by a special train with a private car assigned to him; upon arrival he was accorded an extraordinary reception.

"Dro was well known among the elite of Moscow. Stalin also knew him well, and Dro had been invited to Moscow at his request. They were also well aware of the ARF's past and voluminous revolutionary acts.

"And because Dro was highly valuable and influential, it was necessary to win him over by honoring him.

"Stalin admired Dro first of all for his unique and extraordinary skills, and without forgetting his glorious past.

200

"Stalin was well aware of the role Dro had played in the 1918 Armeno-Georgian inter-ethnic clashes. He also knew, and was grateful, that in 1908, by Dro's unwavering hand, Alikhanov Avarski was shot like a dog in Alexandropol to avenge the Georgians.

"Yes, this was undeniable reality. Dro was of great importance and authority, with promising prospects for implementing the authorities' anticipated horrendous vision.

"Thus, at Moscow's request, Dro accompanied by bodyguards was safely and securely brought to Moscow, and as it turned out, was put at the immediate disposition of Stalin and Dzerzhinski.

"The Moscow authorities settled Dro in one of the neighborhoods around the Nikitinian Arches, in a comfortable house, which was unusual treatment rendered to an exile.

"The role played by Stalin and Dzerzhinski with respect to Dro was primarily notable because what occurred did so in the narrow confines of *Cekist* methods, which meant that the matters were serious and state secrets.

"All of this was designed to win over, persuade, and transform Dro into their reliable agent, while at the same time keeping him isolated from any doubts that might arise from the interior as well as abroad."[53]

In Moscow, Dro was widely respected among the Communist leaders. Here, let us quote Dr. Yervant Khatanasian: "One day Stalin, who already presided over the Politburo, and Dzerzhinski, the chief of CEKA, invited Dro to a meeting. They informed Dro that the ARF, with British imperialist money, had hired two Russians who assassinated Jemal Pasha[9] in Tbilisi, in front of the CEKA headquarters building."[54]

Christopher J. Walker wrote that in 1921, Dro was "amicably" received by Stalin.[55]

---

[9] Jemal Pasha, along with Interior Minister Talaat Pasha and Defense Minister Enver Pasha, was part of the Young Turk (Ittihadist) inner circle troika, ruling Turkey during WWI.

In 1921, Dro's wife, Arpenik Galoyan of Yerevan, with her two sons, Souren and Gourgen, along with Ludwig, the son of Dro's deceased first wife, Nvart, went to Moscow to be with her husband. Accompanying them was Dro's older sister Iskouhi's son, Souren Haroutiunian, who was a student. They resided at #10 Potapovian Street, in the neighborhood of the Lazarian Academy. Souren Haroutiunian returned to Yerevan in 1935; he was eventually exiled to Siberia, where he died.[56]

Four years later, when Dro went to Paris with his firstborn, fourteen-year-old Ludwig, Arpenik returned to Yerevan with her two sons. At first they stayed with Dro's older sister, Iskouhi, in Edjmiadsin, and later in Yerevan.[57]

During the years 1932–1937, Dro's wife, Arpenig, returned to Moscow with her two sons and resided again in the home with which she was familiar, on Potapovian Street.[58]

Dro stayed in Moscow close to five years, under surveillance by CEKA. His social skills and confident nature enabled him to form a large circle of friends among both Armenians and other peoples from the Caucasus, as well as among Russian officers and authorities.[59]

In Moscow Dro enjoyed certain freedoms, but these were limited. He could travel freely within a 60-kilometer radius from his residence, but wherever he went, he had to report within 24 hours. He was under the watch of Sahak Ter Gabrielian.[60]

Life in Moscow was comparatively freer and conditions more bearable. Dro was quickly able to find means of supporting not only himself, but also other exiles. In Moscow resided also Generals Thomas Nazarbekian and Ivan Hakhverdian, who were among the military officers exiled from Armenia, as well as other exiled ARF cadres or community activists, who sustained themselves, although often went hungry. Dro's presence in Moscow became salvation for them.[61]

According to Krzelian, Dro was appointed director of a tobacco factory in Moscow.

For many among the Moscow exiles, another source

of material support was the priest Arsen Simeoniants, who himself had been persecuted by the Bolsheviks of Armenia.[62]

Many among the Armenian and Georgian exiles in Moscow, such as Sahak Ter Gabrielian, Serko Ordjonikidse, Kamo Ter Vahanian, Lukashin (Sargis Srabionian), Alexander Miasnikian, and others, were friends and acquaintances of Dro's from before their exile, from Baku and other places. Dro established relationships with these individuals and expanded his social circles.[63]

From Moscow, Dro established relations also with Georgia's labor movement activists, as well as ARF cadres in Donbas and Kharkov.

On July 21, 1922, on the initiative of ARF's Georgia Central Committee, Jemal Pasha of Ottoman Turkey's ruling Ittihadist troika was assassinated by the hands of Petros Ter Poghosian and Artashes Gevorgian, in front of Tbilisi's CEKA headquarters. CEKA arrested and incarcerated numerous suspects, to no avail. With Stalin's and Dzerzhinski's permission, Dro went to Tbilisi, where all the notable ARF leaders were under arrest. Dro's political capital was so great with both the ARF and the Bolsheviks that he was able to have the majority of those arrested released. On that occasion, the members of Georgia's Central Committee and Dro published a declaration whereby they recognized the Soviet regime and appealed to all ARF cadres to follow their example.[64]

In the Diaspora, at a time when the ARF was waging an "implacable struggle" against Soviet tyranny, Dro's and his comrades' conduct was found to be "impermissible and condemnable," even though that "manifesto" was only skin-deep, surmises S. Vratsian.

Some in the Diaspora viewed the conduct of Dro and his comrades with suspicion, and in 1925 when Dro succeeded in moving abroad and reaching Paris, where the ARF's 10th General Assembly was taking place, there were some responsible comrades who opposed Dro's participation in the General Assembly. During the Assembly and afterward "Dro through his actions shamed those doubters," adds Vratsian.[65]

During his stay in Moscow, Dro exploited any free time he had in pursuit of martial education under the leadership of skilled experts. For a few years he also attended military seminars. He researched Russia's civil wars, the Red Army's methods, and the history of the Russian Communist revolution.[66]

Dro was not interested in theoretical questions. He was a practical man. He did not like to talk about things he did not know. While others philosophized about any subject, he, due to his healthy instincts, would successfully accomplish both his personal and public endeavors.

In the following words, Vratsian again reflects on Dro's unadulterated affinity for Russia:

"His political vision had practical foundations. If love has a place in politics, Dro was a Russophile—as it used to be said, he followed Russian 'orientation.' He understood Russia in two ways: first as a great state close to Armenia, and second as a nation. His rationale was simple and, if you will, elemental; on the one hand Mohammedan Turkism, which was historically hostile to Christianity and the Armenian nation, on the other hand the vast expanse, from sea to sea of this Christian empire, which was historically hostile to Mohammedanism. Small Armenia, with its small Armenian Christian population, had no alternative but to rely on Christian Russia against anti-Armenian Turkey. This is the political ideology which sometimes belatedly is followed by the Armenian citizens of the Diaspora.[67]

"In the Diaspora, Dro gradually liberated himself from the political enchantment which tied him to Russia, but he never renounced his Russophilic sentiments in a populist sense.

"Until the very end Dro kept alive in his soul his love of the great and long-suffering Russian people, and indeed, how is it possible not to love and to hate a nation which has bestowed to humanity the likes of Pushkin, Tolstoy, Dostoyevsky, Chekhov; which has erected splendid cultural monuments; which has not suffered any less and even today does not suffer any less from tyranny than other nations subject to the Bolshevik regime. Not only consciously, but also subconsciously this understanding was very firm in Dro. Perhaps one of the reasons for it was that since childhood Dro had lived and was nurtured in a Russian milieu."[68]

## DRO GOES TO PARIS

When, in 1925, Dro went from Moscow to Paris for a short time, there were still some differences between his and Vratsian's ideological and political perspectives. He was still firm in his "Russian orientation," whereas in the case of Vratsian, the Soviet hegemony over Armenia and his contacts with Europe had begun to "undermine his faith" in Russia.[69]

On the occasion of Dro's departure from Russia, a lot of rumors were circulating to the effect that Stalin had commissioned him to wreck the ARF, or that he had transferred abroad with CEKA's permission to conduct an anti-ARF campaign, etc.

In 1925 Russia's internal and external policies were still moderate; Stalin had not yet consolidated his position in the politburo—for that reason many were allowed to travel abroad.

In the case of Dro, after Jemal Pasha's assassination and the "declaration" by the ARF in Tbilisi, with his well-known Russophilic tendencies he was still trustworthy in the eyes of the Soviets, especially since he had many friends among the elite of the Soviet Union, influential leaders such as Orzhonikidze and Sahak Ter Gabrielian. Even Stalin had treated him well. Without the Soviet government's permission it would have been difficult for Dro to go abroad.[70]

Some suspected that CEKA must have some agenda tied to Dro's trip abroad. Similarly, Stalin could have nurtured covert aims, but Dro himself would assert that he had not assumed any missions to conduct abroad.

When Dro arrived in Paris, through Germany, he went straight to visit Vratsian, who was taken aback and confused, asking sharply:

"What commission have you brought from Stalin?"

"None whatsoever," Dro answered without hesitation.

Living in Moscow for five years had left certain marks on him. His clothes were old and he was still wearing the Russian hat he had taken with him from Armenia to Moscow. In his speech he used Bolshevik expressions. Luminous Paris with its free and lively ambience made a shocking impression on him.

Vratsian's first task was to change the attire of his friend. He bought him a new set of clothes. He took him to the famous Olympia Store on Madeleine Avenue. Everywhere dazzling sights and sounds, crowds, noise, half-naked women with boyish haircuts—Dro was truly shocked and dismayed.[71]

"Is this the free and glamorous France? It makes me sick!"

Postwar Paris was writhing in decadence. He had not seen the other Paris—the Sorbonne, the National Library, the Academy of Sciences, the Opera, and the Comedie Française. Even the Victory Arch of Etoiles and Napoleon's tomb at Invalides, the Louvre, and Versailles could not change his opinion about Paris. The half-naked women of Olympia and effeminate youth had left a negative impression on him. For that reason he did not want to remain in Paris for long and tried to leave France sooner than later.[72]

Dro took part in the ARF's 10th General Assembly. The majority of the delegates were demoralized and depressed. The Treaty of Sevres had entombed the Armenian Question. The Turkish-Soviet friendship and the great states' perfidious stance toward the Armenians resulted in the troubled disposition of the Armenian people and drove many to despair.

The two main resolutions of the 10th Assembly were in ideological opposition to the Soviet regime and unceasing struggle for the sake of a United and Independent Armenia.

Vratsian's careful observation of Dro's mannerisms and expressions led him to conclude that he was tormented by his effort to reconcile the perspective of the Armenians subject to the Soviet regime and those of his comrades in the Diaspora.

At the conclusion of the General Assembly some prominent comrades thought of nominating Dro to the Supreme Council of the Party. He decisively refused and hurried to leave Paris. Despite his lack of financial resources, he refused to accept the Party's offer of assistance. All his life he had been the one assisting others, and now it was difficult for him to receive assistance from others.[73]

## THE HERO SETTLES IN ROMANIA

Dro's stay in Paris was brief. He was able to secure a job as an overseer in the oilfields of the renowned oil industrialist, A. Ghukassian, in Romania.

He departed from Paris with negative impressions. He had received a sum of money from a close friend for his travel expenses and to support himself until he got settled in Romania. After taking his luggage down to the lobby of the hotel, Dro sat down for a moment and rubbed his pants' pocket and then yelled:

"They stole my money. . .!"

Commotion in the hotel. A sharp argument commenced with the Alsatian owner of the hotel, who swore up and down that no such thing could occur in his "honorable establishment." The staff were interrogated, the police intervened, to no avail. He missed his train and had to wait for the next one.

"Damn amoral France!" cursed Dro. "These people need a dose of Bolshevism!"

For a long time there was no news from Romania. A friend from Bucharest let it be known that Dro was not in a mood to correspond.[74]

A. Ghukassian's vast oilfields were located at

Ploeshti, 50 kilometers from Bucharest. Dro's responsibility was to oversee operations everywhere, sometimes through rain or snow, through muddy or icy conditions. He fulfilled his duties conscientiously and was glad that he could earn his livelihood by the sweat of his brow.

At first he did not keep in contact with the outside world except for some correspondence with Vratsian in Paris. His only contacts were the staff of the oil company and some local Armenians.

Over time, he was able to find jobs at the oil company for some of his comrades in arms, such as Kuro, Krikor Amirian, Alexander Sharafian, and others.[75]

In 1919, Lieutenant Kuro Tarkhanian had been an officer in a cavalry regiment under Dro's command. Later he had become chief of staff of the Armenian army, and in the days of the February uprising, he had commanded the armed forces of the Kodaik region.[76]

Krikor Amirian had been Andranik's bodyguard in late 1914. Alexander Sharafian had been a government official of the Republic of Armenia.

## VRATSIAN VISITS DRO

In 1926 Vratsian went to visit Dro in Ploeshti. Dro had already gotten settled and had formed a wide circle of friends and acquaintances. He was active in the community and had become a renowned figure. Materially also he had reached a comfortable level, thanks to the kindness of A. Ghukassian.

Over the years, he prospered and his authority grew. For a while he took leave of his position in the oilfields and engaged in commerce with a Jewish friend. Thanks to his entrepreneurial spirit, he reached an enviable financial status. He took part in the ARF's 11th General Assembly in Paris.

While the Assembly was in session, he stayed at Vratsian's residence on Beacon La Bruyere Street. His disposition was generally good, but sometimes he would fall into grief and melancholy. He would endlessly reminisce about his comrades left behind in the Soviet Union, such as Korun, Tigran, Arsen, and other brothers in arms.[77]

Again they wanted to elect him to the Supreme Council of the ARF, and again he declined.

From 1930 until 1938 Dro resumed his work with Ghukassian as a high-ranking officer and shareholder. Ghukassian's oil refinery company was named *Lumina*. He recruited his long-time friends Nikita Movsesian as director, Alexander Sharafian and Grigor Amirian as financial officers, and Missak Torlakian as an employee. From Constantsa he recruited chemist Yervant Fendekian as director of the research and development department.[78]

In 1922, Fendekian, a native of Trabizon, had settled in Constantsa, a Romanian seaport on the Black Sea. He was a chemistry graduate of Prague's Karlov University. Along with Misak Torlakian he had participated in the assassination of Azerbaijan's Minister of the Interior, Pehput Khan Djivanshir, in 1921.[79]

In 1933, during the ARF's 12th General Assembly, Dro attempted to disenroll from the Party, "but this time the plowshare hit the rock. Conditions were aligned in such a way that Dro felt obligated to enter the Party's active leadership ranks, where he remained until his demise."[80]

In 1938 Dro married Gayané Levonian, the widow of Baruir Levonian, who had died of tuberculosis in 1934. Gayané was Russian-Armenian from Besarabia. From his third wife, Dro had his fourth son, Martiros, named after Dro's close friend Martiros Charukhchian, who had been martyred early on in Persia.[81]

Martiros Kanayan later settled in Sulfur Springs, Texas, where he married and had two sons, Dro and Philip.[82] (By the way, a few years ago, Martiros telephoned me to enquire about the manuscript I was writing about the tumultuous life of his father.)

Dro's firstborn son, Ludwig, who was studying in Germany, returned to Ploeshti in 1937, and settled near his father. He got married to Sona, the daughter of merchant Onnik Korkodian, a native of Amasia. Two years later, Dro's first grandchild was born, who was named Nvart in memory of his first wife. Vartan Zadoyan, a native of Mush and, member of the ARF, who was also a merchant in Ploeshti, became the child's godfather.[83]

In 1838, after Ghukassian's company was liquidated, Dro worked for a German company in Ploeshti, named *Petrolina*.[84] He remained in Romania until the start of World War II.

Dro's enterprising and daring spirit, along with his selfless patriotism, was revealed during World War II. He had many friends outside Romania to whom he was generous with his earnings. For many years he provided a livelihood to comrades or their families who were unable to work, without anyone being aware of his generosity.[85]

## SOVIET ARMENIA EVADES A MAJOR CATASTROPHE DURING WORLD WAR II

British historian Christopher J. Walker relates that "in March and April 1940 Britain and France were seriously studying the possibility of bombing Baku (to which the French attached great importance)—a course of action which would have brought Trans-Caucasus into the war, with fearful consequences for Armenia: Turkey would have invaded from the west, overrunning Armenia, exterminating her people and wrecking her cities more thoroughly than in 1918 and 1920. Lack of enthusiasm on the part of Britain and the fall of France poured cold water on that piece of adventurism."[86]

## ARMENIA'S ROLE IN THE SOVIET UNION'S MOBILIZATION FOR WAR

The invasion of the Soviet Union by Hitler's hordes on June 22, 1941, referred to as the "Great Patriotic War" in Soviet historiography, was very costly for Armenia. How many soldiers did Armenia give to the Red Army? Between

1941 and 1945 around 500,000,[10] which was exceedingly many for one million or a bit more Armenian people. What was the census of Soviet Armenia in the 1940s? Not much more than one million. How many casualties did Armenia give to (what I would call) the "Great *Armenocidal* War?" So many that, in order to maintain the population of Armenia at around one million, they organized repatriation in the late 1940s; because, had the number dropped to below one million, the country would have lost the right to be called a (Soviet) "republic."

By the way, I would not have arrived at this conclusion if during the horrific battle of Berlin in 1945, Armenian soldiers had not been put in the first lines of the Soviet forces. . . .

In Tehran's *Arax* monthly, Armen Ayvazian gives the following statistics about Soviet Armenia's casualties during World War II:

"Of the 600,000 Armenians who took part in WWII from 1941 to 1945, around 300,000 gave their lives. To imagine how horrible this number is for the small Armenian nation, it is enough to say that during WWII the United States and Great Britain gave almost the same number of dead, respectively 281,557 and 357,116 soldiers."[87]

In other words, tiny Soviet Armenia's casualties in World War II were roughly comparable to the casualties of the United States and Great Britain.

What was the reason that Soviet Armenia with a population of around one million gave more casualties than the United States with a population of around 130 million and a bit less than Great Britain with a population of 60 million?

The reason, very likely, was that Armenian soldiers were used as cannon fodder in the frontlines, whereas Russians and Azeris were placed in the second and third

---

[10] This must reflect the number of Armenian soldiers in the Red Army from all across the Soviet Union. At any time, there were up to half as many Armenians in the rest of the Soviet Union as there were in Soviet Armenia. J.C.

lines, as was the case, for example, in the battle of Berlin.

In that war, Armenia gave to the Red Army 50 generals, including the renowned General (later Marshal) Baghramian. Three Soviet admirals were also Armenians, which is all the more surprising when one considers that Armenia has never had a coastline; they included Admiral Isakov, whose account of the Soviet war at sea has been translated into English. Over 32,000 Armenian soldiers were decorated in the war, and over 100 received the "Hero of the Soviet Union" award.[88]

At the end of the war, Diaspora Armenians everywhere bragged that the Armenian soldiers of the Red Army were among the first to enter Berlin. . . .

I wish the Russians, the Tatars, or the soldiers from the other (Soviet) republics had themselves been the first braves to enter Berlin, that is, had been cannon fodder.

# NOTES

1. Hambardzum Terterian, *Memoirs 1920,* December 2, 1921 April 2 (See Vratsian, *Along Life's Pathways,* Vol 6, Beirut, 1967, pp 287–288).
2. Vratsian, *Along Life's Pathways,* Vol 4, pp 200–201.
3. Ibid, pp 201–203.
4. Oliver Baldwin, *Six Prisons and Two Revolutions, Meshag* Publishing, Fresno, CA, 1944, pp 9–10.
5. Ibid, pp 67–68.
6. Ibid, pp 68–69.
7. Ibid, pp 70–71.
8. Ibid, pp 71–72.
9. Ibid, pp 72–73.
10. Ibid, p 76.
11. Richard Hovannisian, *Republic of Armenia, 1919–1920,* Vol 2, 1982, p 44.
12. Oliver Baldwin, *Six Prisons and Two Revolutions, Meshag* Publishing, Fresno, CA, 1944, p 86.
13. Ibid, pp 77–78.
14. Gabriel Lazian, *Portraits From the Armenian Liberation Movement,* Cairo, *Husaber* Publishing, 1949, p 72.
15. Ibid, pp 73–74.
16. Ibid, pp 72–73.
17. Oliver Baldwin, *Six Prisons and Two Revolutions, Meshag* Publishing, Fresno, CA, 1944, pp 80–81.
18. Ibid, pp 82–84.
19. Ibid, pp 96–98.
20. Karpis Djerbashian, *Let Us Not Circumcise History. Nor Kiank,* May 9, 2002, p 30.
21. Christopher J. Walker, p 324.
22. Oliver Baldwin, *Six Prisons and Two Revolutions, Meshag* Publishing, Fresno, CA, 1944, pp 99–100.
23. Ibid, p 101.
24. Christopher J. Walker p 325.
25. Oliver Baldwin, *Six Prisons and Two Revolutions, Meshag* Publishing, Fresno, CA, 1944, p 106.

26. Ibid, pp 106–107.
27. Vratsian, *Along Life's Pathways,* Vol 6, Beirut, 1967, p 19.
28. Ibid, pp 32–33.
29. Richard Hovannisian, *Republic of Armenia,* Vol 4, p 404.
30. Ibid, Vol 3, p 226.
31. Vratsian, *Along Life's Pathways,* Vol 6, p 35.
32. Ibid, pp 38–39.
33. Ibid, p 40.
34. Ibid, pp 46–47.
35. Ibid, pp 55–57.
36. Ibid, pp 79–81.
37. Christopher J. Walker, p 325.
38. Ibid, p 325.
39. S. Vratsian, *Along Life's Pathways,* Vol 6, Beirut, 1967, pp 67–68.
40. Ibid, p 68.
41. Zaven Missirlian, *Three Treaties—of Alexandropol, Moscow and Kars, 1920–1921,* Beirut, 1979, p 111.
42. Ibid, p 116.
43. Ibid, p 116.
44. Ibid, pp 116–117 (See also, Ch. J. Walker, pp 325–326).
45. Christopher J. Walker, p 327.
46. Ibid, p 327.
47. Ibid, pp 327–328.
48. Ibid, p 328.
49. Ibid, pp 328–329.
50. Vratsian, *Along Life's Pathways,* Vol 4, p 204.
51. Ibid, pp 204–205.
52. Armen Tonoyan, *Dro, Navasard* Publishing, 2000, p 30.
53. Manuk Krzelian, *Dro, the Invincible and Immortal Soldier of the Armenian Liberation Struggle, Azbarez,* May 18, 2002, p 13.
54. Armen Tonoyan, p 30.
55. Ch. J. Walker, p 389.
56. Vratsian, *Along Life's Pathways,* Vol 4, p 205.

57. M. Krzelian, *Asbarez*, May 21, 2002, p 6.
58. Ibid, p 6.
59. Ibid, p 6.
60. Hamlet Gevorgian, *Dro*, 2nd ed, 2000, pp 503–504.
61. Vratsian, *Along Life's Pathways*, Vol 4, p 205.
62. Ibid, p 205.
63. Ibid, pp 205–206.
64. Ibid, p 206.
65. Ibid, pp 206–207.
66. Ibid, p 207.
67. Ibid, p 207.
68. Ibid, pp 207–208.
69. Ibid, p 208.
70. Ibid, pp 208–209.
71. Ibid, pp 209–210.
72. Ibid, pp 210–211.
73. Ibid, 211–212.
74. Ibid, p 212.
75. Ibid, pp 212–213.
76. M. Krzelian, *Asbarez*, May 21, 2002, p 6.
77. Vratsian, *Along Life's Pathways*, Vol 4, p. 213.
78. M. Krzelian, *Asbarez*, May 21, 2002, p 7.
79. Ibid, pp 6–7.
80. Vratsian, *Along Life's Pathways*, Vol 4, pp 213–214.
81. M. Krzelian, *Asbarez*, May 21, 2002, p 7.
82. Ibid, p 7.
83. Ibid, p 7.
84. Ibid, p 7.
85. Vratsian, *Along Life's Pathways*, Vol 4, p 214.
86. Ch. J. Walker, p 355.
87. Armen Ayvazian, *Strategic Consequences of the Armenian Genocide*, Tehran, *Arax* Monthly, # 111, May 2002, p 16.
88. Ch. J. Walker, pp 355–356.

Rev. Dr. Clarence T. Ussher

# CHAPTER VII

# OVERSEAS ACTIVITIES

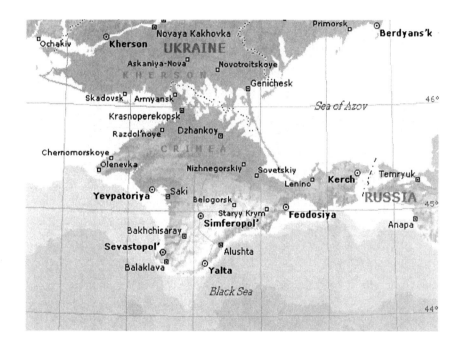

Crimea

## DRO AND WORLD WAR II

World War II changed the course of Dro's life regardless of his will or intention, linking him to the Russian-German struggle as "a collaborator with Nazism."

During WWI he had collaborated with the tsarist regime as commander of the 2nd Volunteer Regiment on the Caucasus front. That does not mean that Dro, Andranik, Vartan, *Keri,* Hamazasp, or others admired the tsar's dictatorship.

Later, when he collaborated with the Bolsheviks, again Dro's only concern was Armenia and the Armenian people.

With the same rationale, it is not possible to accuse Dro of sympathizing with the Nazi ideology. As we shall see in the following pages, in collaborating with Nazism, he was guided solely by the supreme interests of Armenia and the Armenian nation. There is no other way to consider this matter; because, like Andranik, Dro was not an ideologue who understood Bolshevism, Nazism, or the many varieties of socialism. Dro and all the revolutionaries like him, for the most part peasants, knew how to struggle for Armenia and die for the sake of the Armenian people's salvation. Even when those fedayeen were ARF members, they did not understand much about the socialist ideology of that party. For them the ARF was that organization which had trained and molded them to fight against the Turks and other enemies, and if need be, to die for the deliverance of the Armenian people and homeland.

In the years of WWII, the issue that preoccupied Dro's and his comrades' minds, before all and above all, was the physical survival of the Armenian nation, knowing the conditions to which Jewry in all of Europe was subjected.


## "COLLABORATION WITH NAZISM"

Many people threw furious insults at Dro without

understanding why, after living under Bolshevik regime for several years, he would suddenly change color and turn to Nazism, supposedly to "battle" against his much beloved Russia and the Russian people.

The most elemental logic and common sense would make us surmise that the guerilla leader and military commander, still carrying a piece of lead in his lungs from having been wounded on the path of the homeland's salvation, could not have taken such a step if not for the rekindling of patriotism in his heart and soul.

Starting in his adolescence, the elements of Dro's life had been struggle, revolution, war, and adventure.

Thus, simple common sense would reassure us that Dro could not have betrayed his name, his conscience, and his beloved Armenia. For the sake of what purpose would he have taken such a step? For riches or for glory? He was neither materialistic nor ambitious. Surely, he must have had a concealed and supreme goal when he proceeded to "collaborate with Nazism."

The reader remembers that the government of Armenia, during independence, had offered to grant him the rank of colonel when he was military commander of the entire province of Yerevan. Dro had declined that offer.

Years later, when Dro came to Beirut, Lebanon, people everywhere would address him as "General Dro," but he would always demur, saying "just Dro," or "Comrade Dro."[1]

In this present manuscript, did the reader ever get the impression that this man, Dro, the valiant warrior, who at the age of 20 or 21 years had assassinated the tsar's Armenophobe generals and governors, was after riches or glory or rank . . . ? Let the reader answer!

In Igdir, when Dro won a large sum from gambling, he gave away rubles for good causes, then went home with empty pockets. . .

In Moscow, when thanks to his entrepreneurial spirit he prospered, he began to help the needy who were loitering on the streets of Moscow, hungry and unemployed. Among them were those who were exiled from Armenia, such as

General Thomas Nazarbekian, General Hovannes (Ivan) Hakhverdian, Arsen Shahmazian, Smbad Khachaturian, and other ARF exiles and community activists. Dro's presence in Moscow was salvation for those exiles.

In Romania, when Dro was appointed overseer of A. Ghoukasian's oil fields, "he recruited his comrades in arms Kuro (Tarkhanian), Gregory Amirian, Alexander Sharafian, and others."[2] When he left the oil fields for a while to associate with a Jewish merchant and began to earn a good income, Dro's first act was to share his revenue with the needy.

Simon Vratsian writes about Dro:

"Dro never sought glory! Glory always sought him. He never begged for success; success accompanied him in his entire life. He was born under a lucky star and the Armenian nation was lucky to have a scion like him."[3]

An individual with strong character and integrity such as Dro—extremely patriotic, modest, just, left-leaning to his core with a Russophilic orientation, honest and pure to such an extent that he did not like Paris, because he perceived the people's mores to be corrupt and the city's ambience morally adulterated—could such a man, from one dawn to the next, suddenly become a conspirator and betray his conscience and homeland? Absolutely not! There was no motive to drive him to take such a step. Therefore, why did he collaborate with the Nazis?

Simply because he and his comrades perceived the Armenian prisoners of war, the Armenians in the occupied territories, as well as the survival of the Armenians in their homeland to be in grave jeopardy.

Even many of Dro's fellow ARF members and like-minded partisans were unable to comprehend why one of their greatest heroes would take such a step. The ARF Bureau members had diverging opinions about this issue. For example, Ruben Ter-Minasian and Hamo Ohandjanian were decisively against Dro's collaboration with both the Bolsheviks and the Nazis, explaining that both of those regimes were anti-democratic and conducted amoral policies.

Dro's perspective in this regard was that politics itself is amoral, unprincipled, and relativistic. Therefore, for the sake of the salvation of the homeland and the nation, it is necessary, for a period of time and until the storm passes, to forget moral and democratic principles, especially when the anti-democratic regime is mighty.[4]

In the beginning of WWII when Dro's links and contacts with Nazism were publicized, Ruben Ter-Minasian and Hamo Ohandjanian proposed distancing Dro from the ranks of the ARF, but with Vahan Navasardian's active intervention the proposal was rejected. By the way, Navasardian was "Dro's intimate friend and worshipper" and leaned toward collaboration with the Russians.[5]

Before continuing further, let me state that not only did a small group of one faction of the Armenian people collaborate with the Nazis for a specific purpose, but also prisoners of war from all the republics of the Soviet Union did as well, in larger dimensions, were they Russians, Byelorussians, Ukrainians, Caucasians, Tajiks, or any of the rest. Why? Because they all hated Stalin and his bloody regime equally; therefore they did not want to fight and die for Stalin. And if Hitler had behaved a little differently toward the millions of Red Army prisoners of war who willingly surrendered, they could have shaken the anti-populist regime of the Kremlin's dictator and his sycophants from its foundations.

When millions of Russian and non-Russian Red Army soldiers willingly surrendered to the Germans, they hoped to advance side by side with the *Wehrmacht,* that is, with the German armed forces, toward Moscow, and to topple Stalin's hated regime. They were disillusioned—indeed dismayed—because Nazism intended to annihilate all the Slav nations, who, according to Hitler's ideology, were considered sub-human.

Let us now see whether the Armenian nation was endangered when Hitler's armies began to invade Eastern Europe and then the steppes of Russia.

World War II began between the democratic world and Nazi Germany, with the Soviet Union's neutrality.

For as long as the Soviet Union held a neutral position, the Armenians in Armenia and the rest of the Soviet Union did not have an active role in the war.

During WWII, the Armenians in the whole world could be divided into three main parts:

1. The Armenians in Armenia and the Soviet Union, who were obliged to follow the position of the Soviet government;
2. The Armenians in the great countries of the West and the countries more or less subject to them, who similarly were obliged to follow their governments' delineated policies;
3. The Armenians, some 400,000 in all, living in the territory conquered by the *Wehrmacht* in the Balkans and the Ukraine, who naturally were subjected to Nazi dictatorial rule.[6]

Bearing in mind the Nazi Party's chauvinistic and xenophobic ideology and brutal methodology, what would have been the fate of this third group of Armenians? Who would have worried about them?

That individual was to be the brave living in the Balkans, Drastamat Kanayan, *aka* Dro, who would assume the responsibility for the care and safety of the Armenians living in Hitler's imperial domain.

Only a person of extraordinary courage and selflessness would have had the temerity to plunge into such a dangerous political game, in large measure because the supreme leader of Nazism with whom Dro was to deal was not a normal, straightforward man of sound judgment. Excessively eccentric, a skillful trickster with strange ideas, Hitler could have harbored suspicions that Dro served the intelligence services of the Bolsheviks or of the western imperialists and therefore, Dro could have lost his life. I think that Dro's strong personality, sound judgment, and daring enabled him to survive the claws of both Stalin and Hitler, both of whom he dealt with for years.

The work of Dro and his comrades became more difficult when it became evident that Nazism intended to physically annihilate in its entirety the Jewry of Europe.

There was fear that Armenians also could be subjected to the same fate, because according to Nazi ideology (I will submit evidence shortly) Armenians were considered enemies and subject to the same rules. Moreover, in the event of Hitler's divisions invading the TransCaucasus, the existence of the Armenians in Armenia, Georgia, and Azerbaijan would have been greatly imperiled.

The ideology of the Nazi Party was based on Hitler's *Mein Kampf* (My Struggle) and Alfred Rosenberg's *The Myth of the Twentieth Century*. Rosenberg's book, published in 1930, would become the second most popular publication in Germany after Hitler's book. According to Rosenberg, the Nordic race (in Germany, the Scandinavian countries, etc.) was superior to other races. Germany, as the homeland of a superior race, was entitled to expand its borders. The idea of racial superiority was above any other consideration, the feeling of racial pride the greatest virtue; a woman's true function was to breed pure-blooded sons for the state; monogamy was to be retained, but equal honor should be given to unmarried and married mothers of German sons. Jews were considered enemies of the Nordic race and culture, etc.[7]

According to Simon Vratsian, an influential wing of the Nazi Party wanted to classify Armenians as not Indo-European, but to be listed among Asiatic peoples, which meant a race unworthy of living.

Dro and his comrades were able to recognize the danger threatening the existence of the Armenian people in the occupied countries as well as in Armenia. They put forth proofs that Armenians are of Indo-European origin and belong to the Aryan race.[8]

Early on in the War, entire divisions of the Red Army willingly surrendered to the Germans. They were placed in concentration camps surrounded with barbed wire, and died like flies in the winter storms, in open fields, starving and without shelter.

## THE INSTRUCTIONS GIVEN TO THE
## CONCENTRATION CAMP GUARDS

From the first days of the conflict thousands of ex-Soviet soldiers offered to serve in the ranks of the *Wehrmacht*. This willingness to fight their native regime is in part attributable to genuine anti-Stalin conviction, but in greater measure the compelling reason must have been that only through such action could they hope for life itself.[9]

In other words, under Stalinist regime, free and undisturbed life did not exist. There was fear, terror, worry, and insecurity. In order to have any hope of freedom, it was necessary to topple the Stalinist regime.

"Using for sanction the fact that the USSR had not signed the Geneva Convention, Goering quickly pronounced: 'In the care and feeding of Bolshevik prisoners we are, contrary to that of other prisoners, not bound by any international obligations.' And, fearful lest German guards should not be sufficiently severe, the general responsible for the supervision of the Soviet prisoners included in his official regulations the warning that 'any indulgence of even friendly disposition [by German guards] is to be punished very severely . . . Slackness is out of place even with a POW who is obedient and willing to work.' Precisely what this treatment accomplished was later attested to by German officialdom itself. In October 1942 there came from the *Ostministerium* the statement: 'It is no longer a secret from friend or foe that hundreds of thousands [of Soviet prisoners of war] literally have died of hunger or cold in our camps.' "[10]

Even though early in the war Hitler had said that prisoners of war would never be issued weapons, over time this rule was modified. By October 1942, armed prisoners of war were utilized to fight against Russian partisans, and by the end of 1942 around one million Red soldiers were serving in the German *Wehrmacht* as regular forces. Their commander, General Helmich explained that "[t]he use of

225

indigenous units saves German forces and German blood."
On another occasion Helmich expounded:

"The situation therefore demands the utmost increase in the exploitation of the Russian population. They must not only give their strength in the form of work but must be ruthlessly exploited to the last and sacrifice their lives for us."[11]

In October 1943 Heinrich Himmler gave a speech. The terrifying chief of police not only confirmed the aforementioned communiqué, but added that the fundamental reason for the slight softening henceforth of the brutalities against Soviet prisoners was the dearth of the manpower that could be selected from among the prisoners of war, to be exploited for specific purposes.[12]

Dro and his comrades saved the lives of around 40,000 Armenian prisoners of war by enlisting them in the German Army. Otherwise, all of those prisoners would have perished in the inhospitable concentration camps in open fields . . . .[13]

It is in this context that Soviet-Armenian prisoners of war, through the initiative of Dro and his comrades, were absorbed into special detachments to serve as soldiers.

Nazi Germany's *Ostpolitik,* that is, the policy toward the Slavic nations of the East, had been determined by Hitler long before the war. Hitler had classified the Slavic and other races of the East as sub-human.[14]


## RED SOLDIERS WILLINGLY SURRENDER
## TO THE GERMANS

Nazi Germany invaded the Soviet Union on June 22, 1941. From then until November 1, 1941, which is in four and a half months, 2,053,000 Red soldiers had surrendered to the Germans almost without a fight.[15]

By March 1, 1942, 3,600,000 Red soldiers had surrendered to the Germans,[16] simply because they did not want to fight and die for Stalin and his dictatorial regime.

This mentality and political context would change around a year later when the kind of brutality with which the German soldiers treated the Soviet POWs was revealed. Until then, the great terror and massive liquidations orchestrated by Stalin, in 1937–1938, in which millions of innocent people had perished along with countless high-ranking commanders of the Red Army and idealist Communists, were fresh in the minds of Red soldiers and Soviet citizens.

In the 1937–1938 liquidations, three-fifths of all marshals in the Red Army were killed. Thirty-five thousand innocent officers were arrested, imprisoned, or executed. When the war started, The Red Army was in a pitiful condition. The newly appointed officers were inexperienced. Some of the officers who had survived the gulags were brought back and rushed to the frontlines. Examples include Gorbatov, who commanded paratroopers, and Marshal Rokossovski.[17]

German soldiers brutalized the people of the occupied territories, following instructions of their *Fuehrer,* Hitler.

Before the war, when Hitler presented his *Ostpolitik,* not everyone in the Nazi elite approved of it. Rosenberg, Keitel, and even Goebbels understood that in the event of an invasion, the peoples of the Soviet Union would perceive the Nazi armies as liberators; therefore, they could be utilized against Stalin. Hitler, however, opposed this viewpoint to the end.[18]

After the war many displaced Armenians confessed to Sarkis Adamian, "We greeted the Germans as liberators, but then we realized that they had come solely to massacre and pillage. We were forced to fight, not for the sake of Stalin, but to survive."[19]

Early on in the war, of the millions of POWs who crossed over to the German side, around 100,000 were selected to fight as volunteers alongside the Germans against the Red Army. Over time their number rose to 1,000,000. Nominally their commander was General André

A. Vlasov. The movement was called the "Russian Liberation Movement," or simply "Vlasov's Movement."[20]

Aside from the divisions commanded by Vlasov, the Russian National Army of Liberation was formed under the command of General Kaminsky, as well as the Russian National People's Army commanded by General Zhilenkov and Colonel Boyarsky. In Byelorussia an army was formed under the command of Kil-Rotionov Truzhina, and in the Ukraine the liberation army was commanded by Governor Koch. All of these liberation armies collaborated with Hitler, not necessarily to topple the Soviet Union, but to wreck Stalinism.[21]

## VOLUNTEER LEGIONS

These numerous legions originating from various Eastern nations and tribes were called *Osttruppen*.[22]

About the origins of these volunteers who had deserted their military ranks and crossed over to the enemy, a "top secret" memorandum, dated as early as December 30, 1941, states: "The Supreme Command is to set up: (1) A 'Turkestan Legion' consisting of members of the following nationalities: Turkmenians, Uzbeks, Kazakhs, Kirghizes, Karakalpaks, and Tadjiks; (2) A 'Caucasian-Mohammedan Legion' consisting of members of the following nationalities: Azerbaijanis, Daghestanis, Ingushes, Lezghins, and Chechens; (3) A 'Georgian Legion'; (4) An 'Armenian Legion.'"[23]

The term "legion" was applied not to military formations but to training and collection centers for units of each nationality.

Aside from these, the most widely known "Legions" were the Cossack or Kazakh divisions, who had also attained fame in the tsar's divisions as wonderful cavalry.[24]

The German commanders admired the Cossack cavalry and granted them a privileged position, because not only were they superb cavalry, but most importantly, the Cossacks did not belong to the Slavic race. A Cossack division, for example, under the command of the German General von Pannwitz, "was eventually expanded by the *Wehrmacht* to the size of a corps, and before the end of the war transformed into the 25th SS 'Cossack' Cavalry Corps. One of its ex-Soviet regimental commanders had the distinction of being the first *Osttruppen* volunteer to receive the high German decoration of the Iron Cross. In 1945 the entire unit was praised by both Hitler and General Jodl. It might be added that the preferred status accorded the Cossacks was so marked that many other Soviet nationals attempted, and managed, to identify themselves as Cossacks."[25]

"Byelorussians, Ukrainians, and Russian volunteers, fared by no means so well. These peoples were Slavic, and the Slav had long been the Nazi symbol of depravity, cowardice, and disloyalty second only to the Jews."[26]

Although these Eastern volunteers knew that they were fighting against Bolshevism, they were not certain that they would reach their goal. Rosenberg and those who sided with him put forth their idea that the volunteers should constitute independent units, and that in the event of victory, their countries should become independent and anti-Communist. For Hitler though, it did not matter whether the volunteers were Communists or not. For as long as they belonged to the Slavic race, they were not worthy of life. For the time being they would be exploited for Nazi Germany's war effort. As for what could happen to them after the war—of course, if Germany won the war—only Hitler knew that. For that reason, on June 16, 1943, Hitler and his commanders ordered the transfer of most of the volunteer Legions from the Eastern front, and had them dispersed across Europe. Therefore, beginning in the summer of 1943, 70 to 80 percent of the *Osttruppen* were transferred from the warfront to Europe, to labor in factories, to perform police duties, or to fight the underground movements resisting Hitler's regime.[27]

The total number of Caucasians bearing arms for Hitler's Germany was 102,300, and they were spread across different regions of occupied Europe thus:

- The 812th Armenian battalion in Holland.
- The 807th Azeri battalion in St. Rafael.
- The 804th Azeri battalion, temporarily in France.
- The 822nd Georgian battalion in Zandwort.
- The 795th Georgian battalion in Cherbourg.
- The 823rd Georgian battalion in Granville.
- The 798th Georgian battalion in St. Nazareth.
- The 799th Georgian battalion in Perikeo.
- The #II/4, I/9th Georgian battalion in Albi Kaster.
- The 800th, 835th, and 836th North Caucasian battalions in Normandy.
- The 803rd North Caucasian battalion in Holland.[28]

Never had the duties demanded of the *Osttruppen* been of a particularly glorious or honored character. Some units were actually engaged in front-line combat. But far more often they were assigned to rear-area police duties, and, especially, to antipartisan activity.

One of the basic premises of the Vlasovite leaders was that, should Germany lose, an early military conflict between the USSR and the West was inevitable. *"Prompted by this belief, the Vlasov Movement, both during the war and just prior to the German collapse, sent representatives to make contact with high Western officials and arrange with them for the transfer of Soviet opposition forces from German to Allied jurisdiction.* None of the negotiators met with any success. Most of them were interned as ordinary prisoners."[29]

After transferring to the depths of Europe those prisoners of war who had borne arms, the *Wehrmacht* divisions soon arrived at Vladikavkaz, which was the gateway for the invasion of the Caucasus. With the development of this new situation, the masses of Armenians in Tbilisi and Baku were endangered because Hitler classified Armenians as equivalent to the Jews in his list of hatreds, as we shall shortly establish by evidence. The Armenian National Council of the occupied regions appealed to Dro to strive to forestall the holocaust of the Armenians of the Caucasus, if ever Hitler's divisions reached the TransCaucasus.

By the way, the Armenian National Council of the occupied territories was formed in 1942 and consisted of the following members: Professor Artashes Abeghian, President; Abraham Gulkhandanian, Vice-President; and among the members were Garegin Nzhdeh and Vahan Papazian *(Koms)*. From 1942 to the end of 1944, the National Council published a weekly newspaper, *Armenien,* edited by Viken Shant (Levon's son), who broadcast messages from Berlin's radio station.[30]

Dro's negotiations with the Armenian National Council and the German High Command were kept secret.[31]

The Armenian National Council and the Armenian Legion were part of the anti-Stalin liberation movement. George Fisher's description of the Vlasov movement leaves no doubt about their fanatical hatred of the bloody Stalinist dictatorship. The Armenian prisoners of war were transformed into armed battalions—but they never took part in combat; they shared the same Vlasovian orientation toward Stalinism.[32]

When the majority of the Armenian POWs were settled in Holland, the "Liberation Struggle" movement took hold in the ranks, composed of extremist ARF members, with the goal of toppling Stalinism. They accused the ARF of not making concrete efforts to topple Stalin despite having anti-Bolshevik persuasion. The leader of this movement was probably Nzhdeh (who was known as a fiery and rash party member). The more deliberate and calm ARF members responded that if they were to make too much noise, in the event of Germany's defeat how would they escape Stalin's claws,[33] especially since ANCA (Armenian National Committee of America) did not exist yet.

The Vlasovian as well as other liberation movements were based on the premise that in the event of Germany's defeat, the collision would be inevitable between the West and the Soviet Union. This being their presumption, they thought that if Hitler were defeated, the West would gladly greet and collaborate with the Vlasovian and Nzhdehian movements against Bolshevism.[34]

When the war ended, 3,600 Armenian DPs (displaced

231

persons) had remained alive in Germany thanks to Dro, whereas others belonging to different nations had disappeared for eternity. After some Armenians pointed Dro out to the American Military Command, the latter decided to refer Dro to the Nuremberg Tribunal, but when preliminary interrogations revealed the truth, the case was pronounced to be closed. In an interview with Sarkis Adamian, Dro had declared, "If a man becomes a criminal by helping his compatriots, then I am a criminal . . . ."[35]

In late 1999 the government of Armenia resolved to establish an institute in Yerevan for training state officers, and in honor of Dro named it the "Dro Kanayan Leadership Institute." On that occasion, Harout Ter Davidian wrote the following in *Massis* Weekly magazine:

"Let us first acknowledge that if the government of Armenia had decided to build a monument in the name of Dro in Bash-Aparan, we would be one hundred percent in agreement with this decision, because Dro is the meritorious hero of Bash-Aparan. But unfortunately Dro's heroism ended there . . . ."[36]

Harout does not find it fitting to have a state institute named after Dro. But certainly Harout is mistaken because he is not knowledgeable enough about the hero.

Another author, Robert Aramaïsi Martirosian, in his book, *"The ARF's Antidemocratic Activity During WWII,"* explains in detail how ARF activist Artashes Abeghian, professor of Eastern Studies at the University of Berlin and his assistant Dr. Paul Rohrbach, along with the German-Armenian Union formed in 1914, conducted propaganda about the Aryan origin of Armenians, how Nzhdeh was expelled from the ARF in 1937, and how an Austrian citizen, Petros A. Kamsarakan arrived in Sofia from Berlin in 1940 and held a meeting at the home of one-time finance minister of Armenia, Sarkis Araratian, in the presence of Dro, wherein it was decided to collaborate with the German *Reich.*[37]

Among those who joined this group in pursuit of the same goal were Arshak Djamalian, Alexander Khatisian, Abraham Gulkhandanian, *Koms* (Vahan Papazian), David

Davidkhanian of German citizenship, Sahak Ter-Tomassian, and several others.[38]

Here, let me add that the German-Armenian Union was formed in 1914 by Dr. Johannes Lepsius, missionary and expert in matters of the East. The president was Lepsius, and the vice-president was Artashes Abeghian. When Lepsius died in 1926, Dr. Paul Rohrbach became president with Professor Artashes Abeghian remaining vice-president.

Robert A. Martirosian speaks about the "German Fascists" in a tone that implies that the Stalinist Talibanism (referring to the Islamist extremists of Afghanistan in the late 1990s—J. Ch.) had been a loftier, more humane, democratic, and liberal regime. Stalin and Hitler were a match for each other, with one difference: Hitler did to alien nations what Stalin did to his own people, beginning with the Russians. It is said that Hitler subjected six million Jews to the Holocaust, whereas Stalin massacred or subjected to Siberia's ice storms many more of his Union's peoples, in addition to the countless innocents subjected to firing squads in 1937–1938 through forced false confessions.

Just like Andre Andreyevich, as well as Vlasov and Garegin Nzhdeh, Dro also would probably have liked to see the dictator of the Kremlin toppled, despite his extreme Russophilia, having become disillusioned by Stalin's brutality and inhumane acts. But because Dro was an intelligent and deliberate individual, his and his comrades' foremost concern was the security and survival of the Armenian prisoners of war and the Armenian people in the occupied territories, not adventurist acts to topple Stalin.


## ANTI-ARMENIAN PROPAGANDA BY TURKS

Nazi ideologues, in many of their published articles, represented the Armenians as belonging to the Semitic family of peoples-languages; thus, according to their ideology Armenians, as non-Aryans, were condemned to a

233

holocaust like the Jews. This fanciful theory of the Armenians belonging to the Semitic race was put forth during WWI by Germany's then ally and later friend, Turkey, which spread such news everywhere through its agents.[39]

The president of the German-Armenian association, Dr. Paul Rohrbach, and Artashes Abeghian labored to prove the Indo-European origin of the Armenian nation. In 1934 they published a book titled *Armenian-Aryan,* wherein, with input from other German intellectuals along with examples and proofs, they strove to prove that Armenians belong to the Aryan race and the Armenian language to the Indo-European family of languages.

This book had significant influence; however, contradicting this there were newspapers, periodicals, and journals which, influenced by Turkish agents' propaganda, would publish articles suggesting a non-Aryan origin of Armenians.[40]

Now let us see what opinion Hitler himself had about the Armenians, to be able to judge on the basis of the *evidence* whether the Armenians—the prisoners of war in the concentration camps and the people in the occupied territories—were in grave danger.

Kevork Bardakjian, in his *Hitler and the Armenian Genocide,* published in 1985 by the Zoryan Institute, makes notable revelations in this regard.

## HITLER AND THE ARMENIANS

Many Armenians are aware of Hitler's speech given on August 22, 1939, in the presence of the Supreme Commanders of the German army, in which he referred to the massacres of the Armenians. Hitler made this speech a week before the invasion of Poland.

Among other things, the chief of Nazi Germany said the following:

"Our strength consists in our speed and in our

234

brutality. Genghis Khan led millions of women and children to slaughter—with premeditation and a happy heart. History sees in him solely the founder of a state. It's a matter of indifference to me what a weak western European civilization will say about me.

"I have issued a command—and I'll have anybody who utters but one word of criticism executed by a firing squad—that our war aim does not consist in reaching certain lines, but in the physical destruction of the enemy. Accordingly, I have placed my death-head formations in readiness—for the present only in the East—with orders to them to send to death mercilessly and without compassion, men, women, and children of Polish derivation and language. Only thus shall we gain the living space *(Lebensraum)* which we need. *Who, after all, speaks today of the annihilation of the Armenians?"41* (Emphasis added.)

Hitler, of course, must have heard about "the annihilation of the Armenians" during WWI when he served in the army of Kaiser Wilhelm and was awarded the Iron Cross.

The year 1939 was not the first time that Hitler remembered the Armenians and referred to their Genocide as an example that a statesman could massacre peoples, but before long, after one or two decades, everything would be forgotten. Indeed, eight years before the 1939 speech noted above, in 1931 Hitler granted two confidential interviews to Richard Breiting, the editor of the influential newspaper, *Leipziger Neueste Nachrichten,* as well as the chief of Leipzig's powerful bourgeois parties.

In the first interview, on May 4, 1931, Hitler expounded on his future plans, whereas in the second interview in early June of the same year, he detailed his foreign policy to transform Europe.

On that occasion, and among other things, he said the following:

". . . Everywhere there is discontent. Everywhere people are awaiting a new world order. We intend to

235

introduce a great resettlement policy; we do not wish to go on treading on each other's toes in Germany. In 1923 little Greece could resettle a million men. Think of the biblical deportations and the massacres of the Middle Ages (Rosenberg refers to them) and *remember the extermination of the Armenians.* One eventually reaches the conclusion that masses of men are mere biological plasticine."[42] (Emphasis in original.)

The looming danger threatening the Armenian people was indeed great when we keep in mind the following revelations which we read on pages 30–36 of Bardakjian's book.

"It is well known that the Jews headed Hitler's hate-list, followed by the Slavs, Gypsies, and other so-called inferior races. But a cursory search into some Hitler-related documents has revealed that the Armenians too belonged to this group. In fact, in a few documents the Armenians hold the dubious distinction of running not too distant a second to the Jews. The OKH *(Oberkommando des Heeres* or The High Command of the Army), for instance, shared Hitler's utter contempt and held that the *"Armenians were even worse than Jews."*[43] (Emphasis added.)

Alfred Rosenberg, the ideologist of Nazism, classified the Armenians with "the people of the wastes, Jews, Armenians . . . ."[44]

"Jews, Armenians . . . ." You see? On almost equal level. Echoing Rosenberg's racial and racist viewpoints, Hitler on one occasion made the following statement:

"Considering that only a pure consciousness of racism can ensure the survival of our race, we were constrained to introduce racial legislation in such a clear way that such legislation could eliminate all alien racial infection, and this infection is not caused only by Jews. In enlightening the German people with regard to this racial legislation, we should conceive of it as having *the task of protecting the German blood from contamination, not only of the Jewish but also of the Armenian blood.*"[45] (Emphasis added.)

To defend against "contamination" by "Armenian blood"—what was Hitler thinking to do to the Armenians when it was their turn . . . ? Let the reader answer.

After all this evidence, clear as daylight, does the slightest doubt remain in the mind of the reader that Armenians, among the peoples on the list of Hitler's hatreds, were almost on an equivalent position as the Jews? Which indicates on the basis of the evidence that the Armenian prisoners of war, as well as the Armenians in the occupied territories, numbering around 400,000, could have been subjected to holocaust like the Jews if it were not for Dro and his supremely patriotic comrades who, at the price of many sacrifices, forestalled the holocaust of the Armenian POWs and the Armenian people of the occupied territories. . . .

Another observation by Hitler:

". . . They [the Jews] are just pure parasites. In Poland, this state of affairs has been fundamentally cleared up. If the Jews there did not want to work, they were shot. If they could not work, they had to perish. They had to be treated like tuberculosis bacilli, with which a healthy body may become infected. This was not cruel—if one remembers that even innocent creatures of nature, such as hares and deer, have to be killed so that no harm is caused by them. Why should the beasts who wanted to bring us Bolshevism be more preserved? Nations which do not rid themselves of Jews perish. One of the most famous examples is the downfall of that people who were once so proud, the Persians, who now lead a pitiful existence like the Armenians."[46]

Hitler, who had contempt toward Armenians and wanted to defend the German people from "contamination" (mixed marriages) by Jews and Armenians, of course was aware of the Great Atrocity (the Armenian Genocide), because he was a contemporary of the WWI massacres of the Armenians. Not only Hitler, but almost everyone in Germany was informed of the massacres of the Armenians, especially since the tumultuous trial and acquittal of the brave Soghomon Tehlirian (who assassinated Talaat Pasha in the post-WWI years) had taken place in Berlin.

In a speech at Regensburg on June 6, 1937, Hitler said that his National Socialist Party had set itself tasks some of which were:

"1. To create a single people.

"2. To secure to this people, through work, its daily bread.

"3. To protect this people and its work and to restore to it freedom, honor, and power.

"4. Within this people to raise a new and higher social community." [47]

Hitler, who subjected entire peoples with their children and breast-feeding infants to holocaust, concluded with the following prayer:

"May God Almighty give our work His blessing, strengthen our purpose and endow us with wisdom and the trust of our people, for we are fighting not for ourselves, but for Germany!"[48]

Kevork Bardakjian notes in his book that though Hitler knew next to nothing about the history of the Armenians as a whole, he was knowledgeable about their carnage in the years 1915–1916 through such sources as German missionaries, teachers, merchants, doctors, nurses, engineers, military officers, diplomats, books, articles, Soghomon Tehlirian's trial . . . and especially through his best friend, Max Erwin von Scheubner-Richter, who had been standing next to him on November 9, 1923, during the unsuccessful Munich Putsch when he was killed along with sixteen other Nazis, among whom he was distinguished with the finest epitaph by his surviving *Fuehrer:* "All are replaceable but for one: Schuebner-Richter."[49]

This intimate friend of Hitler's, Scheubner-Richter, was Germany's vice-consul in Erzrum from February to late August 1915, when the Armenian Genocide was well underway there.

## ADOLF HITLER SURVIVES A GREAT DANGER

By the way, John Toland, in his voluminous biography of the *Fuehrer,* titled *Adolf Hitler,* 1371 pages long, relates how Hitler himself risked death when at least 17 Nazi leaders and guards among his group—including Scheubner-Richter—fell victim to a rain of bullets. The incident, in a few sentences, was as follows:

On November 9, 1923, the Nazi Party, led by Adolph Hitler, A. Rosenberg, Lieutenant H. Goering, General E. Ludendorff, and others attempted to stage a coup d'état in Germany by occupying Munich. The conspirators' base was a beer hall and thus the incident is known in history as the "Beer-Hall Putsch."

The Nazis set out toward Munich's municipal building, with the supposition that since the renowned General Ludendorff was marching by their side, no one would fire at them. The leaders were followed by around one hundred guards and a mob of party members and sympathizers, armed with bayonets, pistols, and other weapons, always pointing their guns to the ground. Suddenly, a shot was fired, felling a captain. In an instant multiple shots followed. One of the bodyguards threw himself at Hitler, grabbing him firmly to take him down, just as six bullets riddled the guard's body. As he fell, Hitler fell too, dislocating his left arm, causing great pain to the *Fuehrer.* Among the first wounded, Schuebner-Richter helped Hitler to get on the sidewalk, and then expired, having been shot in his lung.

General Ludendorff walked straight toward the oncoming fire, but nobody fired at him. He surrendered to an officer who arrested him and took him away.

Hitler's personal physician, Dr. Walter Schults, reached his side. Hitler stood up with great difficulty and in pain, slowly advancing toward a safe place, the color drained from his face, his hair disheveled over his eyes.[50]

## TURKEY WITH ITS PAN-TURANIAN DREAMS

During WWI, when Turkey joined Germany against the Allies, it was hoping that in the event of Germany's victory, an opportunity would be created for Turkey to accomplish its long-nurtured Pan-Turanian, that is Pan-Turkish, dream by expanding to the East, and along the way wiping out Eastern Armenians.

Similarly, during WWII, when the Pan-Turanian ideal was revived, this time the Turks tied their hope to Hitler's victory against the Soviet Union.

In Nazi Germany, the Foreign Ministry and the army's High Command encouraged Pan-Turanism with the hope that Turkey, siding with Nazi Germany, would invade the Soviet Union, with Hitler himself in favor of this plan. The occupied territories' minister, Alfred Rosenberg, however, was opposed to Pan-Turanism.[51]

On May 8, 1942, a conversation took place between the *Fuehrer* and Rosenberg on the topic of forming divisions from Southern Russia's tribes. On that occasion Rosenberg said:

"If one had not in the beginning, called all those peoples 'Asiatics,' had them shot or left to their fate, there would be more troops at the disposal of the German Reich today." Rosenberg then showed the flags of the divisions formed of Armenians, Azeris, Georgians, and other nations. Hitler did not object, but asked *what his opinion was about the Armenians.* Rosenberg, who was opposed to the Pan-Turanian movement, replied that Armenia was the best wedge inserted between Turkey and Azerbaijan to form an obstacle to the eastward spread of the Pan-Turanian movement. Rosenberg added, *"In general, the Armenian people are stable, a farming people who also have notable industrial skills."*[52]

Meanwhile, when the Nazi armies encountered difficulties in their advance into Southern Russia, Hitler and his men (particularly Germany's ambassador to Turkey, Von Papen) increased their pressure to have Turkey join the Axis powers (Germany, Italy, and Japan) with Pan-Turanian promises, despite Rosenberg's reservations.

The Turks, however, wily and experienced diplomats, waited to ascertain which side would win the war.

To encourage the Turks to lean to their side, the leaders in Berlin arranged to transfer Talaat's remains, by special train, to Constantinople in late February 1943, but the Turks still were not duped.[53]

When the card of Talaat's remains turned out to be useless, one ace remained to play in the Germans' hands, and that was the holocaust of the Armenians. They would have played that ace later on, as we shall see shortly.

Therefore, you can imagine how daring and dangerous was the mission undertaken by Dro, in Nazi Germany's army. By accepting Armenian POWs in the German armies, the Nazis' policy toward Armenians changed entirely. The oppression and persecution which had begun against the Armenians came to an end; the lives of tens of thousands of Armenian POWs were saved, and 400,000 Armenians emerged from the horrors of the war almost unscathed.[54]


## WHEN AND HOW DID DRO'S "COLLABORATION WITH NAZISM" BEGIN

The evidence in the preceding pages suffices, I think, to persuade the reader that great danger threatened the lives of the Armenian POWs, as well as the lives of the Armenians in the occupied territories and the homeland, given that at the top of Hitler's list of races "unworthy of life" were the Jews, immediately followed by, or almost equivalent, were the Armenians, Serbs, Gypsies, etc.

Dro and his associates, sensing the danger threatening the Armenians of Europe and the occupied territories, did not flee overseas from the Balkans, but instead they endeavored, at the cost of great sacrifices, to forestall the tragedy threatening the Armenian nation.

241

Before the invasion of the Soviet Union, at a point when Red Army divisions had crossed the borders of Romania and had occupied advanced positions, the Germans, with active collaboration by the Romanians, expelled the Russians from the borders of Romania. The Germans, surmising that the Jews might have assisted the advance of the Soviet divisions, unleashed massive pogroms against them.[55]

In early summer of 1941, Hitler's divisions invaded the borders of the Soviet Union and with lightning strikes advanced deep into Russia. On that occasion, upon the invitation of Hamo Ohandjanian (the former Minister of Supplies and Finance in the first Republic of Armenia) and Dro, a consultative meeting took place in Bucharest. The aim was to examine the political circumstances and to consider what could be done to render assistance to the Armenian people in the theatres of war, and also how to save the people of Soviet Armenia in the event of Hitler's divisions advancing toward the TransCaucasus.[56]

S. Araratian spoke in general terms about the political context and the condition of the Armenians. Then Dro spoke:

"Fellows, the ARF has been and still is the only salutary force of the Armenians. In all the critical days which our nation has endured, the people turned their gaze to the ARF, and today also, with hope and faith, they anticipate from the ARF the means of their salvation. In these momentous days, we cannot remain silent witnesses and allow our brothers and sisters to drown in a sea of blood. Let us think deliberately and find means of rendering assistance to them, because according to reliable information, like the Jews we Armenians are also endangered."[57]

This meeting was to be the start of Dro's and his comrades' collaboration with Nazism for the sake of saving the Armenians of the occupied territories.

## IN BERLIN

Dro headed to Berlin with some comrades, Misak Torlakian, Hourian (Haroutune Haroutunian), and others. They were well impressed with everything in the city; law and order were notable everywhere. Berlin was peaceful and life was as if normal. Nothing was wrecked and Berliners seemed extraordinarily enthusiastic.

Dro's aim was to establish close ties with the German army commanders, as well as with the members of the German-Armenian Union, particularly Professor Artashes Abeghian, who, along with his associates, toiled ceaselessly to prove to the state elite that Armenians belong to the Aryan race.

Misak Torlakian and Hourian did not remain long in Berlin. They were sent to Warsaw, with two others, from there to go to Russia and assist in the task of defending POWs and AWOL Armenian soldiers. For the same purpose, with the Germans' permission, Simon Piliposian and Tate Petrosian went from Bucharest to Odessa.[58]

The city of Warsaw was wrecked and the citizens were filled with hatred toward the Germans. If the Poles spotted a German soldier at night, they would kill him and grab the weapon from his hand.

The Jews were mostly massacred, or concentrated in their ghetto. All were marked on their chests and backs with symbols to identify them as Jews. They mounted an armed resistance for a while, but the German army and air force bombarded the ghetto and most of them were killed.[59]

Torlakian and the others remained in Warsaw for a month. Hakob Azizian, Poktan Youzbashian, Golia Kevorkian, and others, altogether ten people, arrived from Paris and joined them. They did not do anything in particular. They awaited Dro's arrival.

Dro finally arrived, in a German military vehicle, accompanied by a German officer. The group set out for Crimea.

The roads in Germany were not bad. But when they entered Russian territory, they would often get stuck in mud. It was cold winter and the roads were covered deep with snow. Enduring a lot of difficulties, they reached Crimea in one month.

They entered Simferopol. Having contacts in the city, the first day they met Hovakim Hovakimian and Sarkis Kakosian. They embraced. They had not seen each other since 1919.

The following day they met with Armenak Ter Stepanian. Born in 1876 in the town of Toprak Kala in the Alashkert Region, he had functioned as a courier in the ranks of the ARF. After being imprisoned for three years in Kars, he had managed to escape. He had crossed over to Batum, from there to Feotosia, and then to Simferopol. He became very useful in the task of liberating POWs.

The German division with which they were to collaborate was in Simferopol. They presented themselves to the division, which arranged to have them settled. Hourian and Torlakian were roommates.

Once the news spread that Dro and his associates had arrived in Crimea, many Armenians came to visit, some traveling 4 or 5 hours on foot.

Some of Crimea's Armenians had been imprisoned, together with Armenian POWs from the Red Army.

Dro had come to Crimea to liberate the imprisoned Armenians and the POWs. After the necessary appeals had been made, they were all released to their families within 3 or 4 days, and the POWs joined Dro's legion.[60]

The Crimea was a multiethnic republic where 14 nations had their schools. The dominant elements were the Tatars, numbering around 450,000. There were around 20,000 Armenians in Crimea, the majority having come originally from Trabison. In all of the Soviet Union, schools belonging to ethnic minorities were shut down in 1937–1938. Crimea's 3,000 Armenian students were transferred to "reconstructed" Russian schools.[61]

Within a few months of Dro's group's arrival in Crimea, the Germans registered the region's Jews, Gypsies, and Crimchaks, altogether 15,000 people. Before long, they took them in groups to a pre-designated place, then drove them outside Simferopol on the way to Feotosia to trenches dug by Russians and massacred them all. People were not allowed to go anywhere near those trenches. But when Dro's group passed by these locations, they saw that the SS had finished their grim work. Having filled the trenches with cadavers, they were covering them with earth. It appeared that they had first disrobed their victims, because there were clothes lying in piles on the side. "It was a heart-wrenching picture of human brutality and cruelty. We went on to Stari, Crimea, where we met Vagharshak Minasian, then went to Feodosia. Along the way we saw similar heart-rending scenes, except that the numbers of victims in subsequent trenches were smaller."[62]

Here it is necessary to record how, thanks to Dro's contacts, the Armenian population of Crimea was saved from ending up in those trenches. If it were not for those contacts, today there would not be a single Armenian in Crimea; because the Tatars of Crimea, numbering around a half million, were spreading propaganda everywhere that Armenians were as bad as Jews, that they were worse usurers, and most of all that they were inveterate Germanophobes and fanatical Russophiles. These Tatars had provided the Germans with special divisions and were directly allied with them, and so they could have succeeded if it were not for Dro.[63]

When Dro was in Crimea, the Cekists of Moscow tried to entrap him. To execute that devilish plot, they brought Dro's 22-year-old son, Kourken, from Siberia to Moscow and provided him with a group of experienced saboteurs, and assigned to him the mission of going to Crimea to strike his own father in the back as his "patriotic duty." This group was able to capture Dro, but he managed to find an opportunity to escape.[64]

Kourken Kanayan returned to Siberia and decided to settle there, where his older brother, Souren and his unfortunate mother, Arpenik Galoyan, were buried. Some time later he moved to Omski in Siberia, where he got married and had three offspring: Souren, Irina, and Rouben.[65]

## THE ARMENIAN COMMUNITY OF POLAND

In 1939 when Hitler occupied Poland, the Armenians there did not suffer; this was not because they were Armenians, but because they were typically citizens of Iran, a neutral country.[66]

## A GOOD SAMARITAN ARMENIAN WOMAN

Near Poland's Eastern border, next to the town of Rovno, was a concentration camp wherein there were Armenian POWs. The only Armenian inhabitant of the town, the baker's wife, took it upon herself to approach the camp, and by offering some cigarettes—a most precious commodity in those days—to the guards, found out that the majority of the 35–40 Armenian POWs had already starved to death, with some 15 prisoners remaining. Every day, this compassionate woman, with the help of her two sons, 10 and 12 years old, would deliver sufficient food to these prisoners at a prearranged time.

This heart-rending story was told to Aram Dabaghian by one of the prisoners when the two met a few months later at another camp, where the prisoner had managed to find a horse's tail and kept it under his pillow, gnawing at it for days afterward. The prisoner had witnessed a Kalmik from Tajikistan smash the skull of his just deceased friend with a rock, in order to extract the brain and eat it.[67]

One day the Good Samaritan woman asked the Armenian POWs, "Let me have your change of clothes, your underwear, for me to wash and return to you."

"We do not have any. We sold them all for a few potatoes or a piece of sausage, when the peasants would approach the barbed wire under cover of darkness."

The Good Samaritan quickly went home and returned with her husband's clean underwear and distributed it to the POWs.[68]

246

## DRO AGAIN SERVES AS SAVIOR

After a while, Hitler's administration decided to conscript the healthier inmates among the POWs from Caucasian nations as "volunteers." These divisions were concentrated in the small town of Poulava, located 50 kilometers from Warsaw. Altogether they numbered 5,000, of whom 1,800 were Armenians.[69]

Although it was early spring, the winter cold continued. Aram Dabaghian of Warsaw received a telegram from Berlin that Artashes Abeghian would be coming to Warsaw. The physically frail Abeghian was the president of the National Council of the Armenian Community of Berlin.

Artashes Abeghian had appealed to the leadership in Berlin in an effort to keep the Armenian volunteers from being sent to the front, but to no avail.[70]

For this reason, Abeghian had telegrammed Dro to come to Warsaw for consultation.

Dro came to Warsaw from the East and had a secret meeting with Abeghian at Aram Dabaghian's home. We do not know what was said at this meeting, but the private conference lasted more than one hour. When they emerged from the room, the facial complexion of both had changed. The thin Abeghian's pale face was all red, whereas Dro, who had traveled at length through the cold and wind, had turned pale.[71]

They took leave of each other in disagreement. The issue was horrendous and momentous. Had it not been resolved in our favor, the Armenians also would have been subjected to the fate of the Jews.

Days later, Dro told Aram:

"I am sorry that Artashes was vexed when he took leave of me. But I could not have done otherwise. I could not and would not set foot where, supposedly, there are volunteer divisions being formed to go to fight Russians as well as Armenians in the ranks of Russian forces.

"Abeghian got upset when I decisively told him, 'Would my not visiting Poulava cause the Armenians of Europe to be massacred as non-Aryans? I do not think so.

247

But Aram, let me tell you, in this matter there is the hand of the Turks.' "[72]

In 1933, during the Nazis' Nuremberg conference, Goebbels had formally declared that the Armenians were Aryan. What had happened to negate that resolution?

Until 1942–1943, Armenians had been exempted from holocaust thanks to the efforts of Dro, Professor Artashes Abeghian, Johannes Lepsius, and others. Now, however, something seemed to have changed in Berlin's political-military sphere and the Armenians of the occupied territories were no longer considered to belong to the Aryan race. What had happened? Probably, as Dro had guessed, the Turks had stirred the issue.

The German ambassador in Ankara, von Papen, the old and shrewd diplomat, had spent every effort to hitch Turkey to the Nazis' wagon to fight together against the Soviet Union. But Turkey's Prime Minister, Sarajoghlu, was not any less experienced and shrewd than von Papen in the art of playing international politics. On the one hand, he would inspire hope in von Papen that Turkey was with the Germans, and on the other hand, he would delay and procrastinate in this matter to see which way the war's outcome was leaning. For the impatient Germans, there was one means left to sway Turkey to their side—to subject the Armenian people to holocaust like the Jews. To do so, Hitler's government would first have to officially declare the Armenians non-Aryans. When rumors started circulating about a possible holocaust of the Armenians, Artashes Abeghian, panicking, braved the winter weather on his frail body, and rushed to Warsaw to meet with Dro to persuade him to allow the Armenian POWs to fight against the Soviet Union, in order to forestall the intended holocaust of the Armenians. Dro, himself intelligent and shrewd, was not persuaded, despite Artashes's hour-long rationalizations, reasoning that if Berlin had decided to annihilate the Armenians, the decision would not be reversed by the POWs going to the front. The panicked Abeghian, having failed in his mission and thinking that catastrophe would befall the Armenians, returned to Berlin worried and riled.

In the meantime, the Armenophobe Sarajoghlu was procrastinating and delaying signing a Turkish-German treaty, while at the same time carefully following the status of the German advance in the East, which was beginning to falter . . . .[73]

The fact that the German divisions were faltering in the East and had failed to hold Stalingrad undermined the *Wehmacht's* barbaric plot to sell a collaboration agreement to Turkey by subjecting the Armenians to holocaust; it also discouraged the Turkish hordes, lying in wait at the border, from invading the TransCaucasus, which would have been disastrous for Armenia.

The volunteer divisions of Caucasian POWs were sent to the front. As for the Armenian divisions, their departure was delayed for the following reason:

The high-ranking commander of the German Eastern front's Southern section was named Braun, a good friend of Dro's. Thanks to his intervention, the Armenian divisions, instead of being sent to the East, were sent to Normandy, where they did not take part in fighting.[74]

Once again, Drastamat Kanayan, the supremely patriotic Armenian and the commander with a Russophilic orientation—excepting of course Stalinism—saved the Armenian divisions from engaging in combat.


## DRO'S ILLNESS

It was sometime in March 1943, a little after midnight, when Dabaghian's telephone rang. It was Dro, his voice faint, hoarse. Aram asked, "Are you ill, General? How are you doing?"

"Do not worry, nothing serious. I have a bad cold. Do you have something to keep me warm? Grab a bottle and come over."

With the bottle in his pocket, Aram went to see Dro.

It was a cold night. Dro was pacing the floor of his cold hotel room, his lambskin hat on his head, his boots on his feet, wearing his coat plus a comforter on his shoulders.

When he saw Aram, he blurted out curses in Russian at the hotel manager, who had put him up in that freezing room.

Dro downed a large glass of liquor.

"Enough," he said, "let us sit down. I have been walking for the past three hours. I was afraid to undress and get in the cold bed. First, as a reward for bringing you here in this cold night, let me give you good news. The issue of our being non-Aryan is resolved, done. Do you recall I told you, in this matter there is the hand of the Turks? Anyway, now tell me, how is your work in rendering assistance to the POWs and refugees proceeding?

[Did you notice that as soon as Dro gave the "good news," he changed the subject because he did not want to brag about how he resolved the matter? Who else . . . .?]

Regarding the POWs and refugees, Aram replied that 120 refugee families had arrived from Baranovich, a Polish town on the Polish-Russian border.

Aram had barely spoken, when Dro let out another common Russian curse at "pumpkin-head Valodia," the overseer of the refugees. Valodia was an Armenian from Crimea who spoke Armenian mixed with Tatar words.

"I told that idiot," continued Dro, "to stay put. I am going to arrange in Berlin about where they should go."

When Aram proceeded to talk about the local Ministry of Labor, Dro got up and said, "Let's go."

They went downstairs. The only means of transportation remaining in Warsaw was the "carriage," nicknamed "beast-cart." Behind a bicycle was finagled a box-like cart which was called a *"richk"* (sounds like a derivative of rickshaw. J.C.), wherein two passengers could sit. Aram called a *richk* and gave an address, but Dro said, "Let us first visit the refugee camp."

When they arrived there, everyone—children and grown-ups—was already up and about. When they saw Dro, the children cried, *"Diada* Dro" (Uncle Dro).

After making some arrangements there, when Aram again called a *richk* to take them to his house, Dro objected, saying, "First let us go to the municipality. I want to meet with Mayor Chicherin. After that you go home and I will meet you there in one hour."

Within the hour, Dro arrived at Aram's home in a good disposition and greeted Aram's wife like family.

"Set it out, sister, whatever delicious foods and drinks you have. It has been two days since I had a good meal.[75]

## MEETING WITH POWs

In the fall of 1942, a meeting was held in Berlin with Armenian POWs. Dro made a speech:

"Hard fate has dispersed our brothers and sisters all over the world. The sun does not set on the Armenian individual, because Armenians are everywhere, on all continents. We have one faith, one language, and one homeland. Today's Armenia, which is approximately 28,000 square kilometers, is but one sacred and precious piece of our vast homeland.

"We should not forget that our age-old enemy is Turkey, which has concentrated two million troops on our borders and is ever ready to invade the Caucasus; of course, in the first place, Armenia. The Turks are intently following the bloody battles in Central Russia. If the Russians lose Stalingrad, Turkey will invade the Caucasus."[76]

(By the way, Vahan Sarkisian, a native of the Boujakan Village in the region of Aparan, was present at this Berlin meeting and heard Dro's speech noted above. His memoir, *Meeting With Dro,* was published in the March 21, 2000, edition of the *Hayastani Hanrapetutiun* [Republic of Armenia] newspaper. Also in existence is Vahan Sarkisian's audiotape regarding that meeting.)

Among Armenian political circles in the Diaspora there were those who advocated the viewpoint that in the event of Hitler's divisions invading the Caucasus, the people of Armenia, utilizing the opportunity, should raise the banner of uprising to shake off the vile Bolshevik yoke.

Dro opposed this idea. He had confidence in the

251

Russian people and did not believe that the Soviet Union would be defeated. Even if the German forces were at the gates of Moscow and Stalingrad, Dro was convinced that the Russians would win.[77]

On the other hand, he had succeeded in establishing firm links with some eminent people in the German government, earning their trust and admiration through contacts made in the years of his work in the oilfields of Ploeshti.

## LEAVING ROMANIA

In 1944 the Russians were advancing on Romania. General Dro knew, through his international contacts, that Romania would fall to the Russians. He arranged for the Germans to provide 6 railroad cars for any Armenians who wished transport out of Romania. Very few Armenians left because they couldn't imagine that the Russians would be as brutal as they proved to be. None of Gayane's family left. Simon Sarkissian's family was typical; they chose to stay in Romania and his father was sent to Siberia.

Enroute from Romania, the train suffered many bombardments. They arrived in Austria, where Dro's family stayed for a short time. They then moved to Heidelberg because Dro knew (through his contacts) that they would be safer there. Dro had access to the outside world and knew how Germany would be broken up after the war.[78]

## AUSTRIA AND THE GOOD LUCK PIG

While still in Austria, Dro had to travel to Berlin via airplane. Marty gave his father a small pig that he owned, which was considered a good luck charm. It was supposed to bring good luck for his trip. Dro was seated in the front of the plane as befitted his position. A German officer made a big fuss about the seating. To avoid controversy, Dro gave up his seat to the officer and sat in the back of the plane.

The plane crashed on takeoff and all who had sat in the front of the plane—including the German officer—were killed. Dro was fine, but the pig broke a leg.[79]

## DRO'S IMPRISONMENT

In early 1945 the Americans entered Heidelberg, where the Kanayans were living. A Mrs. Steinmayer had designs on their apartment. She went to the American military police and told them that a high-ranking Nazi was living there. Because of her complaint to the police, the Americans apprehended Dro, a decision supported by his also being very high on the Russians' most wanted list.

Lieutenant John Dean was one of the young officers investigating the allegations against Dro. He befriended Gayane after hearing her story. Nothing made sense to Lt. Dean—including Mrs. Steinmayer and her allegations.

Dro and his cousin Vazken were imprisoned. While he was there, the Americans were making arrangements to repatriate him to the USSR. The Armenian community and Western intelligence sources were looking for him, knowing that the Russians would want to have him repatriated if at all possible. At this time, a French officer, Hrant Agonayan, who was a member of the ARF Central Committee, came to the Heidelberg/Mannheim area looking for Dro. He had thought that Dro might possibly be there. In late April or early May 1945, the Americans took Dro from his cell (where the living conditions were awful) to transport him to the train which would take him to the USSR. Vazken Kanayan was left behind in the prison. One of the military officers escorting Dro to the train was Lieutenant Dean. Agonayan came to the prison and discovered that Dro was in a car going to the train station. Based on his credentials, he and his driver were allowed to go to the train station. On the platform he saw the MPs escorting a man to the train. He recognized Dro. He went to the MPs, presented his credentials, fell to his knees, and kissed Dro's hand. Lieutenant Dean and the MPs recognized that they could not send Dro to the USSR, when someone with Agonayan's credentials was vouching for him. Instead, they sent him to Mannheim, to a retention center for high-ranking German commanders who were not considered Nazis. The retention center was a former palace/estate, and the accommodations were very comfortable. Dro had Vazken Kanayan brought there also.[80]

Dro had succeeded in obtaining a razor blade and had decided to cut his wrists if he were to be delivered to the Bolsheviks.[81]

Within a couple of weeks, probably late May, Defense Intelligence and the OSS flew Dro to the United States. Vazken Kanayan was released but had no idea what had happened to Dro. Dro was flown to Hanscom Air Base in Massachusetts. They landed in the middle of the night—between 2:00 a.m. and 4:00 a.m. Three civilians from the ARF Central Committee met him: Levon K. Daghlian, Hamo Paraghamian, and Garabed Lachinian. They were allowed to briefly speak with him. After their meetings, Dro was flown to Washington, D.C., for debriefing by United States intelligence.

## ALLEN DULLES

After the war, Dro was meeting in Washington with Allen Dulles, head of American Intelligence, regarding Armenian affairs. Dr. Levon K. Daghlian was Dro's translator. Dro was disturbed that the United States had not lived up to its commitments while the Armenians had fulfilled all the Americans' requests. Dro, who did not really speak English, told Dr. Daghlian, in Armenian, to say exactly, "You son of a bitch. We kept our end of the bargain. You haven't kept yours." Dr. Daghlian was trying to soften Dro's words to be polite when suddenly the non-English speaking Dro said, in English, "No, no, no, Levon, say son of a bitch."[82]

Before returning to Heidelberg, Dro was having lunch at the old Stattler Hilton Hotel in Boston with several friends. A few tables away sat the *Ramgavar* (Armenian Democratic Liberal) editor of the *Baikar* (Struggle) newspaper. That morning's headline in the *Baikar* had screamed, "Where is the great traitor Dro? When will the Americans catch him?" Dr. Daghlian and others recognized him and laughed.

When Dro returned to Heidelberg, the family had had no idea where he had been or what had happened to him. In late summer of 1945 Gayane, Martin, and Gayane's daughter, Olga Levonian, had been sharing an apartment with a Frau Witte in Heidelberg. The family was in the dining room. Martin, aged 7, said, "I hear Papa's voice." Everyone else thought, "Oh, the poor boy. He's missing his father." Dro walked in the door from America with two large suitcases. One was filled with travel items and the other was filled with fruit for his young son who tasted bananas for the first time.

From the time Dro was arrested, Gayane's strength and dedication to Dro and the family were unparalleled. In the early days of Dro's capture and until the return of Vazken Kanayan to Heidelberg, all Armenians ran away from Gayane and refused to help her or the family. Included in this group were all the Armenians who had been saved by Dro and the entire Armenian leadership. The only people who were of any support, that is, with food, etc., were three German families. One of those was the Emic family in Gaiberg, who were farmers and with whom the Kanayan family had summered before. They took care of Martin and Olga. Frau Witte shared her apartment with Gayane. Elizabeth Lehmans, an artist and friend of Darvish, a famous Armenian artist who later lived in Persia, also helped. Lehmans painted the Heidelberg picture, which disappeared and later reappeared in Olga's house.

Gayane would walk to Gaiberg through the fields and mountains twice a week to check on her children. Martin remembers how Gayane would arrive with bleeding feet but still dressed as a lady.[83]

As an adult and as an American military officer in Germany between 1963 and 1965, Martin had the chance to visit and renew his acquaintance with Elizabeth Lehmans, Frau Witte and her family, and the Emic family. He also saw Darvish, who was living in Stuttgart at that time.

Through Darvish, Martin also had the opportunity to meet and visit with Captain Baum, the son of the man who was one of the key architects of the German reconstruction in 1945. In addition to being extremely instrumental in the German reconstruction, Baum was a close friend of Dro's.

During Dro's imprisonment, Gayane prayed a great deal, especially to St. Anthony. As was the custom, she had a large brick with an inscription placed in the church in Heidelberg. Martin knew this story and when he was in the Army, he found the Church and brought the stone back to the United States.[84]

## LEAVING GERMANY

Gayane and Dro had to decide where to go and where to live. They considered having the family live in Switzerland with Dro based in the Middle East, where he was involved in Armenian affairs. Gayane wanted the family together. Therefore, they decided the family would go to Beirut, Lebanon, where Dro would join them.

Gayane, Martin, and Olga left Germany by train in late April 1946, escorted by an American officer. Their destination was Milan, Italy. The American military had given them transit documents but the Kanayan name was still on the Russian most wanted list. Dro had been exonerated on a high level, but his name was still on the list. Just prior to crossing the Russian zone, the Russians announced that they would not allow an American officer to continue accompanying the family. This part of the journey was particularly perilous because, against all advice Gayane had sewn jewelry and money (gold) in her clothes. An American officer met the family again after they passed through the Russian zone. The family stayed in Italy for 7 to 9 months, and in 1947 they established residency in

Beirut, where Dro joined them.

In 1951, Dro recognized the instability in the Middle East and he wanted his son to get an education. The family moved to Watertown, MA. They obtained permanent residency in the United States on a Russian quota. They joined Olga, who had married Paul O. Proudian and had moved to the United States in 1950.[85]

## VLASOV'S TRAGIC DEMISE

Through providential intervention, Dro was saved. The intrepid commander of the Russian liberation armies, General Vlasov, was not so lucky.

Near the end of WWII, when Red Army units began penetrating deep into Germany, Vlasov, his subcommanders, and his troops were thrown into disarray. On one side was the Red Army, on the other the Soviet Union's ally, the American military.

On May 12, 1945, General S. K. Pouniachenko of Vlasov's army, with his followers, found refuge in the Schlozelburg fortress, which was the headquarters of the Americans. American officers told the Russian general that they sympathized with Vlasov's movement, but they could not permit the Russian rebels to enter their zone of occupation. Furthermore, they were going to evacuate the Schlozelburg fortress—where Vlasov also found refuge with his followers—because that region would fall under the Soviet zone of occupation.

That news was a fatal blow to the Vlasovian division. Pouniachenko instructed his troops to disperse, with everyone to fend for himself.[86]

It is assumed that half of the division's troops, around 10,000 in number, were either captured by the Red Army, or were captured by Czech partisans and handed over to the Soviets. The rest of the troops crossed over to the Americans, but they were also handed over to Russian commanders later. General Pouniachenko sought permission to join with Vlasov in the fortress, but both of them ultimately were captured by the Soviets.[87]

There are a few versions of Vlasov's capture, with minor differences. I will skip those.

After staying in the fortress for a while, Vlasov and his followers emerged and headed toward the American occupation zone, but they were captured by the Red Army. Vlasov's identity being well known, he was put under arrest. There was no news about him until May 2, 1946, when the *Izvestia* newspaper announced that Vlasov and eleven others were interrogated by a military tribunal, condemned to death, and hanged on the gallows.[88]

Vlasov, who, in the days of the Soviets, had been pronounced to be an "enemy of the people, traitor, Nazist, bandit, and fanatical nationalist," is today recognized in the Ukraine as a national hero, having earned pan-national respect. The sculpture immortalizing his memory has become a symbol of the Ukrainian people's liberation struggle through the centuries, despite the fact that Vlasov was not Ukrainian; he was Russian.[89]

# NOTES

1. A. Tonoyan, p 48.
2. Vratsian, *Along Life's Pathways,* Vol 4, p 213.
3. A. Tonoyan, p 49.
4. Hamlet Gevorgian, 2nd ed, p 514.
5. Ibid, p 514.
6. Vratsian, *Along Life's Pathways,* Vol 4, pp 216–217.
7. *Collier's Encyclopedia,* 1950, Vol 14, p 391.
8. Vratsian, *Along Life's Pathways,* Vol 4, p 217.
9. George Fischer, *Soviet Opposition to Stalin,* Harvard University Press, Cambridge, MA, 1952, p 44.
10. Ibid, p 44.
11. Ibid, pp 45–47.
12. Ibid, pp 44–45.
13. Vratsian, *Along Life's Pathways,* Vol 4, p 218.
14. Sarkis Adamian, *The Armenian Community,* New York, Philosophical Library, 1955, pp 396–397.
15. George Fischer, p 3.
16. Ibid, p 3.
17. Catherine Andreyev, *Vlasov and the Russian Liberation Movement,* Cambridge University Press, 1987, p 33.
18. Sarkis Adamian, p 397.
19. Ibid, p 397.
20. Ibid p 397.
21. George Fischer, pp 42–43.
22. Sarkis Adamian, p 397.
23. George Fischer, p 48.
24. Ibid, p 49.
25. Ibid, p 49.
26. Ibid, p 49.
27. Ibid, pp 50–51.
28. Ibid, p 51.
29. Ibid, pp 106-107.
30. Christopher J. Walker, p 357.
31. Sarkis Adamian, p 399.
32. Ibid, p 399.

33. Ibid, pp 399–400.
34. George Fischer, pp 106–107.
35. Sarkis Adamian, p 402.
36. Harout Ter Davidian, *Who Understands Dro? Masis Weekly*, October 16, 1999, p 6.
37. Robert Aramaïsi Martirosian, *The ARF's Anti-Populist Activity During WWII*. 2nd ed, Yerevan, 1986, pp 47–50.
38. Ibid, p 50.
39. Hamlet Gevorgian, 2nd ed. p 508.
40. Ibid, p 510.
41. Kevork B. Bardakjian, *Hitler and the Armenian Genocide,* The Zoryan Institute, Cambridge, MA, 1985, p 6.
42. Ibid, pp 25–28.
43. Ibid, p 30. (See Robert Cecil, *The Myth of the Master Race: Alfred Rosenberg and Nazi Ideology,* London, 1972, p 200.)
44. Ibid, p 30. (See Alfred Rosenberg, *Der Mythus des zwanzigsten Jahrhunderts.* Munich, 1930, p 213.)
45. Ibid, p 30. (See Henry Picker, *Hitlers Tischgesprächeim Führerhauptquartier,* 3rd ed, Stuttgart: Seewald, 1977, p 422.)
46. Ibid, p 31.
47. Norman H. Baunes, *The Speeches of Adolf Hitler,* April 1922–August 1939. Vol I, Oxford University Press, 1942, p 118.
48. Ibid, p 115.
49. K. B. Bardakjian, p 32.
50. John Toland, *Adolf Hitler,* Ballantine Books, New York, 1976, pp 224–233.
51. K. B. Bardakjian, p 33.
52. Ibid, p 34.
53. Ibid, p 35.
54. Vratsian, *Along Life's Pathways,* Vol 4, pp 218–219.
55. H. Kevorkian, 2nd ed, p 512.
56. Tate Petrosian, *Dro (1884–1956), Hairenik* (Homeland) Monthly, 1956, #10, October, p 29.
57. Ibid, p 29.

58. Misak Torlakian, *My Memoirs,* 2nd ed, Beirut, 1963, p 515.
59. Ibid, pp 515–516.
60. Ibid, pp 516–518.
61. Ibid, p 519.
62. Ibid, pp 519–521.
63. Ibid, p 521.
64. Manuk Krzelian, *Asparez,* May 24, 2002, p 6.
65. Ibid, p 6.
66. Aram Tabaghian, *My Meetings With Dro, Hairenik* (Homeland) Monthly, 1967, #5, May, p 3.
67. Ibid, p 5.
68. Ibid, p 5.
69. Ibid, p 6.
70. Ibid, p 6.
71. Ibid, p 6.
72. Ibid, p 6.
73. Ibid, p 7.
74. Ibid, p 7.
75. Ibid, pp 7–8.
76. H. Kevorkian, 2nd ed, p 517.
77. Ibid, p 518.
78. Martin M. Kanayan, Personal communication with the author, February 9, 2006.
79. Ibid.
80. Ibid.
81. Misak Torlakian, 2nd ed, p 545.
82. Martin M. Kanayan, personal communication with the author, February 9, 2006.
83. Ibid.
84. Ibid.
85. Ibid.
86. Katherine Andreyev, pp 76–77.
87. Ibid, p 77.
88. Ibid, p 77.
89. Manuk Kezerlian, *Asparez,* May 24, 2002, p 6.

# CHAPTER VIII

## LAUDATORY TESTIMONIALS ABOUT DRO
## AND THE HERO'S DEMISE

Dro at the dusk of his fleeting life and the
dawn of his eternal glory

## FROM A. KOCHARIAN'S MEMOIRS
(Kotaik district, village of Kasakh)

In late 1941, the Red Army commenced military operations to defend the Crimean Peninsula against the onslaught of the German divisions. As a result of the failure of one of those military operations, a Red Army soldier named Vazgen Kocharian was captured by the Germans, in an unconscious state. With thousands of other prisoners of war, Kocharian was transported to the Zanko camp in Crimea (mentioned by Misak Torlakian), where, due to starvation, extreme cold, and awful conditions, thousands of POWs were dying every day.

Vazgen Kocharian, who survived the ordeal, relates:

"In Zanko concentration camp, conditions were grim. Every day the Germans filled pits with a few thousand corpses. I don't know what would have happened to us if not for the Armenians' assistance reaching us. The Armenian liaison, Muratian, arrived at the camp accompanied by Dro, whom he introduced as 'General Dro.' Both were dressed in civilian clothes, with black coats, of medium stature, broad-shouldered, having come to rescue us from our predicament. From January until March, the Germans had not given the POWs any provisions."[1]

In late March, Dro and his associates transported the Armenian prisoners of war rescued from the Zanko death camps to Simferopol.

Kocharian continues the narrative of his experiences:

"We made the three-day journey from Zanko to Simferopol on foot. An automobile and carts transported the wounded, the sick, and the provisions. Every 3–4 kilometers we would pause, rest, and then continue our journey. All along the way, Muratian and Dro walked with us. The former introduced me to Dro. The General was exceedingly modest and patriotic.

"We reached Simferopol, where there were many POWs. Immediately they took away our clothes to delouse them.

"With me were Mamikon Grigorian, who now lives in

the 5th Section of Nork, Misak from the village of Kasakh in Aparan, *Tornik* (Grandson) Hovsep, Amro, Ruben, Haik from Martuni, Paul from Yerevan, Amasik, and others. . . . Later on they all found their way home by various routes.

"Conditions in Simferopol were incomparably better. I can surely assert that thanks to Dro and Muratian, more than 300 Armenians, among them myself, were saved from the threat of certain death in the Zanko concentration camp."[2]

At the same time that Dro was saving Armenian prisoners of war from the claws of death in the concentration camps, he was also exerting a lot of effort to caution and prevent the people of Armenia from rebelling against the Soviet regime. When he and his comrades reached Northern Caucasus, he sent Misak Torlakian along with some comrades in arms to Armenia to prevent the outbreak of such uprisings.

## FROM THE MEMOIRS OF THADEUS PETROSIAN

Taté relates:

"I befriended Dro in 1900 when we were classmates and shared the same ideology in our student days in Yerevan."[3]

[February 1905, in Baku, the early days of the one-and-a-half-year-long Armeno-Tatar War.]

"On the evening of February 6, 1905, at the Mantashevian factory in Zabrad, I was attending a Party conference when unexpectedly I received a phone call from the Petroleum Industry Council. The speaker was Haroutune Shahrikian. He related that Douman would be going to the city [Baku] in the evening and instructed that I, along with some activists, go to the city to meet at Melikian's photo studio.

"It goes without saying that I immediately complied with the order and with some comrades went by carriage to the city, all of us armed with 'barabelum' pistols and a hundred bullets each.

265

"We arrived at the Melikian studio, which Douman had transformed into his command post. Inside, Douman, G. Gulkhandanian, Father Abraham, and Dashnakist Khecho had gathered around a table to develop a self-defense plan. Near the entrance stood a group of impatient, intrepid young men. Among them were Martiros Charukhjian, Mekerdich Aghamalian, A. Djanpoladian, *Aruids* (Lionheart) Avag, and Thaddeus Amirian. We had barely greeted each other, when in walked Drastamat Kanayan, in military uniform. He had been serving in the tsarist Akhuldinski regiment when, hearing about the Baku Armenians' grave predicament, he had asked for leave and come to Baku."[4]

By the time Nikol Douman arrived in Baku and organized a counterstrike, the Azeris had already killed around one hundred Armenians. In those days Andranik had gone to Geneva as the guest of Avetis Aharonian, the editor of *Droshag* (Flag), to seek treatment for his arthritis. I will not delve further into this matter, as I have written about it in the past.

The Armenian braves gathered in Melikian's studio. Douman approached them and kissed their brows. When he approached Dro, he hugged him and said:

"In this bloody struggle I have made a new discovery. That is Drastamat. He will have a great future if he remains in a suitable milieu. Bravo, my son, I have great hopes for you."

Dro cried with immense joy. The great warrior's praise was the biggest reward for Dro.

"Mr. Douman, I will strive to justify your hopes," was Dro's reply.[5]

A couple of excerpts regarding World War II:

"The victorious advance of Hitler's armies and the 'liberator' appeals published every day could have stirred the people of Mother Armenia, which had drunk to the lees the bitter cup of the Soviet regime. Especially after the fall of Kerch, where the Armenian forces of the Red Army sustained heavy losses, the Nazis reached the gates of the

TransCaucasus. Among the prisoners of war we rescued from the Novorosisk, Alagir, and Armavir concentration camps there were many intellectuals and officers who related the Armenian people's great discontent with the Soviet regime. According to our information, anti-Soviet sentiment was very strong among responsible officers. All this made it necessary for us to caution the Armenian masses against untimely uprisings. The slightest movement in the country against the Soviets and in favor of Nazism could have led to tragic consequences.

"It was not an easy task. Even a snake on its belly, a bird with its wings, were incapable of penetrating the bloody iron curtain. Nevertheless, Dro created the means to do so, and through trustworthy selfless individuals from Feodosia, Taman, and Armavir, he sent word simultaneously to anti-Soviet groups in the homeland to absolutely refrain from any demonstrations, be it anti-Soviet or pro-Nazi."[6]

## CHRISTOPHER J. WALKER ABOUT DRO'S BATTALION
(Excerpt from Walker's "Armenia . . .")

"In December 1941 an Armenian battalion was created by a decision of the *Wehrmacht,* known as the 'Armenian 812th Battalion.' It was commanded by Dro, and was made up of a small number of committed recruits, and a larger number of Armenians from the prisoners of war taken by the Nazis in their sweep eastward. Early on the total number was 8,000; this number later grew to 20,000. The 812th Battalion operated in the Crimea and the North Caucasus."[7]

Christopher J. Walker continues:

"Except for Nzhdeh, no Armenian has ever been an ideological Fascist. So what was the motive of the collaboration in the occupied areas?"

The British historian speculates, "It is possible to see it as a purely vengeful desire to retake Armenia from the

Bolsheviks. . . ." But in the end he arrives at two conclusions:

"1. Dashnaks such as Dro remembered—and the memory has been an overwhelming constituent of their policy in the preceding two decades—the events of 1917–18, when the strength and organization of their party apparatus was the only guarantee against the final extermination of the children of Haik[11] from the Armenian plateau. With Russia again threatened with break-up, it made sense to prepare to enter Yerevan with the forces that might supplant Bolshevism, in order to assure public security before the Turks swept in from the west."

"2. *[Dro's and his comrades'] immediate and overwhelming concern was to secure the safety of the Armenians in the occupied territories."*[8] (Emphasis added.)

## A REMARKABLE INTERVIEW WITH AVETIK ISAHAKIAN

(As recorded by *Edjmiadsnetsi* [Native of Edjmiadsin—pen name])

One year before the demise of Avetik Isahakian in 1956, one of my close acquaintances who had gone to visit Armenia, upon my request met with the Master Poet a few times. I had wanted to benefit from those *tête-à-tête* meetings to learn about the Master's authoritative opinion on a few hot topics unsettling our lives. What follows are excerpts from those interviews:

Question: Master, why did they execute or exile the Armenian intellectuals and scientists?

Answer: Because they were good and patriotic Armenians.

Q: Master, how did you manage to survive that slaughter?

---

[11] Mythic progenitor of the Armenian nation. The Armenians refer to themselves as *Hai's* and their homeland as *"Haiastan."*

A: By applauding the murderers.

Q: The anti-ARF press in the Diaspora wrote at length about Dro being an agent of the Nazis. What is your opinion?

A: I have known Dro for a long time. We were close friends in the past. He is a great patriot, a bold revolutionary, has accomplished heroic deeds. But his greatest service to Armenia and the Armenian people was indeed during the war, when he appeared to be collaborating with Germany.

Sensing the defeat of the Nazis, he had gone to the Northern Caucasus with the German army, and cautioned the people of Armenia against any uprising against the Bolshevik regime, which would have been the death of Armenia, as it was for the Crimea, the autonomous regions of the Kalmuks and Chechens, whose natives had gladly welcomed the German forces. After the retreat of the Nazis, the Bolsheviks not only put an end to those three autonomous regions, but also exiled their people en masse into the depths of Siberia and filled their homelands with Russians. The same grim fate was reserved for Armenia, if not for Dro's forewarning. Now you be the judge: was Dro a traitor or a patriot? Only the future historian will be able to properly appraise this great service by Dro.[9]

Q: In the pro-Soviet press in the Diaspora, we would often read about the love and motherly feelings that Stalin and Beria manifested towards Armenia. How much truth was there in those praises?

A: That press you mentioned was, unknowingly, or it would be more correct to say, cynically, lying. By Soviet law, if a people in their homeland are less than one million strong, they cannot constitute an independent republic, but only an autonomous region which would be attached to a neighboring republic. Stalin and Beria exerted all efforts to lower the number of the people in Armenia to below one million, to be able to divide it up between Georgia and Azerbaijan. To execute their diabolical scheme, they tried all means: beginning in 1934 massive deportations to Siberia and the steppes of Turkmenistan; the slaughter and

269

liquidation of that segment of the Armenian intelligentsia which was exerting passive resistance to the realization of that diabolical scheme; but, most importantly, the vast majority of the Armenian Communist leaders, headed by Sahak Ter Gabrielian, Lukashin, Aghasi Khandjian, Sasha Pekzadian, and others, openly struggled against those two Georgians, who wanted to dig Armenia's and the Armenian people's grave. They sacrificed their lives to abort that diabolical scheme. It was true that among the white sheep there were to be found also black sheep. For example, among the writers were to be found Nairi Zarian and some hide-bound like-minded few, as well as Communist Aroutiunov and his sycophants. But those were a contemptible minority unworthy of having Armenian identity.[10]

## ANDRANIK DSARUKIAN ABOUT DRO

Andranik Dsarukian's appraisal or personal observations of Dro as man, hero, commander, or national figure are generally objective and positive, except for his perspective on Dro's collaboration with Nazism, whereby it is revealed that Andranik himself was not adequately informed about this complex topic. He should not be blamed for this, because this talented poet and literary figure possibly had not read the works of Sarkis Adamian, George Fisher, Kevork Bardakjian, Christopher Walker, Oliver Baldwin, and others, who have shed sufficient light on these otherwise cryptic and inadequately explained adventures. Dsarukian sometimes reflects the opinions of Soviet Armenia's writers who were not free-thinking intellectuals but wrote whatever could please their masters in the Kremlin. Thus:

"In Armenia, Dro's name did not ring well. People had not forgotten his complicity in Hitler's army. [To reverse this] it was necessary for Marshall Baghramian to write his memoirs wherein it can be read that the main commander of the Bash-Aparan battle was Drastamat Kanayan among the leaders of the ARF."[11]

These Armenian intellectuals who considered Dro to be a "traitor"—Kevork Abov, for one—were simply trying to curry favor with the masters of the Kremlin by trying to please and demonstrate their "loyalty."

Dsarukian publicizes some anecdotes having to do with the final years of Dro's life, thus:

"One day I heard Dro saying, 'money is nothing for me, but if I am unable to give money to others, I would be unfortunate'."[12]

Also:

"Above all else Dro was an intrepid and fearless warrior, a selfless fedayee, though not of the same stock as Andranik or Murat, who personified the fedayee who embraces his rifle instead of his sweetheart, who did not have comfort anywhere, but a fedayee who loved to embrace his sweetheart along with his rifle, loved to indulge in luxurious living like a tsarist aristocrat. His taste for that lavish lifestyle became the reason for our national Achilles to have a vulnerable heel. Two irredeemable stains will contaminate his otherwise magnificently masculine figure. The first was his formation of Armenian collaborator brigades to fight alongside the German army against the Soviet forces, which was to be more a moral stain on him than any actual harm to Armenia, and the second was his organization of a spy network in Syria-Lebanon for America, as a result of which, a prosperous Armenian community in the Diaspora was undermined, with scores of Armenians arrested in Aleppo, some tortured in prisons, others having to flee the country, starting a flow of thousands migrating from Aleppo to Beirut. . . .[13]

"In both cases, whether the paymaster was Germany or America, large sums were involved and the administrator was Dro himself.

"Money is nothing for me but . . . ."[14]

Aside from the two "stains," Dsarukian makes the following inappropriate remark about Dro's marital life:

"Dro was a selfless fedayee, though not of the same

271

stock as Andranik or Murat, who personified the fedayee who embraces his rifle instead of his sweetheart, but a fedayee who loved to embrace his sweetheart along with his rifle."

I said "inappropriate" because Dro's first wife, Nvart, died a year after their wedding from tuberculosis, orphaning the baby boy, Ludwig.

Twelve long years later, Dro married 26-year-old Arpenik Galoyan in Yerevan.

A few years after his second wedding, Dro was exiled to Moscow in early December 1920. Shortly thereafter, in 1921, Arpenik with her two sons, Souren and Kurken, as well as the deceased Nvart's son, Ludwig, went to Moscow to be with her husband.

Four years later, in 1925, when Dro went from Moscow to Paris, he took with him only his firstborn, Ludwig. Arpenik with her two boys returned to Yerevan.

Dro's stay in Paris was brief. He took part in the ARF's 10th General Assembly and then settled in Romania. After settling in Romania and obtaining the position of general overseer of Ghoukasian's oilfields, why did he not seek his wife and two boys behind the Iron Curtain? Because in those days, communications were nonexistent between Romania and the Soviet Union, when an "iron curtain" had descended on the borders of the Soviet Union, which "not even a bird could fly through," per popular expression. Moreover, Dro, who had left behind his friends and acquaintances in Moscow and Yerevan and gone overseas, perhaps did not wish to reveal his whereabouts to the Communist elite of Moscow and Yerevan.

I still suspect that Dro really did not like Paris, the "City of Light," and wanted to settle in the less luminous Balkan Peninsula.

Ten years after settling in Romania, in 1935, Dro got married for the third time, to Russian-Armenian Gayané Levonian, the widow of Paruir Levonian, who had died of tuberculosis.

By the way, Mrs. Gayané, until recently, early 21st century, was still living in Boston, as a centenarian.

272

In all this history, where does one conclude that "Dro loved to embrace his sweetheart along with his rifle"? That was never the case, as the reader can see. Between his first and second marriages, for twelve years, Dro was unattached. Similarly, between his second and third marriages, for ten years, Dro was a bachelor.

Let us now address the two "stains" on Dro's name.

The first, that during World War II Dro formed Armenian collaborator brigades to fight alongside the German army against the Soviet forces:

Hitler did not need Dro's "collaborator brigades." By forming brigades from prisoners of war, Dro saved their lives. Otherwise, they would all have died like flies in the concentration camps. In addition, with the pretext of "collaborating" with Hitler, Dro also saved the lives of the 400,000 Armenians in the occupied territories, who could have been subjected to holocaust, because, as we saw, Armenians were classified as almost equal to Jews on the list of Hitler's hatreds.

Whatever Dro did during World War II, it was for the sake of the Armenian prisoners of war, the Armenians of the occupied territories, and the homeland.

Instead of critiquing Dro and searching for a "stain" on the hero, I wish others also . . . had conceived of something, or had done something for the sake of the Armenians endangered during World War II.

As for the second "stain," that Dro organized "a spy network in Syria-Lebanon for America, as a result of which a prosperous Armenian community in the Diaspora was undermined, with scores of Armenians arrested in Aleppo, some tortured in prisons, others having to flee the country, starting a flow of thousands migrating from Aleppo to Beirut . . . ."

In the summer of 1945, a few months after the tragic death of my younger sister, my family settled in Beirut. I am aware that some bad things happened in Syria in the early '50s. A couple of my brother (ARF member) Hovannes's friends lost their lives; and if Hovannes evaded being tortured in prison, it was only because of the

273

intervention of his business associate who was a Damascene colonel. If Dro was behind this affair, as some speculate, I am not certain why he took this step. I would speculate that when the Americans arrested Dro in Heidelberg and were going to hand him over to their allies, the Bolsheviks, but fortuitously did not and instead released him (details noted elsewhere in this book), the American administration may then have asked or pressured Dro to go to the Middle East and, as a military man and a United States citizen, to form anti-Bolshevik cells and spy networks. Could he have refused? Let us not forget that it was the cold war's hottest days, when it was rumored that the Red Army would march south, toward the Arab states.

## DRO IN ALEPPO

Dsarukian relates:

The first time Dro came to Aleppo was in late Spring of 1948. His purpose was not tourism, of course—Aleppo does not have scenic sites except for its historic fortress and covered bazaars—but to resolve a sharp disagreement among the Party leadership.

The first Arab-Jewish war had started as a consequence of the founding of Israel and the city was mobilized, displaying a tense stir. The Arab "National Party" (Nationalist) with whom we had close relations and were electoral allies had requested that we form a 500-man Armenian Volunteer legion which they were willing to arm with their own treasury. There were those among us who were ready to respond positively to this proposal, others who were firmly opposed to it. Dro was called as judge.

"Pretend I am not here and express yourselves freely" were his first words.

He listened to both sides, without revealing his perspective. He even allowed sharp and bitter words to the point of hurtful exchanges. Adour, who had been liaison

274

with the Arabs, along with Hrach, had already promised them and kept saying like a refrain, "To save the fifty-thousand strong Armenian community I would concede five hundred."

"We are at the poker table beginning to draw on your bet" mocked Herardian, addressing the assembly in general without looking at Adour (a new opportunity for Herardian to allude to Adour's gambling habit).

These two, with fundamentally opposite temperaments, could hardly tolerate each other. If, during the assembly, one of them was first to speak, the other one would remain quiet and withdrawn as if sulking. Both were committed, experienced nationalist activists; even their contradictions complemented each other and they were necessary cadres for the Party. Adour, with his soft temperament, was much liked by all, respected by even his opponents, and among his friends he was called "soft thorn." Herardian, with his sharp personality and dry manner, was barely tolerated even by his friends. It was left up to us, the younger members, to keep the balance between the two. But that day, against the given agenda, we were siding with Herardian. Only Onnik, as always, sided with Adour and Hrach. If it was left up to them, we should have already started the registration of the volunteers days ago. And it was because of our opposition that this was delayed, and now Dro had arrived to resolve the dispute.

He let everyone speak at length in presenting the rationale for their opinions and listened patiently without interrupting. Fearing that Herardian with his rough words could bring the disagreement to a boil, I spoke up, with a little conciliatory spirit:

"The problem has two aspects, moral and practical. I find it unbecoming that our lads fight against the people who have suffered like us and shared our fate, who want to survive. And then, the practical aspect: If we consider that in this city of half a million population the Armenian community numbers fifty thousand, then compared to the number of Arabs, our share would be fifty people and not five hundred, that is, if we have to, due to circumstances, respond to the proposal . . . ."

Hrach interrupted me:

"You see, Comrade Dro, didn't I tell you? Our young man here is not only a poet, editor, and orator, but now he is becoming a strategist."

"It is not a matter of strategy, but of accounting," I said, but could not continue. What did he say? "Didn't I tell you?" he said . . . . That meant that in my absence he had already spoken with Dro about me and of course "praised" me according to his good custom. Under these circumstances, it was not necessary to be polite and hide from Dro the tension in our relationship. On the contrary, I should speak as harshly as I could, so that our guest would realize that in this context, Hrach's "intimate conversations" could not have been objective . . . . When it is revealed that your relationship with someone is not good, then what you say about him will be taken with a grain of salt.

But Dro did not allow more time. Considering himself enlightened enough, he began to speak:

"The comrade is correct, Hrach. The strongest Arab force, the Jordanian army, organized by Glubb Pasha, numbers ten thousand men. The Syrian army, I do not know, could be double that, but not of the same quality. The Egyptian, numbering the most, lacks martial spirit. This much about the military forces. As for providing volunteers, Armenians do not have to provide volunteers. Let the Syrian Government declare mobilization and the Armenian lads along with the Arabs will go to fulfill their duty. When a country is at war, it is the responsibility of the government to declare mobilization and not that of the political parties, be they Armenian or Arab. That is my opinion."

Have you had occasion to drink a glass of cold spring water when very thirsty? Oh, How pleasing! I was that pleased.

After that day, for many years, I have been with Dro, at meetings or during *tête-à-tête* conversations, but at no other time did he seem to me to be as logical as he was during that Aleppo Assembly. On the contrary, after that I have seen Dro to be partial, sometimes simply delusional, and I have thought, "Is this the same man or someone else?"

As for the issue of volunteers, fortunately or unfortunately, events pre-empted it quickly. Israel won and that was the end of the topic. Only Herardian had not forgotten, and once in a while he would repeat, with a mischievous smirk, "Adour lost his bet."[15]

## DRO VISITS ALEPPO'S FORTRESS
(Excerpts from Dsarukian's *The Great Men and the Others*.)

Over the wide moat surrounding the fortress there is a stone bridge which ends at the entrance. An honor guard of soldiers with their rifles was lined up along the bridge saluting the Armenian General. Dro, with the seriousness of a state minister, passed in front of the soldiers, nodding slightly, and then shook the commanding officer's hand. He then mingled with the soldiers as if he was their comrade. Not just the Armenians, but also the Arab soldiers were taken in by Dro and were following our footsteps en masse.

Dro had a surprise for us.

"Ask the officer if we can arrange for a marksmanship contest here."

The officer gladly accepted the challenge. At a distance of 25–30 paces, six beer bottles were placed on an elevation. Dro's competitor was chosen, evidently their best marksman. Dro, without delay, picked up a rifle, checked it out, and suddenly, while standing, took quick aim and shot three times. Three bottles disappeared. The other marksman took his time, knelt with one foot behind, and shot three times with only one hit. The soldiers' excitement was indescribable. *"Ta'ish janaral Armen"* (long live the Armenian General) they shouted, excited and happy. The trip to the fortress was transformed into a joyful picnic. In two hours, Dro had won the hearts of the soldiers, become their friend. The Armenian lads' happiness was boundless. They were proud. The whole detachment, in disarray, accompanied us to the street and sent us on our way with claps and hoorays.[16]

Dro had amazing charisma. He would quickly generate admiration, wherever he might be. A ray of warmth flowed from him and enveloped those around him.[17]

## WHEN THE DRIVER REFUSES
## TO ACCEPT PAYMENT

A day before returning to Lebanon, upon leaving a restaurant in the Cybil neighborhood, Dro asked his companions:

"Is there a good shop around here where I could buy a watch?"

They headed toward Levon Babigian's shop. The vehicle stopped in front of Aleppo's best watchmaker's shop. Dro entered and said: "I want a good, man's watch; the best and most valuable."

Levon demonstrated the best watch found in his shop, a Zenith, which cost 250.00 Syrian pounds. Since the watch was for Dro, he gave a notable discount, crossing out the price on its label with a pencil. Dro left behind its attractive case, picked up the watch, paid for it, and left the store.

Dsarukian surmised that the watch was for Dro's son Martin. As soon as he got in the car, Dro pulled the driver's arm and put the watch on his wrist, saying, "You refused my payment, you cannot refuse Dro's gift."

It was revealed that several times he had tried to pay the driver, Sahak, but encountering resistance, had changed the way of making payment.[18]

## RETURN TO THE COUNTRY OF THE CEDARS

Dro stayed one week in Aleppo. After meeting with comrades in the city and *Nor Guigh* (New Village) and going

on a few excursions, he set out toward Beirut one morning
before sunrise. The driver of the vehicle was Martiros, next
to whom sat Dro. In the back were Neshan and Andranik
Dsarukian.

At sunrise, they reached Ma'ara, the birthplace of
Abou Lala. Dro expressed his desire to visit the newly
constructed tomb of Abou Lala, to see "how is Avo's (the
poet Avetik Isahakian's) man doing?"

After a brief pause in Ma'ara, Martiros sped toward
Beirut.

Shtora, in Lebanon, had become the Summer resort
of the elite. Nikol Aghbalian had built a private residence
there. Being close to the purely Armenian-populated town
of Anjar,[12] Shtora had a distinct advantage and attraction.
Dro had also fallen in love with the place, seeing a
resemblance to Armenia's Dilijan region in the surrounding
forests. He had given his daughter in matrimony to Dr.
Broutian there. He was considering building a home there
as well.[19]

Before Dsarukian finally settled in Lebanon, he had
come to Beirut with Holy Father Zareh. The last evening
they were invited to Dro's house for dinner, along with two
Iranian-Armenian families. The guest of honor at the lavish
table was, of course, the Holy Father. Dsarukian and the
Holy Father were seeing and tasting caviar for the first time
at Dro's table.

The next morning when Dsarukian and the Holy
Father were in front of Shahinian's pharmacy waiting for
their ride to Aleppo, Dro reached them with two porters in
tow, each one carrying a crate of apples, plums, bananas,
etc. When the Holy Father and Dsarukian objected, saying
"This wasn't necessary," Dro answered, "What are you
saying, Holy Father? This is a tradition as sacred as the
Holy Mass for us. In Igdir, when the Holy Father would

---

[12] The survivors of the fabled uprising of the Armenian villagers of Musa Dagh
(the story depicted in Franz Werfel's *Forty Days of Musa Dagh*) against the
Ottoman government's order of deportation into the desert were rescued by the
French and eventually resettled in Anjar.

honor us with his visit, it was impossible to let him go without gifts. The town's honor was on the line. . . ."[20]

## DRO'S DISSILLUSIONMENT WITH HIS FORMER PASSIONS

At the ARF's 14th General Assembly in 1947, as well as at the 15th General Assembly in 1951, Dro had become one of the Party's strongest and most galvanizing leaders. By then he was an established figure, having earned respect and trust, and freed of his former passions— Russophilia, socialism, revolution, and other dreams.[21]

Foremost among Dro's passions was his plain, sincere, and unadulterated love of the Russian people, but never of dictatorship, be it tsarist or Bolshevik. Dro's love of the Russian people was natural and spontaneous because, until the overthrow of the Romanov Dynasty in March of 1917, Igdir and the province of Surmalu were part of the Russian Empire, where Dro was born and raised in a milieu influenced by Russian culture. The province of Surmalu, where Mount Ararat and the ruins of the ancient city of Ani are located, were "only intermittently part of Turkey in the 18th century."[22]

Dro's love of the Russian people did not restrain him from assassinating the overtly Tatarophile and Armenophobe officials of Tsar Nicholas II.

Inevitably, Dro was also disillusioned with the Bolshevik regime. How could one forget the nauseating purges of 1937–1938: the forced confessions; the great terror among the masses; the cutting down of the intelligentsia, starting with Yeghishé Charents; the execution of countless innocent, sincere, and patriotic Communist leaders, high-ranking military officers, and political cadres, such as Aghasi Khandjian and others; the horrible murder of His Holiness Khoren I, the Catholicos of All Armenians, at midnight on April 19, 1938, hacked to death by four beastly communist thugs;[23] the exile of millions of ordinary citizens to the ice storms of Siberia; the

280

terrible atmosphere of fear and suspicion among the people, wherein a man could not trust his wife, a sister her brother, when in the same family one betrayed the other in order to save himself? In other words, the dictator of Moscow had transformed his own country into a Dantéesque hell. A sad panorama, the true extent of which was revealed only years after the war.

Stepan Aladjadjian relates the psychology prevalent in the Soviet Union in those days:

"On the outside, the country is being built magnificently, whereas on the inside, a man's psyche is collapsing in misery."[24]

Before expiring his last breath, the dictator of Kremlin had begun to persecute the Union's doctors, to cut down some of them, probably the elite, with trumped-up and false accusations. After that, who knows whose turn would have been next?


## DRO'S LAST DAYS IN BEIRUT

Aside from his political activities in Europe, America, and the Middle East, Dro had become a family man. "He did not like the noisy restaurants. Sitting at length in a café or restaurant was torture to him. He liked to be home, his own or at his friends'. There, during family pastimes and parties, he was unmatched with his joyful nature, quick wit, captivating stories, songs, and dance. His speech was unadorned, but could touch sensitive chords in a person's soul."[26]

After 1950, Dro and Vratsian lived under the same roof for five years in Beirut. Before that they had traveled together to America a few times. In New York they would stay at Vratsian's residence. In San Francisco they would stay at the home of Avetis and Anahit Garageuzian; in Los Angeles, at the home of Mark and Gladys Vartanian; in Washington, at the home of Khachik and Gohar Haroutiunian; in Boston, at the home of Dr. Levon and Lucine Daghlian. Wherever they went, Dro and Vratsian were surrounded with love and caring.[27]

In Beirut, the five-year cohabitation of these two close friends was often the subject of humor among their friends. This duo was called bride and groom. Dro reserved for himself the role of bride, but in reality, Vratsian would say he played the role of mother-in-law.

In Beirut Dro had formed a wide circle of friends among whom he felt at home. He relied on them in times of pain and illness.[28]


## THE HERO'S DEATH

"When did 'the cursed illness' begin in Dro's body?" asks Vratsian.

He could not recall Dro ever being ill in the Caucasus, aside from the lead he had received in war, which remained lodged in his lung. He became very ill once in Romania and underwent surgery, but that did not have any lasting effect on his overall health. When he came to America the first time, he complained of arthralgia. Was it just arthritis? Neither he nor his doctors seemed to know.

When Vratsian relocated to Beirut in late 1951, Dro had begun to receive treatments. He suffered from severe pain. His doctors were unable to determine the etiology of his illness. He ascribed his aches to arthralgia.

"This rheumatism is killing me," he would complain.

The specialist physicians of Beirut and Europe were torturing him with different tests and trials. Maybe they suspected malignancy. They offered various remedies and procedures, but the damned illness always eluded their grasp.

Dro was suffering and with him suffered those around him. He especially hurt at night. And yet in all this he kept his mental lucidity and his willpower. His illness and aches did not impair his daily activities.[29]

Simon Vratsian

When the doctors in Beirut and Europe were unable to find a remedy, he went to America for medical tests. The specialists at Boston's famous Leahy Hospital diagnosed cancer and began treatment. With the treatment leading to a positive outcome, he returned to Beirut. Convinced that he was in remission, he enthusiastically resumed his partisan and public activities. Sometimes, though, doubt would gnaw at his mind, when the "arthralgia" would cause acute shoulder pains. He also complained that he felt weak and lacked appetite. He had also developed diabetes, which he kept to himself, fearing restrictions on his diet. Generally, he was a gourmand.[30]

In those days he often recalled his military mentor, Nikol Duman, under whose command he had fought in the 1905–06 Armeno-Tatar War. "Duman also had cancer," writes Vratsian, but I know that Duman suffered from arthritis and tuberculosis in the years before World War I. In September of 1914 when he heard that Armenian volunteer regiments were being formed in Tbilisi and he would not be able to take part, he tried to commit suicide with his pistol. But the bullet missed his heart and instead pierced his lung. He did not die immediately but passed away a few days later in the hospital.

Vratsian was afraid that Dro might follow Duman's example. To pre-empt such peril, he would spend time with Dro, reminiscing about his comrades Martiros Charukhjian and Dashnakist Khecho and others until the early morning hours.

In the fall of 1955 Dro's condition deteriorated and his aches became more severe. His close friends in Beirut tried to convince him to depart to America for treatment. The specialists at Leahy Hospital also found it necessary to have their patient undergo new tests. Dro was himself finally convinced that he should go.

Before departing for America, Dro was in a nervous state. He had sleepless nights. He would enter Vratsian's room and sit on his bed. Sometimes he spoke of past events, sometimes he would become melancholic and begin to sing sad songs.

The night before his departure for America, Dro again entered Vratsian's room and sat on the bed.

"Go to your room so I can catch some sleep."

Dro did not heed and said softly, "You know what? We will not meet again."

"Don't be silly. You will go, get well, and return."

"Of course I will return, but I am afraid . . . ."

"Go, get some rest."

Dro did not leave. They lay side by side under the same comforter.[31]

284

When they went to the airport the next day, Vratsian was in a sad mood. Many friends and comrades had come to bid farewell. They were all sad. Dro tried to lighten the atmosphere, joking around, but he was not the same Dro. Last embraces, kisses, and he flew away, was gone.

For some time after he went to America, there was no news from Dro. It was evident that his illness had become graver. And indeed, the Leahy specialists' diagnosis had confirmed everyone's fears. The cancer had metastasized, causing severe pains. The diagnosis was kept hidden from him. He was told that he had osteomyelitis, curable by radiation. He also wanted to believe that his illness was osteomyelitis and curable.

After that, Dro's letters to Beirut revolved around "osteomyelitis." He complained of pain but was hopeful about an imminent cure. He continued to show interest in partisan and public affairs. Despite being in America, his mind and heart were in Lebanon.

In Lebanon, foreboding news were arriving from America, but no one knew the truth. One day word arrived that Dro's condition was terminal.

People in Beirut wanted to know the truth and details about his condition.

Finally, a letter dated February 3, 1956, arrived from the ARF Central Committee of America:

"After approximately a one-week hospital stay, comrade Dro is discharged home. Today he went to the Leahy Clinic where he underwent some tests. Just now his doctor, who was with him, telephoned us.

"The X-Rays indicate that the 5th vertebra of his spinal column and his right and left shoulders are afflicted with the known illness. For the time being, the specialists are wary of saying anything decisive about a cure or prognosis.

"They will administer eight radiation treatments to at least noticeably ameliorate his pains. After that, X-Rays of his afflicted tissues will be taken again to compare with previous ones.

"If the pains are relieved or noticeably ameliorated,

then his doctors will be more hopeful about the condition of their patient.

"You know that comrade Dro also has diabetes.

"When he came to America, his weight was 204 lbs. It is now 179 lbs. Worried about his condition, Dro has lost his appetite and does not sleep well. These factors of course also impact his weight loss.

"When you write to him, encourage him and lift his spirits; do not burden him with any tasks. To assume any responsibility and to be unable to fulfill it due to his condition would make him more stressed and anxious.

"Regarding his illness, we have said that it is osteomyelitis. When you write, you as well should not name his illness."[32]

While Dro was in Boston undergoing treatment, various comrades would drive him to his appointments. Dr. Levon Daghlian and Hamo Baraghamian were often the drivers. One day, Daghlian and Baraghamian drove Dro by a lovely house in Watertown called Campbell Residence. It was located at the corner of and School Streets and was an old and imposing residence. They asked Dro how he liked the house and he replied that it was very nice. They handed Dro some documents (probably a purchase and sale agreement) and told him it was a gift from his comrades. Dro tore up the documents and told them in an angry voice that funds collected from Armenians should never be spent on an individual, but should be used only for the good of all Armenians. That was the end of the house.[33]

In his letter of February 4, Hamo Baraghamian wrote:

"After a four-day stay in the hospital we brought Dro home.

"The outcome was that the cursed illness has metastasized to his ribs. There is no cure. His condition is grave. We have not told him anything. I beg of you or any of our comrades out there, if you write letters to him, do not reveal the truth. So many times he has said, 'Dear Hamo, are you going to allow your brother to die in bed?'

"The other day we edited the Leahy 'Report' as we

saw fit and transmitted it to him through Dr. Touzjian. He telephoned and said, 'Brother, the report is very good, it is only bone pain, which could be treated with X-Rays.'

"We are living through grave times. Levon and myself witness every day his wasting away. His appetite is completely cut off. Imagine, he has lost around 35 pounds. It is unlikely that he will survive much longer."[34]

Dr. Levon Daghlian, in his letter dated February 23, relates Dro's condition in darker colors:

"Last Thursday, the night of February 16, we took Dro to the hospital. Gayane heard a noise and got up to find Dro fallen on his face in the bathroom, passed out. He had gotten up to void, felt nauseous, and leaned over to vomit when he lost consciousness and fell; luckily he did not injure himself when he fell. He had diarrhea, mostly blood, and also vomited blood. Touzjian alerted me around 3:00 a.m.; we called an ambulance to take him to the hospital. He received blood transfusion continuously, and bled lightly a couple of times. Finally, the bleeding stopped. He had some fever, was heavily medicated, sometimes delirious—calling the names of Simon, Martiros, Adour— next moment he would be awake and lucid, wanting to write letters to Adour, Vahan. Luckily, he is not fully informed of his condition; he has some suspicions but, like most patients, he is inclined to hope. He is concerned about his progress.

"With 'they will give this medicine,' 'take that X-ray,' 'we will get a report tomorrow,' 'we will then find out,' and such routine worries, the hours passed.

"How long he will last like this, nobody knows. Before this blood loss, they estimated three months; now they are talking about weeks. He gets the best care; besides the nurses and doctors, one or two comrades are with him 24 hours a day."[35]

On March 8, Dr. Daghlian mailed to Simon Vratsian his last letter to Beirut:

"Dro underwent surgery on Monday morning. His whole body was jaundiced. His bile duct was blocked and instead of emptying into the gut, bile was spreading in the body. If not for emergency surgery, he would have died of poisoning. Considering his condition—diabetes, stomach ulcer, metastatic cancer, etc.—the surgery was very risky. The doctor said he may not come out alive from the operating room. According to the doctors, the surgery was successful and Dro held out well. I visited him yesterday and today. He is not conscious. He is under the influence of drugs; sometimes he opens his eyes. They hope that in a day or two there will be a turn for the better. His jaundice is as before. There was no cancer in the gall bladder though his pancreas was afflicted and growing in size, and had pressed on the bile duct. They cleared this blockage and opened a bypass for the bile. He is not in a position to read letters though sometimes he asks that we send you telegrams that the crisis has passed, etc."[36]

It was evident that his days were numbered.

Finally, that same evening, at 8:45 p.m. on March 8, Dro expelled his last breath, under an alien sky, far from his beloved homeland.

Telegraphic networks everywhere relayed the following brief news: "Dro died."

In distant Beirut, Vratsian waited impatiently for news of Dro's last hours. Finally, he received this letter from Baraghamian:

"I am deeply sorry that the letter you requested may not be sufficient for you, but nevertheless I will try to respond to the extent I can. Dro did not think about death much. Sometimes he would become aware that his condition was grave, other times he would say, 'This too shall pass'; for that reason he did not say much, nor did he give deathbed requests or instructions. Nonetheless, I would like to write about a few distinct incidents in the last 4–5 weeks.

"For me the most interesting was that when I would drive him to the Leahy Clinic for treatment, he would often sing on the way and always the same song, 'Girl fleeing to Zangezur, I am your soul mate; I wish I could see Armenia one last time, and then die,' or else, 'See Yerevan one last time,' etc.[37]

288

"The night he vomited blood and was transported to the hospital, Hamastegh and his wife had come, and Levon and I were there as well. The topic of conversation was the election of the Catholicos of All Armenians. Hamastegh as usual opposed our support of Zareh as candidate, that we should concede and appoint their candidate. Levon and I were silent. We let Dro speak, and the sick man arose like a lion. He began to give a speech about how important this election was for the Armenian people. And finally, he said the following word for word:

" 'Comrades, be proud to be a member of an organization that strikes fear in both the Turk and the Bolshevik; that is why they want to destroy it. Foreigners respect us and take us into consideration because though we are small in numbers, our strength is great in quality. Be proud, I say.'

"And we, we all rose in honor of our organization.

"Afterward, that night, Dro vomited blood. They called me at 3:00 a.m. We informed Touzjian and took him to the hospital.

"In the hospital his condition was grave. His whole body was jaundiced. You could feel that the giant was slowly fading away. Sometimes he was lucid and articulate. Other times he was incoherent and delirious. Despite the fact that I was at the hospital three times a day and stayed with him for some time, he said to Paul Nahapetian one day, 'Dear Paul, where is Hamo? He does not come around; is he upset? Why is he not coming by? Tell him that I have important things and assignments to talk with him about. It is essential that he come.'

"The morning of the day he died, we went again with Gayane and entered his room. The first thing he said was 'Gayane, I am in a coma' and then he turned to me 'Dear Hamo, any news from Beirut or elsewhere?' and then he fell into a coma again. He had said the same thing to Levon one day. Levon had stayed by his side for a long time, but he did not say another word."[38]

## THE FUNERAL AND BURIAL

From Saturday evening until past midnight on Sunday, March 9, 10, and 11, Dro's open casket was placed in the hall of the *Hairenik* publishing house surrounded with many floral wreaths and comrades standing in honor guard. From Boston and the environs some 2,000 male and female comrades and compatriots passed by his casket, "in silent columns and grateful reverence," to pay their respects to the revered hero.

The burial took place on Sunday, March 18. There was a severe storm that day—strong winds, chill, snow, and ice. A lot of roads were impassable. Vehicles and trains were inching forward with difficulty. A large crowd of mourners waited to bid their last farewell to the hero, from New England, New York, and other states. Many were stuck on the way, mired in snow.

After the formal and moving ceremony in the Holy Trinity Cathedral of Boston, the burial took place in Watertown's Mt. Auburn Cemetery. On this sad occasion one of those present wrote the following to the hero's close friend, Simon Vratsian:

"You cannot imagine what happened. It was a terrible storm, windy and cold. The roads were impassable. Countless vehicles were stuck in snow. Many were unable to make it to the burial. I came close to missing it myself.

"And imagine the miracle that took place. We were already at the grave when suddenly the storm dissipated. The sky cleared and the cemetery which was covered with snow was flooded with the sun's dazzling rays. And that fantastic interlude lasted until the casket was lowered to the ground. Then the storm resumed with a vengeance.

"When the heartrending melody, 'To Jerusalem Above,' was heard, I raised my eyes up; in the sky, high above, a plane was visible with silver wings, which was soaring up as if taking with it Dro's illuminated soul. The illusion was so unexpected and its impact so moving that I almost passed out."[39]

Without a doubt it was Dro's soul—"Tempestuous

290

Dro" himself, who was born in a tempest and departed this world in a tempest.

Moreover, according to Ned (Nshan) Abikian's report, not only were Tempestuous Dro's birth and burial days stormy, but also the day of his reburial, which occurred on May 28, 2002, in Bash-Aparan, Armenia.

Dro's Mausoleum in Aparan, Armenia

# NOTES

1. Hamlet Gevorgian, 2nd ed, pp 531–532.
2. Ibid, pp 532-533.
3. Tate Petrossian, *Dro (1884-1956), Hairenik* (Homeland) monthly, 1956, #10, October, p 17.
4. Ibid, p18.
5. Ibid, pp 18–19.
6. Ibid, pp 29–30.
7. Christopher J. Walker, p 357.
8. Ibid, p 357.
9. Ibid, pp 357–358.
10. Of Edjmiadsin, *Avetik Isahakian About the Ardent Issues of Our Times, Hairenik* Monthly, 1960, # 5, May, p 94.
11. Ibid, pp 94–5.
12. Andranik Dsarukian, *The Greats and the Others,* Beirut, 1992, p 181.
13. Ibid, p 182.
14. Ibid, pp 182–183.
15. Ibid, p 183.
16. Ibid, pp 183–186.
17. Ibid, pp 188–189.
18. Ibid, p 193.
19. Ibid, pp 190–191.
20. Ibid, p 193.
21. Ibid, pp 194–195.
22. Simon Vratsian, *Along Life's Pathways,* Vol 4, p 222.
23. Christopher J. Walker, pp 325–326.
24. Torgom Vehapetian, *The True Clergyman,* Beirut, 1987, pp 29–36.
25. Stepan Aladjadjian, *Sixtieth, Nor Gyank* (New Life) weekly, July 5, 2001, p 3.
26. Vratsian, *Along Life's Pathways,* Vol 4, p 222.
27. Ibid, p 223.
28. Ibid, p 223.
29. Ibid, pp 223–224.

30. Ibid, p 224.
31. Ibid, pp 224–225.
32. Ibid, pp 225–227.
33. Martin Kanayan, unpublished family stories submitted to the author, dated February 9, 2006.
34. Vratsian, *Along Life's Pathways,* Vol 4, p 227.
35. Ibid, pp 227–228.
36. Ibid, p 228.
37. Ibid, pp 228–229.
38. Ibid, pp 229–230.
39. Ibid, pp 231–232.

# POST-MORTEM REFLECTIONS
# ABOUT DRO

## PRESS, INDIVIDUALS

(The majority of these excerpts are from
Hamlet Gevorgian's *Dro* volume's
appendix. Yerevan, 1991.)

# PRESS

## FIRST PRESS RELEASE

With immense grief we announce the death of our great and beloved comrade, Dro, which took place on Thursday, the 8th of March, 1956, at 7:45 p.m. at the New England Deaconess Hospital, after a prolonged and torturous illness.

This fatal blow, which wrests from this people one of its heroic sons, deeply grieves all Armenians, from the Diaspora to Armenia, where the memory of the heroic acts of this progeny of the mythical Vahagn remains alive and glowing in the hearts of the Armenian masses.

With Dro's demise, passes one of the most glorious martial figures of the Armenian Liberation Struggle, one of the braves of the last guard who adorned the history of Armenians with light and victories.

He was one of the rare and distinguished figures who constructed Armenia's Liberty and Independence on all fronts, most notably in the heroic battles of Bash-Aparan, as a leader who, with his high martial skills, knew how to inspire and lead the Armenian army to victory.

Dro, who inspired spirit and daring in the struggling masses, is today lifeless, though his memory moves all Armenians.

We have had few leaders whose names could move the masses. Dro was one of those names which became the flag of Liberty and daring acts. His boldness, his instinctive and acquired martial skills, besides his extraordinary daring, his immense goodness, classify him as one of Armenian history's greatest figures, unforgettable and revered.

*Hairenik*
(March 10, 1956)

# THE "MAGICALLY BRAVE"

On the evening of March 8, 1956, at 8:45, in distant America, the last page was closed on fifty plus years of *active* history, whose first page was adorned with a single, short name—DRO.

Until yesterday, he was *alive*, today he becomes *history*.

Until yesterday he was *action*. Now he is *spirit*.

Just before his demise he was mortal. Right after his demise he became a symbol.

He left this earth to enter that Golden Volume which is called Modern Armenian History.

Serob, Kevork *Chavush, Keri,* Khecho, Murat, Andranik, Sebuh, Dro, and many others—volunteers for the homeland and nation—all of them wrote with their own hands the epic story of Armenian heroes in the last 60 years.

Tomorrow, March 18, a fifty-year history will be laid to rest in distant America.

An era ends with him; another era opens again with him.

Furthermore, his mortal body died *outside,* but with his spirit he remains *inside.* His body was laid to rest in this hospitable *foreign* land, but his heart remains in the *homeland.*

He was an Armenian. He loved his people passionately.

He was an Armenian. Not one of those in whose presence it is possible to malign Armenians, but one of those in whose presence no one would dare utter an unfavorable word against Armenians.

The famous author, Hovannes Tumanian, on one occasion wrote the following about Alexander Khatisian: "He was such a patriot, uniquely so among Armenians, that even I was wary of saying anything negative about Armenians in his presence."

If Alexander Khatisian was such a patriot, Dro Kanayan was more so, not only in whose presence, but also in whose absence it was not possible "to malign the Armenian people."

He was Armenian and Mamikonian, perhaps of the last offshoot of that legendary dynasty which "recorded acts of daring in Armenian History."

Dro Kanayan? No! Dro Mamikonian—intrepid, bold, his hand always on his sword, always ready to die for the sake of the Armenian nation.

He was not one of many, but One among many.

He was great when he was living; his greatness seems to have grown upon his demise.

His arm was merciless against the enemy, but would become nurturing to the compatriot and friend.

How many times was his daring arm raised to punish mercilessly the Armenophobe and Armenocidal rulers, be they gendarmes, princes, or viceroys?

His stormy life was an endless dedication and sacrifice for the sake of his people and homeland.

He was modest, humble, avoided the limelight.

But he would become talkative, loquacious, almost an orator if others were the subject.

He was sweet in his everyday life, but stern and hard against those who could, who wanted, to harm or malign his people.

He was all smiles with his intimates. "I am going to swoon" he would joke or say mockingly if he would hear—despite himself—praise or admiration about his name, his fame, or about his past. He would then change the subject.

His world was his homeland, his country, his comrades in arms. With such pleasure and immense admiration he would speak especially about his "great teacher," Nikol Duman.

Nikol Duman was an idol for him, just as he is an idol now for us and others.

He was a warrior. The dominant characteristic of his personality, temperament, preferences, capabilities, talents, perhaps even his genius could be summed up by repeating those two words: a warrior.

Without hesitation we can say that this

"characteristic" could have earned him a marshal's baton, had he lived and worked among other nations. But he preferred to be a "soldier" for his people, rather than a "marshal" for others.

We believe though that our word would neither increase nor decrease the hero's glory. Because the glory which he obtained in his lifetime, to which he reaches now also after his death, is greater than the marshal's baton, more than any bestowed or received medals.

For us, his comrades and friends, for his loved ones, for the Armenian homeland and its people, Dro, now absent, but always present, is a fifty-year history, a fifty-year epic, a fifty-year victory song. What was mortal in him will go to join the earth. What was spiritual in him will remain and extend beyond him in time and space.

He vanquished time and space.

And that is the glory, great, real, permanent glory.

Now that his coffin is sealed and his grave filled in, it seems to us that his old comrades, who fought together but did not die together, would tell him:

"Was it necessary for you to die, especially you, when we are still alive . . . ?

*HOUSABER*

## THE BRAVE DRO'S DEMISE IN BOSTON

How frequent have the sad news become? Along with the modest ones, the mighty oak trees are also toppling, leaving behind grief and desolation.

With immense grief we bring to you the sad news of the last, irreplaceable loss of the lionhearted Dro, after a torturous illness in Boston.

The Saturday paper was in print when we received the following two telegrams:

"Cairo, March 9—Comrade Dro died March 8, at 8:45 p.m. in Boston."

"Boston, March 9—Comrade Dro died on Thursday, March 8, at 8:45 p.m."

This bitter blow was not a surprise. The doctors had given up any hope for some weeks now and considered the end inevitable. Every time the postman appeared with a telegram in hand, we were filled with fear.

*HARADJ*


## IN GRIEF

Dro enjoyed reverential love and admiration because he belonged to the phalanx of the selfless.

Our deceased comrade was an apostolic figure of that organization known as the ARF, whose ideals he personified. In him we recognize not just an individual, but an era, a page in our history; one could say some glorious pages.

From his adolescence until his death, he never lived for himself; he gave of himself to his homeland, his nation, soldier and citizen. He had opportunities for immense riches, but whatever he had he shared, gave without expectation.

From 1903 to 1953 he struggled against all calamities that threatened to topple our nation from its existential bearings. He became a punishing arm and inspired warrior, magical in his martial skills, among the bravest of braves. Our contemporary history would not be exaggerating if it were to draw a parallel between the two wars for existence, in 451 and in 1918, in the plains of Avaraïr and Ararat respectively, between Vartan in 451 and Dro in 1918, the two luminous warriors of the Armenian faith and homeland, who had spellbound their soldiers with the same determination to fight against impossible odds.

In 1903, when the tsarist regime began expropriating our ecclesiastical estates, and in 1905 when the Armeno-Tatar clashes threatened to deprive us of out sacred rights, it was Dro's punishing arm which relayed our nation's vitality and will to live. It is not we who will write history, but we can be confident that one day the History of Armenians will proudly etch his name in the pantheon of immortals.

The memorials and various expressions of grief and loss would cease to have meaning if the vanishing figures' life and work do not become a compass for the newcomers. With this awareness we mourn the irreplaceable loss of our great comrade.

*AREVELK*

# INDIVIDUALS

## VAHAN PAPAZIAN

aka *Koms* (Count), *Bjishk* (Doctor)

### DEDICATION

(Note: the subject of this article is not entirely news; some of it is mentioned in my book; however, the form of its presentation, its style is new. The author has given a theatrical touch to his article—especially in the last part. I retain it in honor of my Beirut neighbor, to the immortal memory of the gentleman, *Koms*.)

The years 1905–1906.

The blood of the martyred people of Taron and Sasun and that of the revolutionary fighters had not dried yet; the anguish had not ceased in the wounded Turkish-Armenian heart; the grief over the annihilation of the volunteer teams from the Caucasus rushing assistance to Sasun was still raw, annihilation by both Russian and Turkish forces at once. . . . It was in that era when tsarist Russia with cynical willfulness conceded to all the demands of its neighbor, Turkey. It wanted to wrest from Germany its supremacy and its attendant spoils.

Russia also had its own reasons to have a jaundiced view of the Armenians of the Caucasus. The Armenians, through the ARF, had adopted the way of struggle against the Russian dictatorship.

The Armenians of the Caucasus were prominent in the country's entire industrial and mercantile spheres. They had created a rich cultural life—Armenian schools, publishing, philanthropic and other civil institutions. All of this was intolerable, especially because in that era the Armenian element was becoming allied with Russia's revolutionary organizations.

Russia schemed and conceived the diabolical idea of quickly provoking interethnic clashes—with the years'-long Armeno-Tatar war as the result.

The Turkish Tatar beks and aghas were the convenient tools of this enterprise.

Right under the noses of the Russian authorities, with the Cossacks' moral, and sometimes direct, material support, the Tatar mob exploited the element of surprise and rushed the Armenian villages and towns. The atrocities committed by the agitated Tatars were awful—massacre, looting, arson, and destruction. The barbarism reached the point where Armenians cowering behind their doors were hunted down and slaughtered.

Baku was constructed through Armenian enterprise. Gandzak (Gyandja), Tbilisi, Gharabagh, and the Erevan provinces had large Armenian populations. The blows were primarily aimed against these points. Hundreds of Armenian villages endured agonizing critical times.

This Russo-Tatar blow was a terrifying one.

But the Armenian people reacted quickly. The ARF quickly grasped the moment's magnitude. It immediately created self-defense and later offensive teams. The Armenian people stood by the ARF and engaged in a life-and-death struggle.

Our people got armed with superhuman and extraordinary efforts. Resistance fronts and punitive bands were formed; mobilization of young and old took place. All the veteran and experienced fighters were fielded.

The fighters from Taron and Sasun who had gone through "fire and sword" and miraculously survived, from Vaspurakan and the other provinces, as well as the veteran fedayeen in the Caucasus, assumed the leadership of the regions. Activity, enthusiasm, selflessness. After that stunning blows were delivered to the Turk and Tatar mob.

The counterstrike was so heavy and awesome that the Tatar Khans holding olive branches would attempt to approach and shed crocodile tears, blaming the *sheytan* (devil), that is, the Russians, for the hellish situation.

302

The general commander of the self-defense of the large province of Yerevan was Nikol Duman, one of our greatest martial leaders.

He was merciless against the enemy. His orders were stern, which he issued without even moving a muscle in his face. "Only through terror can we bring these barbarians to their senses." He had firmly forbidden raising a hand on women and children. But if an Armenian was killed treacherously, he would make certain three to five Turks were killed for each.

Heavy crises confronted specially Gharabagh, Baku, Old Nakhidjevan, and Sharur. The dearth of experienced and capable leaders was noticeable.

By early 1906, the clashes had reached the point of tearing each other apart mercilessly.

Nikol Duman, like a programmed machine, was at the head of his command day and night. Any unpleasant or dangerous news or threatening situation did not perturb his calm, cool, and collected decisiveness; at such times he would get up, pace from one corner to another and then suddenly, joining his thumb and forefinger, he would issue his orders distinctly and decisively; not one objection; his orders were to be carried out.

In those days, taking advantage of his leave of absence, a young, bold martial leader much favored by Duman got married in a provincial town.

The town enjoyed a great feast. The team leader was the scion of a prominent local family and much loved by all.

The wedding took place in the evening. The chapel was illuminated; the locals crowded the entrance in their best attire.

And, aha, the bridegroom entered the chapel accompanied by his comrades in arms.

The bride also arrived with her bridesmaids. The ceremony ended. The bride and groom slowly headed to the exit; at that moment a courier approached the groom and delivered a note to him.

It was a telegram. Nikol Duman ordered the groom to immediately depart to Zangezur . . . .

The captain groom, momentarily stunned, froze. Those around him got unsettled. The captain, deliberately and unperturbed, continued his walk by his bride. When they reached home, their intimate family members surrounded the newlyweds. The groom approached his father and said, "Father, I have received orders from Duman, I have to depart forthwith. . . . I entrust my wife to you, to safeguard as your own offspring."

The father, a traditional, conservative man, was at a loss, as if not grasping the meaning of his son's words, then murmured, "It is not the time, it is a shame . . . go tomorrow."

"No, father, it cannot be; an order is an order."

Then, turning to his comrades, "Let's get going, my friends; saddle the horses."

He then quickly approached his father and mother; he kissed their trembling hands, caressed his bride's head, and then emerged.

The groom went from his wedding straight to sacrifice himself, unperturbed. That is how that generation was then.

The groom was our unforgettable comrade, Dro.


## REINTERMENT OF THE HERO'S REMAINS IN BASH-APARAN

(Excerpts from Manuk Krzelian's *The Armenian Liberation Struggle's Invincible and Immortal Soldier, Dro,* article in *Asparez,* May 25, 2002, p 15.)

Forty-four years after the interment of Dro's remains in the Mt. Auburn Cemetery at Watertown, one of Boston's suburbs, on May 24, 2002, headed by a special delegation from Armenia (which comprised of Deputy Defense Minister Colonel Michael Grigorian, Colonel Astvadzatur Petrosian, the military attaché of Armenia's Embassy in the U.S.,

Colonel Haik Kotandjian, the Ambassador of Armenia to the U.S., Arman Kirakosian, the delegate of Armenia to the U.N., Movses Abelian, and three military honor guards), Dro's remains were brought from Boston to Yerevan's Zvartnots Airport; they were greeted by a vast crowd, military and civilian state officials, public and political formal delegations, headed by Prime Minister Hrand Margarian, and the Catholicos of All Armenians, Karekin II.

The general ambience was so moving. The immortal hero's remains returning to the homeland after 44 years in foreign earth. After lowering his coffin with appropriate protocol, it was transported with armored vehicles to Yerevan's Republican Sports and Concerts Center where people were granted an opportunity to say their final farewell to the immortal hero.

On Saturday, May 27, the General's remains were transported to the See of Edjmiadsin for a memorial ceremony. On May 28, Armenia's Independence Day forged through fire and blood, near the memorial sculpture symbolizing for eternity the battle of Bash-Aparan, an official memorial ceremony took place, which was attended by President Robert Kocharian, Chair of the National Assembly Armen Khachaturian, the Defense Minister who was the M.C., high-ranking state officials, military officers, delegates of youth and student organizations, members of the ARF Bureau and Supreme Council Hrand Margarian, Albert Ajemian, Vahan Hovannisian, the editor of *Droshak* (the ARF Bureau's press organ), Nazaret Berberian, high-ranking clerics headed by the Catholicos of All Armenians, and thousands of Armenians.

From the General's family were present Kanayans living in Armenia, from the United States his younger son Martiros Kanayan with his wife and two sons, Drastamat-Dro and Philip, the General's 102-year-old widow, Gayané Kanayan.

In his speech, the delegate of the ARF Bureau, Hrand Margarian, notably said:

"Comrade Dro did not have rest in his entire life; he moved and lived wherever his duty called, where there were

ARF missions, and lived as every ARF cadre enlisted to serve his nation should. . . ." Then he underlined, "Finally, Dro returns home, not just as sacred remains, but as a revitalized heritage having vanquished decades of denials."

With this profound speech by the honorable Hrand Margarian of the ARF Bureau, I conclude my manuscript about the immortal Dro's tempestuous yet heroic life.

A. Ch.

# BIBLIOGRAPHY

Adamian, Sarkis. *The Armenian Community.* New York, Philosophical Library, 1955.

Afanasyan, Serge. *La Victoires de Sardarabad, Arménie, 21–29 Mai, 1918.* Éditions l'Harmattan, Paris, 1985.

Aharonian Gersam. *On the Way to Our Grand Vision.* 2nd ed, Beirut, 1964.

Aharonian, Vardges. *Andranik.* Boston, 1959.

Aladjadjian, Stepan. *Sixtieth. Nor Gyank* (New Life) Weekly, July 5, 2001.

*Alik* (Wave). Special Edition. May 4, 1956.

———. Extra Edition. *In Memory of Dro.* 1956.

Allen, W.E.D., and Muratoff, Paul. *Caucasian Battlefields.* Cambridge University Press, 1953. Reprinted by permission, The Barry Press, Inc., Nashville, TN, 1999.

Andreyev, Catherine. *Vlasov and the Russian Liberation Movement.* Cambridge University Press, 1987.

Avetian, Lieutenant M. *Armenian National Liberation Movement's Jubilee (1870–1920) Album and General Andranik.* Paris, 1954.

Avetisian, Hrand A. *The Victory Achieved by Armenian National Unity in May 1918.* Yerevan, 1998.

Ayvazian, Armen. *Strategic Consequences of the Armenian Genocide.* Tehran, *Arax* Monthly, #111, May 2002.

*Asbarez* Daily. Los Angeles, May 28, 1980.

Bagramina. *Memoirs.*

Baldwin, Oliver. *Six Prisons and Two Revolutions. Meshag* Publishing, Fresno, CA, 1944.

Bardakjian, Kevork B. *Hitler and the Armenian Genocide.* The Zoryan Institute, Cambridge, MA, 1985.

Baunes, Norman H. *The Speeches of Adolf Hitler, April 1922–August 1939.* Vol I, Oxford University Press, 1942.

Cecil, Robert. *The Myth of the Master Race: Alfred Rosenberg and Nazi Ideology.* London, 1972.

Chalabian, Antranig. *Revolutionary Figures.*

———. *General Andranik and the Armenian Revolutionary Movement.* 3rd ed, Michigan, 1988.

*Collier's Encyclopedia.* 1950, Vol 14.

Djerbashian Karpis. *Let Us Not Circumcise History.* Nor Kiank (New Life), May 9, 2002.

Dsarukian, Andranik. *The Greats and the Others.* Beirut, 1992.

*Encyclopedia Britannica.* 1958, Vol 19.

———. 1958, Vol 25.

Fischer, George. *Soviet Opposition to Stalin.* Harvard University Press, Cambridge, MA, 1952.

*General Andranik Speaks and Additional Articles.* Los Angeles, 1974.

*General Andranik's Historic Diary of the Caucasus Front.*

Gevorgian, Hamlet. *Dro.* 2nd ed, 2002.

Grzlian, Manuk. *Dro, The Immortal Soldier of the Armenian Liberation Struggle.* Asbarez, May 21, 2002.

Gutulian, Gr. *General Andranik and His Life and Wars.* 2nd ed, Beirut, 1929.

Haigal. *We Will Not Bow.* Horizon Weekly, Montreal, June 21, 1982.

*Hairenik* (Homeland) Monthly. July 1959.

*Hairenik* (Homeland) Monthly. January 1934.

*Hairenik* (Homeland) Monthly. May 1967.

*Hairenik* (Homeland) Newspaper. August 30, 1977.

*Hairenik* (Homeland) Daily. May 28, 1956.

*Hairenik* (Homeland) Daily. November 29, 1978.

Hovannisian, Richard. *Republic of Armenia, 1919–1920.* Vol 2, 1982.

———. *Republic of Armenia, 1919–1920.* Vol 4.

———. *The Republic of Armenia, Feb–Aug 1920.* Vol 3, 1996.

————. *The Republic of Armenia.* Vol 2.

————. *The Survival of Armenia.* Vol 3.

————. *The Republic of Armenia, Between the Crescent and the Sickle.* Vol 4, 1996.

————. *The Republic of Armenia, 1918–1919.* Vol 1. The University of California Press, Berkeley, Los Angeles, London.

————. *The Republic of Armenia.* Vol 4.

Hovsepian, Archbishop Garegin S. *The Most Calamotous Day of my Life (The Fall of Kars).* Cairo, 1945.


Kadjaznuni, Hovhannes. *The ARF Has Nothing Left To Do.* Cairo, 1954.

Kanayan, Martin. *Unpublished Family Stories.* Submitted to the author, February 9, 2006.

Kayaloff, Jacques. *The Battle of Sardarabad.* Mouton, The Hague, Paris, 1973.

Khadisian, Alexander. *The Beginning and Development of the Republic of Armenia.* 2nd ed, Beirut, 1968.

————. *Asbarez,* May 21, 2002.

————. *Asbarez,* May 24, 2002.

————. *Dro, The Invincible and Immortal Soldier of the Armenianb Liberation Struggle. Asbarez,* May 18, 2002.


Lazian, Gabriel. *Portraits From the Armenian Liberation Movement.* Cairo, Husaber Publishing, 1949.

Leo (Arakel Babakhanian). *Border Disputes.* Tbilisi, 1919.


Martirosian, L. *A Life's Album.* Beirut, 1959.

Martisrosian, Robert Aramaïsi. *The ARF's Anti-Populist Activity During WWII.* 2nd ed, Yerevan, 1986.

Missirlian, Zaven. *Three Treaties—of Alexandropol, Moscow and Kars, 1920–1921.* Beirut, 1979.


Of Edjmiadsin. Avedik Isahakian About the Ardent Issues of Our Times. Hairenik Monthly, #5, May 1960.


Papazian, Vahan. *My Recollections.* Vol 2, Beirut, 1952.

Petrossian, Taté. *Dro (1884–1956). Hairenik* (Homeland) Monthly, #10, October 1956.

Picker, Henry. *Hitlers Tischgesprächen Führerhauptquartier.* 3rd ed, Stuttgart: Seewald, 1977.

Poghosian, A. M. *Socio-Economic Relationships in the Province of Kars, 1878–1920.* Yerevan, 1961.

Raffi (Hakop Melik-Hakobian). *Collected Works.* Vol 3, Djalaleddin, Yerevan, 1962.

Rosenberg, Alfred. *Der Mythus des Zwanzigten Jahrhunderts.* Munich, 1930.

Ruben. *Memoirs of an Armenian Revolutionary.* Vol 7, Beirut, 1979.

Sassuni, Karo. *The Armenian-Turkish War. Hairenik* Monthly, July 1926.

———. *History of Taron.* Beirut, 1957.

Sebuh. *Pages From My Memories.* 1st ed, Boston, 1925.

Serobian, M. *On the Occasion of the Independence of Armenia.* Cairo, 1950.

Shahan. *Another Addendum, on the "How" and "Why" of the Treaty of Alexandropol.* Boston, 1945.

Tabaghian, Aram. *My Meeting With Dro. Hairenik* Monthly, #5, May 1967.

Ter Davidian, Harout. *Who Understands Dro? Masis* Weekly, October 16, 1999.

Terterian Hambardzum. *Memoirs.* December 2, 1921.

Terzibashian, Avetis. *Andranik.* Paris, 1942.

———. *Nubar.* Paris, 1939.

Toland, John. *Adolf Hitler.* Ballantine Books, New York, 1976.

Tonoyan, Armen. *Dro.* Navasard Publishing, 2000.

Torlakian, Misak. *My Memoirs.* 2nd ed, Beirut, 1963.

Turshian, H. G. *The Heroic Battle of Sartarapt.* Yerevan, 1969.

Tutunjian, Levon. *The Tragedy of Karin's Fall. See Memorial Book of the Great Atrocity,* Beirut, 1975.

Varandian, Michael. *A. R. Federation History.* 1st Printing. Paris, 1932.

Vartan, Levon. *Chronicle of the Armenian 1915–1923.* Beirut, 1975.

Vehapetian, torgom. *The True Clergyman.* Beirut, 1987.

Vratsian, Simon. *Along Life's Pathways.* Vol 3, Beirut, 1965.

————. *Along Life's Pathways.* Vol 4.

————. *Along Life's Pathways.* Vol 5, Beirut, 1996.

————. *Along Life's Pathways.* Vol 6, Beirut, 1967.

————. *Armenia Between the Bolshevik Hammer and the Turkish Anvil.* Beirut, 1953.

————. *Independent and United Armenia.* Boston, 1920.

————. *Republic of Armenia.* 2nd ed, Beirut, 1958.


Walker, Christopher J. Armenia, *The Survival of a Nation.* Croom Helm, London, St. Martin's Press, New York, 1980.


Yapujian, Avetis. *And the Armenian Nation Resurrected From the Fire and the Sword.* Cairo, 1971.

————. *The Political, Military, Economic, and Social Conditions of the Republic of Armenia.* Cairo, 1972.